Legal Aspects of Certification
and Accreditation

Contributors to this Volume

Jerome S. Beigler, M.D.
Chairman, Committee on Confidentiality, American Psychoanalytic Assn.; Former Chairman, Committee on Confidentiality, American Psychiatric Assn.; Private Practice of Psychiatry & Psychoanalysis, Chicago

John A. Benson, Jr., M.D.
President, American Board of Internal Medicine, Portland and Philadelphia; Professor of Medicine, Oregon Health Sciences University

Henry G. Cramblett, M.D.
Warner M. and Lora Kays Pomerene Chair in Medicine, Ohio State University, Columbus

James B. Erdmann, Ph.D.
Director, Division of Educational Measurement and Research, Association of American Medical Colleges, Washington

Joseph Neff Ewing, Jr., J.D.
Saul, Ewing, Remick & Saul, Philadelphia

Albert J. Feldman, L.L.B.
Wolf, Block, Schorr and Solis-Cohen, Philadelphia

Thomas B. Ferguson, M.D.
President, American Board of Medical Specialties

Jerald A. Jacobs, J.D.
Leighton, Conklin, Lemov, Jacobs and Buckley, Washington, D.C.

Joel I. Klein, J.D.
Onek, Klein and Farr, Washington, D.C.

Donald G. Langsley, M.D.
Executive Vice President, American Board of Medical Specialties

John S. Lloyd, Ph.D.
Director, Education and Research, American Board of Medical Specialties

James W. Rankin, J.D.
ABMS Counsel; Kirkland and Ellis, Chicago

Daniel W. Vittum, Jr., J.D.
Kirkland and Ellis, Chicago

Peyton E. Weary, M.D.
Professor & Chairman, Department of Dermatology, University of Virginia School of Medicine, Charlottesville

David E. Willett, J.D.
Hassard, Bonnington, Rogers and Huber, San Francisco

Legal Aspects of Certification and Accreditation

Donald G. Langsley, M.D., Editor

American Board of Medical Specialties
Evanston, Illinois

Other Books Published by the American Board
of Medical Specialties

Evaluation of Noncognitive Skills and Clinical Performance, Edited by John S. Lloyd, Ph.D., 1982.

Evaluating the Skills of Medical Specialists, Edited by John S. Lloyd, Ph.D., and Donald G. Langsley, M.D., 1983.

Oral Examinations in Medical Specialty Board Certification, Edited by John S. Lloyd, Ph.D., 1983.

Computer Applications in the Evaluation of Physician Competence, Edited by John S. Lloyd, Ph.D., to be published 1984.

KF
2905.1
.L43
1983

Library of Congress Number: 83-72022

Copyright © 1983 American Board of Medical Specialties.
All rights reserved.

Design/typesetting: North Coast Associates.
Printed in the United States of America.

Contents

Introduction
Thomas B. Ferguson, M.D. xi

Overview: Legal Aspects of Certification and Accreditation and Current Developments Affecting Hospital Staff Privileges
James W. Rankin, J.D. 1

The Antitrust Laws and Medical Specialty Certification
Joel I. Klein, J.D. 17

Due Process in Certification and Accreditation
Albert J. Feldman, L.L.B. 27

The Principle of Reasonableness
Jerald A. Jacobs, J.D. 45

Validity and Reasonableness
John S. Lloyd, Ph.D. 65

Standards Affecting Training Programs
Joseph Neff Ewing, Jr., J.D. 87

Judicial Review: Liability in Tort for Certification or Accreditation Activities
David E. Willet, J.D. 103

The Role of Trade Names and Trademarks in Medical Specialty Certification
Daniel W. Vittum, Jr., J.D. 111

Standardized Testing Legislation: Consumer Protection or Consumer Fraud?
  James B. Erdmann, Ph.D. 127
Disclosure of Confidential Information
  Jerome S. Beigler, M.D. 137
Challenges to Licensing Boards—1983
  Henry G. Cramblett, M.D. 153
Recertification
  John A. Benson, Jr., M.D. 163
Establishing New Specialties
  Peyton E. Weary, M.D. 175
Appendix
  Antitrust Issues in Health Care Law
    Onek, Klein & Farr 183
Index 285
Index to Cases Cited 301

Acknowledgments

The papers in this book have been derived from a conference by the same name as the book, but are edited and extended from the addresses given at the conference. The conference was sponsored by the American Board of Medical Specialties and took place on April 15-16, 1983 in Chicago.

ABMS is especially grateful to Mr. James W. Rankin, ABMS Counsel, for his aid in planning the conference and this volume.

American Board of Medical Specialties
One American Plaza, Suite 805
Evanston, Illinois 60201

Introduction

Thomas B. Ferguson, M.D.

There is an ancient Chinese curse that says, "May there be a lawyer in your life." Many centuries ago this may have been uttered in earnest or may merely have been the first in a long line of jokes about lawyers. We will never know.

One thing *is* certain: Lawyers are with us to stay, and this is not a curse, but a blessing. For as civilization has evolved and become increasingly complex, we have looked to the judicial system and its caretakers—the members of the bar—to maintain and nurture the orderly growth of this civilization. And if we occasionally become impatient with the pace that at times characterizes the mills of the gods, we need only to recall that in any other direction lie anarchy and chaos.

There has never been a time in history when it was so important for the legal profession and the medical profession to work together, and each to understand the other's point of view. A misstep in any number of directions may jeopardize the target of our concern—the individual citizen and his right to health in an orderly society.

The processes of certification and accreditation have evolved over a long period, but basically are the result of the knowledge explosion in medicine during the past 100 years. Specialty medicine began when practitioners, all recipients of the same M.D. degree, began *voluntarily* to limit their practice to a particular compartment of medicine. Specialty societies, that is, organizations of medicine with interests in the same disease processes, then proliferated rapidly. The next development was the introduction of a formal training program after graduation, designed to prepare the physician for his chosen specialty field. The system that evolved to assure the prospective trainee of uniform standards among specialty training programs is the accreditation process

There soon followed the final logical step in this sequence, that of assuring the public that the *individual* trainees from accredited programs were themselves of a uniformly high quality. This is done by testing, scrutiny, and, ultimately, approval of the physician specialist by a group of recognized leaders in that specialty—the process of certification.

Accreditation of training programs is performed by the residency review committees, individuals drawn from many areas of medicine who are willing to undertake this at times burdensome task. Certification is the responsibility of the medical board in each of the specialties.

Both systems, accreditation and certification, have evolved wholly within the house of medicine, and, however they may be viewed by the world at large in 1983, I think without fear of contradiction it may be stated that the impetus for their development was and is a single-minded goal—a high-quality medical specialist.

It is true that both systems have arborized and become complex and for valid reasons are experiencing intense scrutiny from without. Our hope is that these probings—always keeping our target John. Q. Citizen in mind—will work toward building a taller and better structure on the existing foundation rather than digging a new hole in the ground to start anew. There is real danger in the latter.

We hope that this book will expand your awareness of the interaction between law and medicine, between the physicians who protect the health and enhance the quality of life and the lawyers, who protect and enhance life in another fashion.

This year the American Board of Medical Specialties celebrates its 50th anniversary. A half-century ago it was organized as the Advisory Board for Medical Specialties and at the time recognized only four specialty boards: ophthalmology, otolaryngology, obstetrics/gynecology, and dermatology. In 1970 the Advisory Board was reorganized as the American Board of Medical Specialties, and today the ABMS is a *federation* of 23 boards which are authorized to issue 32 types of general certificates and 40 types of certificates recognizing special qualifications. This book is one way to demonstrate the responsibility that ABMS feels toward high-quality health care.

Overview: Legal Aspects of Certification and Accreditation and Current Developments Affecting Hospital Staff Privileges

James W. Rankin, J.D.

Part One will touch on due process, trademarks, insurance EEOC and FTC investigations, and a number of additional topics such as truth-in-testing and recertification.

Thereafter, in Part Two of this chapter, three key issues impacting on hospital staff privileges will be reviewed, as follows: the proposed JCAH revisions pertaining to "medical staff," questions raised by closed medical staffs at hospitals, and litigation involving exclusive contracts between physicians and hospitals. Although the individual factual issues raised with respect to each of these topics vary widely, they have in common recurring federal antitrust scrutiny.

Although one cannot generalize in the absence of the unique circumstances raised in each instance, we have recently had occasion to analyze each of these three subjects in detail, and have reached the conclusion in every instance that the judiciary and the enforcement agencies should view these arrangements as ones involving nonprice vertical restraints, judging the relationships created thereby under the "rule of reason." As a matter of sound analysis and proper medical and hospital practice, we believe that in most instances the judiciary should ultimately reject antitrust challenges raised in these three instances, taking into account the importance of the reasonable medical and practical consideration underlying the developments in each case. Before proceeding to a more

2 Legal Aspects of Certification and Accreditation

detailed analysis of the rationale supporting these conclusions in Part Two below, let us first review the last several years.

Part One: Legal aspects of certification and accreditation

When reviewing the topics on this program, I was struck by the importance of the historical development over the last decade of the legal issues facing the medical specialties. In the early 1970s, the three principal legal issues confronting ABMS and its member boards were:

1. The importance of due process to a member board's orderly functioning. Typically, a disgruntled applicant might challenge his or her failure to be certified by attacking the board's procedures. This issue remains with us to this date. Although the field has undergone a number of refinements, the basic contours of due process that existed ten or fifteen years ago remain unchanged.

At the same time, a disgruntled applicant a decade ago might have attempted to raise antitrust issues, but the antitrust law had not developed anywhere near as much as it has today, and, typically, such allegations at that time were merely tag-along contentions. Today, the antitrust issues involved in certification and accreditation are quite significant.

2. The protection of the boards' trade names and trademarks. In the early 1970s, there would occasionally be a thinly financed operation, sometimes resembling a diploma mill, that would attempt to set itself up as the American Board of Whatever and to certify applicants in return for significant monetary payments. Boards found this problem amenable to redress by invoking trade names or trademark legal doctrines in those cases in which the board had obtained this protection. During the last decade, there has been substantially increased sophistication among the boards and their counsel with respect to the copyright protections that are available.

3. Ten years ago, there was substantial debate about the possibility of obtaining insurance to cover the cost of litigation that might be filed against ABMS or its member boards. It was deemed important by some to have this kind of insurance in light of the perceived astronomical costs of potential litigation, including legal fees and related expenses. With the advent of the so-called medical malpractice crisis in the mid-1970s, it became difficult and inordinately expensive to obtain any reasonable insurance covering the broad risks in this arena. By the late 1970s and early 1980s, ABMS and many member boards had an assortment of insurance policies that covered some, but by no means all, risks that might be involved. The ultimate resolution of this issue was far less encompassing than originally envisioned ten years ago.

Now, leaving the legal arena of a decade ago and turning to the developments during the mid-to-latter 1970s, ABMS and its member boards were confronted with the joys of increasing federal regulation, or attempts at it, by agencies like the Equal Employment Opportunity Commission (EEOC) and the Federal Trade Commission (FTC). *First,* the Equal Employment Opportunity Coordinating Council (only one of whose members was the EEOC) proposed to issue regulations that could have had a disastrous effect on the examinations administered by the boards. The asserted impetus for the proposed regulations was a concern for increased validity and reliability of examinations throughout the country, typically in day-to-day blue-collar job settings where, it was perceived, traditional examining procedures had tended to discriminate against certain segments of society. The proposed regulations, however, were not limited to those job settings; they were so sweeping that they would have had a stifling impact on member boards' operations, as well as most other professions throughout the nation.

In response to this challenge, ABMS took the lead in organizing an ad hoc committee, which included representatives of most professions in the United States. After submission of a number of position papers to the federal government, there was a meeting in Washington, D.C. with the Deputy Attorney General of the United States at which this issue was discussed fully and frankly. The Department of Justice did not respond at that time to the positions that were expressed, but in the draft guidelines ultimately issued there was created, in effect, an exception so that the guidelines did not read directly on the boards' examining procedures. Of course, the end result of this episode—which continued over several years—was a heightened awareness among the medical specialties of the importance of validity and reliability to the examining process. ABMS has been instrumental (along with others) in sponsoring a number of conferences addressing these issues in recent years.

Second, and also in the mid-to-late 1970s, the Federal Trade Commission embarked on a series of investigations involving the health care field, beginning with the so-called AMA I proceeding which challenged restrictions on physicians' advertising. The investigations continued thereafter with AMA II, which focused on medical education generally, including many more narrowly focused studies of particular aspects of medical education, such as the medical specialties.

The FTC issued subpoenas to all the boards, as well as ABMS. ABMS coordinated the responses among the boards. ABMS sponsored a conference of board representatives, legal counsel, and others in which

4 Legal Aspects of Certification and Accreditation

the various facets of the FTC's investigations were reviewed in detail. In due course, the FTC counsel in charge of this investigation met in our offices. Once again—after not months but years of effort—the FTC staff was apparently satisfied that the mainstream of the medical specialty credentialing activities posed no significant anticompetitive restraints, and no action was taken with respect to ABMS or most of the boards. On the other hand, the result of the FTC's investigation was a heightened concern about the activities in a few particular specialties, particularly one or two of the specialty societies. In one instance—involving plastic surgery—there was an adversary proceeding that extended over a lengthy period of time.

The FTC was not limited in its scrutiny of health care to AMA or the medical specialties, but embarked on a host of related investigations and initiatives among them Blue Cross and Blue Shield, dentistry, veterinary medicine, and other professions, including law. These investigations led to a spate of symposia and articles by commentators, especially in the academic world. Nonetheless, there have recently been articles in this arena including Kissam, *Applying Antitrust Law to Medical Credentialing*, 7 AM. J. L. & MED. 1 (1980).

In addition to the foregoing areas, there has been during the past decade a number of additional issues that have become prominent from time to time. For example, the truth-in-testing area was at the forefront for a time following the enactment by New York State of rigid legislation in this area, which impinged on not only the medical specialties but on organizations such as ETS. As this issue ultimately evolved, most of the truth-in-testing legislation did not pose an insurmountable problem for the specialty boards. The Association of American Medical Colleges (AAMC) deserves credit for having been in the forefront of the dialogue with the state legislators, as well as the Congress, with respect to this and other issues.

Likewise, numerous questions were raised with respect to the entire field of recertification. There appeared to be a time in the late 1970s when this issue had gained great momentum, and numerous pressing legal issues were likely to impact on all the boards. However, the recertification question began to be perceived by some as a political issue, among other things, and changes were implemented within the past several years that some commentators characterized as a relaxation of the original proposals. In any event, the pressing urgency of legal analysis in this area subsided.

In addition, the topic of establishing new specialties gained prominence from time to time as groups such as emergency medicine petitioned for the creation of new boards with membership in ABMS. The FTC's investigation, mentioned earlier, focused in part on the liaison between ABMS, AMA, and others with respect to this area.

Likewise, the activities of the various state licensing boards continued to be important during the last decade. Recently, as numerous medical schools have been appearing in the Caribbean area, the licensing boards in the various states, including the Federation of State Medical Boards, have been instrumental in addressing this challenge.

Part Two: Current developments affecting hospital staff privileges

As many are undoubtedly aware, the questions raised by hospital privileges have become topical during the past several months. Rather than attempt to review exhaustively all the issues currently under discussion, I will simply touch on three key developments this morning, concluding that in most instances the judiciary should evaluate antitrust challenges in this arena under the "rule of reason," with the expectation that, if proper procedures have been followed, these three developments should be justified by reasonable medical and practicable considerations and hence withstand federal antitrust scrutiny. Of course, one can still expect a host of antitrust concerns to be raised in each of these arenas in the months and years ahead.

First, the Joint Commission on Accreditation of Hospitals (JCAH) has proposed to revise extensively its standards pertaining to the "medical staff." In essence, the proposed revision discusses an "organized staff," rather than a "medical staff," and appears to provide that hospitals may properly grant staff privileges to nearly all licensed health care practitioners, perhaps including midwives, chiropractors, and others. Also, the proposal would appear to sanction having all those with staff privileges represented on the executive committee of the organized staff and in other areas. One of the stated reasons for this proposed sweeping change was a concern about the potential antitrust exposure of the existing standards dealing with the medical staff. We recently have been asked by one of our clients to examine this area in depth and have earlier this week delivered a written opinion which concludes, among other things, that the federal antitrust laws do not mandate the wholesale revisions previously proposed, although more limited changes might be appropriate. In addition, we question whether this type of sweeping change is likely to be of material assistance in the pending cases around the country. Rather, we suggest that the JCAH's proposal be returned for further study. Informally, we have been advised that the JCAH is in the process of

6 Legal Aspects of Certification and Accreditation

preparing an alternative to its current proposal for discussion purposes, and that by the summer there should be in general circulation at least one additional approach to this subject.

Second, there has been renewed scrutiny in recent months of closed medical staffs at hospitals. Some have questioned whether a closed staff may be anticompetitive for a variety of reasons. On the other hand, as the FTC and other federal enforcement agencies have gained increasing sophistication in this area, they have begun to appreciate the complexities and challenges of medical care. Within the past few months, for example, the FTC issued an advisory opinion in essence sanctioning the closed medical staff at the Burham Hospital in Illinois.

Third, there has been increased litigation involving exclusive contracts between physicians and hospitals. A prominent illustration involves a contract in Louisiana whereby a group of anesthesiologists had the exclusive right to furnish the anesthesia services at the Jefferson Parish Hospital, notwithstanding the recommendation by the medical staff that other anesthesiologists be permitted access to the hospital. In that case, the federal appellate court invalidated this contract on antitrust grounds, notwithstanding the fact that the federal appellate court for the Seventh Circuit—which includes Illinois and the surrounding area—had reversed a lower court's order enjoining comparable arrangements in the *Dos Santos* case. Thereafter, the Department of Justice and the FTC filed a "friend of the court" brief urging the U.S. Supreme Court to review this case and to reverse it, arguing in part that exclusive contracts in proper circumstances may promote competition, the patients' welfare, and the public interest generally. The Supreme Court now has accepted this case, and we can anticipate that within the next year there will be an authoritative ruling resolving some of the issues in this field.

Each of these three current developments affecting hospital staff privileges presents widely varying factual situations, but in turn each can be analyzed based on a common approach to the antitrust issues that have already been raised and that are likely to be raised in the months and years ahead. Thus, persons challenging the current developments will typically claim that the practices in question are "horizontal," in the sense that competitors have allegedly banded together to limit the competition from others. For example, disgruntled applicants for hospital staff privileges have often claimed that their failure to obtain those privileges is the result of the existing medical staff precluding additional physicians from competing with them. Likewise, exclusive contracts between hospitals and groups of physicians have led to claims that such agreements preclude competition from other physicians who should have an equal opportunity to furnish comparable services to the hospital.

In addition, antitrust challenges to hospital staff arrangements typically include the claim that there is an attempt to "monopolize" the market in question. To illustrate, plaintiffs regularly argue that the hospital is the only one within a given community or region that can furnish the required health care services, that the hospital working together with the medical staff and others is attempting to preclude any competition from other hospitals or any other health care providers, thus contending that Section 2 of the Sherman Act should be invoked to strike down the challenged relationships.

As many are undoubtedly aware, responding to these types of allegations can often be a complex process, requiring a detailed step-by-step analysis of Sections 1 and 2 of the Sherman Act, the relevant markets involved, the potential for "economic power," and a host of other factors. Nonetheless, in our opinion, in most instances the current developments should be defended successfully against federal antitrust challenges. This conclusion is based upon the antitrust analysis set forth below, which is divided into six sections:

  I. Accreditation Standards and Other Restraints
 II. Section 1 of the Sherman Act
III. Vertical v. Horizontal Restraints
 IV. Rule of Reason Analysis
  V. Section 2 of the Sherman Act
 VI. Recent Antitrust/Health Care Developments

It should be noted that, notwithstanding the complexity of this area, a wealth of additional written materials is available to illustrate and reinforce the analytical discussion that follows.

I. *Accreditation standards and other restraints.* Accreditation standards, which, in practical effect, may limit the number and the type of health care providers who may use a hospital's facilities and who may admit patients to a hospital obviously are restrictions on the ability of others to enjoy that same access and those same privileges. The question whether such limitations constitute unlawful anticompetitive conduct under federal laws is quite complex, as illustrated in a 1983 study (nearly 200 pages in length) by Professor Sallyanne Payton of the University of Michigan entitled "Antitrust and Hospital Staff Privileges: A Window Onto the Contest for Control of the Practice of Medicine."

Of course, one of the cases factually similar to the issues raised in this area is *Wilk v. American Medical Association,* No.76 C 3777 (N.D. Ill.), *appeal pending,* No. 81-1331 (7th Cir.), a lawsuit in which several chiropractors sued the American Medical Association, the American Hospital Association, the American College of Surgeons, the American College of Physicians, the JCAH, and others under § 1 and § 2 of the Sherman Act alleging unlawful restraints of trade and monopolization. The lawsuit included allegations that defendants had conspired to prevent chiropractors from having access to hospitals. After trial, a verdict was entered in favor of all defendants on January 30, 1981. An appeal of the judgment was argued on January 20, 1982, and a decision should be rendered sometime this year by the Seventh Circuit Court of Appeals.

At the outset, it should be noted that a few years ago, in *Goldfarb v. Virginia State Bar,* 421 U.S. 773, 788-89 (1975), the United States Supreme Court rejected the idea that persons engaged in professional occupations were totally exempted from the antitrust laws but suggested in a footnote that a different standard be applied to professional services in judging their legality under the antitrust laws:

It would be unrealistic to view the practice of professions as interchangeable with other business activities, and automatically to apply to the professions antitrust concepts which originated in other areas.

In a subsequent case, the Supreme Court stated that the footnote in *Goldfarb* "cannot be read as fashioning a broad exemption under the Rule of Reason for learned professions." *National Society of Professional Engineers v. United States,* 435 U.S. 679, 696 (1978). Nevertheless, the Court adhered to the view expressed in *Goldfarb* that professional services by nature may differ significantly from other business services, and that, as a result, the competitive nature of such services may vary. The Court concluded that "ethical norms may serve to regulate and promote this competition, and thus fall within the Rule of Reason." *Id.* See also, *American Society of Mechanical Engineers v. Hydrolevel Corp.,* 72 L.Ed.2d 330 (1982) (not-for-profit organization setting engineering standards liable under antitrust laws for acts of its agents). There is some justification, therefore, for believing that hospital staff privileges will be judged by standards appropriate to the individual professional setting (as contrasted with the traditional business or industrial scene), particularly where the challenged conduct or practice does not involve pricing considerations.

Moreover, courts have held that properly motivated standard making is a legitimate function and one that is recognized by the antitrust laws. See, e.g., *Eliason Corp. v. National Sanitation Foundation,* 614 F.2d 126,

128-29 (6th Cir. 1980), *cert. denied,* 449 U.S. 826 (1980); *Neeld v. National Hockey League,* 594 F.2d 1297 (9th Cir. 1979); *Hatley v. American Quarter Horse Ass'n,* 552 F.2d 646, 653 (5th Cir. 1977) (self-regulatory actions taken by industries that necessarily require a high degree of interdependence and cooperation should not be governed by per se rules of Sherman Act illegality absent "at least minimal indicia of anticompetitive purpose or effect"); *E. A. McQuade Tours, Inc. v. Consolidated Air Tour Manual Committee,* 467 F.2d 178 (5th Cir. 1970), *cert. denied,* 409 U.S. 1109 (1973); *Marjorie Webster Junior College, Inc. v. Middle States Ass'n of Colleges and Secondary Schools, Inc.,* 432 F.2d 650, 654-66 (D.C. Cir. 1970), *cert. denied,* 400 U.S. 965 (1970) ("an incidental restraint of trade, absent an intent or purpose to affect the commercial aspects of the profession, is not sufficient to warrant application of the antitrust laws"). There is no doubt, however, that the federal antitrust laws relate to the procurement of medical and hospital services. *American Medical Association v. United States,* 317 U.S. 519 (1943).

II. *Section 1 of the Sherman Act.* Of principal concern for purposes of this general discussion, the *Wilk* case illustrates, is the Sherman Act, 15 U.S.C. § 1 and § 2. Focusing first on § 1, the Sherman Act outlaws "every" contract, combination, or conspiracy in restraint of trade or commerce among the several states or with foreign nations. Violation of this provision is a felony punishable by a fine, by imprisonment, or both. Suits may be brought by the government or by private parties, including treble damage actions through § 4 of the Clayton Act, 15 U.S.C. § 15. In addition, the Federal Trade Commission may challenge acts violative of § 1 of the Sherman Act under § 5 of the Federal Trade Commission Act, 15 U.S.C. § 45, as "unfair methods of competition."

Despite the express statutory language, as a result of the landmark decision in *Standard Oil Co. of New Jersey v. United States,* 221 U.S. 1 (1911), the term "every" as used in § 1 of the Sherman Act has been interpreted to prohibit only unreasonable contracts, combinations or conspiracies in restraint of trade. Moreover, certain restraints of trade have been further classified as unreasonable *per se.*

Our conclusions with respect to hospital staff privileges depend upon an analysis of two distinctions that are critical to the Sherman Act § 1 issues:

(a) Should these privileges be viewed as a vertical or a horizontal arrangement?
(b) Should the analysis be conducted pursuant to the rule of reason or as a *per se* practice?

These two questions are discussed more fully below.

III. *Vertical v. horizontal restraints.* Suits brought under § 1 of the Sherman Act and alleging a restraint of trade usually require the courts or the juries to determine whether the particular restraint at issue is "horizontal" or "vertical." This distinction is meaningful in a traditional industrial or commercial situation where business activities can be divided, for example, into manufacturing processes and distribution. These distinctions do not as readily lend themselves to professional groups and organizations, however, such as the health care field. Indeed, even industrial or commercial contexts, such determinations have become subject to much dispute and controversy recently. See, e.g., *Red Diamond Supply, Inc. v. Liquid Carbonic Corp.*, 637 F.2d 1001 (5th Cir.), *cert. denied*, 454 U.S. 827 (1981).

No one can predict how litigation will arise or, more importantly, how it will terminate. Antitrust analysis concerning the manner in which hospital staff privileges might be judged under the federal antitrust laws depends, in part, on certain assumptions made concerning the parties to potential future litigation and the substantive allegations raised in that litigation. At the present time, any number of parties conceivably could be foreseen as being involved in such suits. Potential plaintiffs could include, for example, government agencies that might bring suit as a result of a social or political decision to try to change health care industry practices, as well as to enforce federal antitrust laws. Disgruntled health care professionals (and others) who have been foreclosed from access to a hospital because of the hospital's adherence to accreditation and other standards also could sue. So, too, could patients who want particular health care providers to treat them at a particular hospital.

Quite recently, in *Smith v. North Michigan Hospital*, No. 81-1513 (6th Cir. 3/25/83), the Court of Appeals for the Sixth Circuit considered a case in which a hospital and a clinic had been charged with violating § 1 and § 2 of the Sherman Act. Plaintiff physicians sued the hospital for, among other things, granting an exclusive contract to the clinic to staff the hospital's emergency room. The lower court granted summary judgment in favor of defendants. On appeal, the Sixth Circuit held that plaintiffs had failed to rebut the medical justifications for the exclusive arrangement with any showing of a conspiracy to implement restrictive practices in the hospital's emergency room. The court held that the exclusive contract was a vertical relationship to be judged by the rule of reason:

[This case] does not involve a group of horizontal competitors whose joint control over some essential facility produces an unreasonable restraint on trade. Rather, [the defendant hospital], as the coordinator and supplier of an essential but limited public service, stands in a vertical relationship to both the [defendant clinic] and the [plaintiffs]. [The defendant hospital] not only may, but also is obliged to, staff its limited facilities in the manner which best serves the public interest. The evidence is overwhelming that it has done just that. There is nothing which would permit a jury to infer that the [defendant hospital's] [b]oard adopted the exclusive contract concept to force [plaintiffs] out of any market.

The court also upheld summary judgment as to most of the § 2 claims, but reversed and remanded as to the monopolization and attempt to monopolize charges against the clinic. The court stated that the clinic "has an obvious, but legitimately obtained monopoly . . . over the delivery of acute care medicine to the extent it is delivered through an emergency room. If this is a submarket and if the [clinic] has utilized this monopoly power unfairly to either exclude competition for emergency room referrals or in an attempt to gain monopoly power in primary care or the 'overlap' market alleged to exist by the [plaintiffs], liability under [§ 2] might be established." The Court of Appeals therefore ordered the lower court to consider fully the issue of relevant market prior to final disposition of the § 2 claim.

IV. *Rule of reason analysis.* As a second and far more crucial step in analyzing any alleged Sherman Act § 1 restraint, one must examine whether the restraint would be judged by the so-called rule of reason or the *per se* rules. Under the federal antitrust laws, some practices or combinations are considered so nefariously anticompetitive that they are declared illegal *per se*. As the United States Supreme Court stated in *Northern Pacific Railway v. United States*, 356 U.S. 1, 5 (1958):

There are certain agreements or practices which because of their pernicious effect on competition and lack of any redeeming virtue are conclusively presumed to be unreasonable and therefore illegal without elaborate inquiry as to the precise harm they have caused or the business excuse for their use.

Principal among those restraints treated as *per se* unlawful are horizontal agreements among competitors to fix prices. *United States v. United States Gypsum Co.*, 438 U.S. 422 (1978); *United States v. Trenton Potteries Co.*, 273 U.S. 392 (1927). At least some types of group boycotts also have been considered *per se* illegal where they are "naked restraints of trade"—plainly anticompetitive and lacking any redeeming value. *Klor's, Inc. v. Broadway-Hale Stores, Inc.*, 359 U.S. 207 (1950); *Fashion Originators' Guild of America, Inc. v. Federal Trade Commission*, 312 U.S. 457 (1941). Recently, in *Arizona v. Maricopa County Medical Society*, 102 S.Ct. 2466 (1982), the United States Supreme Court applied the *per se* standard to an agreement among physicians and their medical society as to the maximum fees that they would claim as reimbursement for services rendered to insured groups. Imposition of the *per se* standard is, in our view, not normally proper in the context of hospital staff privileges, however, since neither pricing concerns nor purely commerical activities are usually at the heart of the issues.

The rule of reason test, in contrast to the *per se* rule, is "the standard traditionally applied for the majority of anticompetitive practices challenged under § 1 of the [Sherman] Act." *Continental T.V., Inc. v. GTE Sylvania, Inc.,* 433 U.S. 36, 59 (1977). Assessment of the accreditation and other standards at issue in this instance under the rule of reason analysis permits consideration of the purpose, operation and effect of those standards to determine whether the restraint, if any, is such as "merely regulates and perhaps thereby promotes competition or whether it is such as may suppress or even destroy competition." *Chicago Board of Trade v. United States,* 246 U.S. 231, 238 (1918). The classic statement of the rule of reason was made by the United States Supreme Court in the *Chicago Board of Trade* case:

The true test of legality is whether the restraint imposed is such as merely regulates and perhaps thereby promotes competition, or whether it is such as may suppress or even destroy competition. To determine that question the court must ordinarily consider the facts peculiar to the business to which the restraint is applied; its condition before and after the restraint, and its effect, actual or probable. The history of the restraint, the evil believed to exist, the reason for adopting the particular remedy, the purpose or end sought to be obtained, are all relevant facts.

The rule of reason analysis normally imposes on the plaintiff the burden of demonstrating that the purported anticompetitive effects are unreasonable and the defendant has the opportunity to justify the conduct in question in light of existing market conditions. Thus, the court must examine carefully the particular arrangements or practices at issue. In evaluating allegedly anticompetitive market effect, the following factors usually are considered:

1. The market area involved;
2. The nature of the particular industry, product, or service involved;
3. The nature of the alleged restraint and its effect, actual or probable;
4. The reasons for adopting the particular practice which is alleged to constitute the restraint; and
5. The condition of the business before and after the restraint was imposed. *Chicago Board of Trade, supra,* at 238.

In numerous cases brought under § 1 of the Sherman Act, the dispute focuses primarily on the pivotal question of whether the court will apply the *per se* standard or the rule of reason test. It is not useful to attempt at this time to summarize the instances in which one standard will be applied as opposed to the other because this area of the antitrust law has been analyzed repeatedly and at length, and literally hundreds of significant and complex decisions have been generated on this subject. The issue of which standard will be applied varies with the particular industry involved; the type of allegations raised by the complaint; the types of plaintiffs and defendants themselves; the conduct or practice at issue; the factual context; the specific time in which the case is brought; the political atmosphere concerning antitrust enforcement; the social, economic, and political climate surrounding the practices under consideration; and so forth

The question whether the rule of reason test or the *per se* approach should be applied in cases involving professional organizations and service industries is currently a subject of substantial debate. Generally, nonprice or noncommercial vertical restraints in traditional areas of industry and commerce have been judged under the rule of reason. Thus, exclusive franchise agreements and areas of primary responsibility, for example, typically are analyzed in terms of the reasonableness of the particular vertical restraints imposed. In a recent policy paper prepared by the Economic Policy Office of the Antitrust Division of the United States Department of Justice, the government itself recommended a more tolerant treatment of vertical restraints across the board:

> . . . Overall, a more tolerant legal treatment of vertical restraints it highly desirable as a matter of rational economic policy. The law has been far harsher on intermediate forms of vertical control such as resale price maintenance, tie-ins, and exclusive territories than on complete control through vertical integration. If the latter is generally viewed as economically beneficial or benign (as we believe it should be), logic requires a more positive view of vertical restraints. *Vertical Restraints*, EPO 82-8, December 2, 1982.

There is abundant logic to applying the rule of reason instead of the *per se* test to service industries. Market mechanisms in such industries, including the health care field, are different from those in traditional industries and commerce. For example, tying arrangements prohibited in manufacturing sectors are often the essence of service industries. In sharp contrast to most traditional industries, there are few capital barriers to entry in service industries, although the creation of a new hospital can obviously be a major undertaking. Moreover, the existence of an underlying regulatory network in services and professional organizations makes the usual application of antitrust principles particularly challenging. Clashes inevitably will result between pertinent regulations and the federal antitrust laws. The health care field in particular does not readily lend itself to traditional concepts under federal antitrust laws because of the pervasiveness of regulation, the number and various kinds of parties involved, the difficulties of defining relevant markets, the diversity and breadth of the health care field itself, and similar factors. Analysis of any alleged antitrust violation involving nonprice restraints in the health care field, therefore, is particularly well suited to a rule of reason analysis.

V. *Section 2 of the Sherman Act.* Focusing next on § 2, the Sherman Act condemns "every person who shall monopolize, or attempt to monopolize, or combine or conspire . . . to monopolize. . . ." The Act thus defines three separate and distinct felony crimes, punishable by a monetary fine or by imprisonment or by both. In addition, any person injured in his business or property by reason of any of the three offenses specified in § 2 may bring a private treble damage action under § 4 of the Clayton Act, 15 U.S.C. § 15. The § 2 monopolizing offense requires more than the existence of monopoly power. For example, it is unlawful to achieve or maintain monopoly by a combination, by a restraint of trade, or by conduct that is predatory.

Under the pertinent case law, courts have defined monopolization as the purposeful acquisition or maintenance of monopoly power in a relevant market that is a part of trade or commerce among the several States or with foreign nations. The definition of the relevant market is a pivotal issue in cases brought under § 2. For that reason, as well as for the reason that monopolization itself is an economic concept, a monopolization case usually requires complex expert analysis and evidence. The law concerning monopolization and attempts to monopolize under § 2 of the Sherman Act is vague in comparison to certain other areas of the antitrust laws precisely because the cases typically involve intricate discussions of markets and economic power in a particular area.

Violations of § 2 of the Sherman Act are commonly alleged in antitrust cases and should be expected in any challenge relating to hospital staff privileges. To illustrate, in a recent case, *Weiss v. York Hospital,* 548 F. Supp. 1048 (M.D.Pa. 1982), a class action was brought on behalf of osteopathic physicians against a hospital and its staff, alleging violations of § 2 of the Sherman Act. The lower court held that the staff conspired to deny or at least to impede access to staff privileges by osteopaths and

and that the hospital committed the offenses of monopolization and attempt to monopolize. Consequently, the court entered an injunction ordering defendants to give osteopaths free access to hospitals. Procedures also were outlined for seeking money damages from defendants in later proceedings.

VI. *Recent antitrust/health care developments.* Several current court proceedings illustrate the importance of market definition, the increased prominence of the rule of reason in antitrust/health care analysis, and the vertical aspects of medical staff arrangements.

Thus, the Department of Justice's recent *amicus curiae* brief in the United States Supreme Court urging the Court to consider the petition for certiorari in *Jefferson Parish Hospital District No. 2 v. Hyde*, No. 82-1031, took the position that a hospital's exclusive contract with a professional medical corporation to provide anesthesia services to the hospital was a vertical combination that should be judged by a rule of reason analysis. The government argued in its brief that the hospital's exclusive dealing with a single professional medical corporation in fact promoted competition and was lawful.

Likewise illustrative of the government's attitude toward arrangements peculiar to the health care field is the Federal Trade Commission's recent order in *Michigan State Medical Society*, FTC No. 9129 (2/18/83). That case involved allegations of an attempt by the Michigan State Medical Society to fix fees and to influence Blue Cross/Blue Shield and Medicaid policies by negotiating collective agreements with insurers. The administrative law judge had issued an order that would have prohibited the medical society from initiating any communications whatsoever with insurers about reimbursement. The medical society argued that this order would prevent it from adequately representing its members. In response to this concern, the Federal Trade Commission (in a sharply divided vote) applied the rule of reason analysis to the alleged restraint and issued a less-stringent order, still condemning any attempt to fix prices, but nevertheless allowing the society to discuss reimbursement and other issues with insurers, provided that such discussions fell short of actually entering into agreements on behalf of members.

In *Feminist Women's Health Center, Inc. v. Mohammed*, 586 F.2d 530 (5th Cir. 1978), *cert. denied*, 444 U.S. 924 (1979), the Fifth Circuit Court of Appeals reversed in part the grant of summary judgment for most defendants in an antitrust action brought by an abortion clinic against physicians who allegedly interfered in the clinic's business. The Court of

Appeals held that the lower court had to examine the facts of the case to determine, among other things, whether the defendants were merely enforcing professional standards—in which case the rule of reason should be applied—or whether the defendants had engaged in intimidation and coercion.

More recently, in *Hospital Building Co. v. Trustees of Rex Hospital*, 691 F.2d 678 (4th Cir. 1982), the Fourth Circuit Court of Appeals reversed a judgment of $7.8 million against the largest hospital in Raleigh, North Carolina. The plaintiff had proven damages from the efforts of the defendant hospital and Blue Cross, through the local health planning committee, to prevent the plaintiff proprietary chain from expanding into a larger general hospital in a different location. The Court of Appeals held that planning activities of private health care providers are not unreasonable restraints of trade under the Sherman Act if undertaken in good faith. It remanded the case for a new trial on the question of whether the defendant hospital's motivation was really concern for an existing oversupply of hospital beds in the area and an effort to avoid needless duplication of facilities, or rather, a desire to exclude a more viable competitor.

Conclusion

For the foregoing reasons, with respect to the three current developments involving hospital staff privileges, in each instance our legal analysis has led to the conclusion that normally a rule of reason antitrust analysis should be applied, viewing the developments as vertical nonprice arrangements, with the expectation that in most instances they should withstand antitrust challenge. Of course, the individual circumstances surrounding any particular lawsuit, or enforcement action, would have to be taken into account since each case will ultimately depend on its own factual setting.

The Antitrust Laws and Medical Specialty Certification

Joel I. Klein, J.D.

The antitrust laws are a series of federal statutes aimed at protecting robust competition in the American economy. These laws announce broad principles prohibiting anticompetitive practices, which may generally be described as business practices that restrain the free play of market forces. For almost a century, the courts have given detailed substance to these basic statutory principles through the issuance of numerous case-law decisions. This body of law now stands as the backbone of laissez faire economics in our society, establishing a variety of requirements to regulate business practices and providing comprehensive mechanisms to ensure effective enforcement.

The antitrust laws are intended to be a potent form of market regulation. A violator can be enjoined from further unlawful activity and/or assessed money damages at three times the economic harm resulting from the anticompetitive practices. A losing defendant must also pay the cost of the plaintiffs' attorneys fees. And in especially serious cases, the United States Department of Justice may file criminal charges, punishable by up to five years' imprisonment and/or a stiff fine. To ensure rigorous enforcement, moreover, several individuals and groups are given designated roles. Depending on the circumstances, competitors, consumers, the Justice Department, and the Federal Trade Commission can institute a variety of actions. In addition, virtually every state has its own antitrust laws, many of which mirror the federal laws in large part.

Until very recently, the antitrust laws have had little impact on medical practice. Initially, the courts ruled that they were not intended to apply to the provision of "professional" services such as medicine, law, engineering, and teaching because these services were not considered "commercial" in the same sense as business dealings were. This somewhat amorphous doctrine, generally referred to as the "learned professions exemption," was firmly rejected in 1975, by the Supreme Court's landmark decision in *Goldfarb v. Virginia State Bar*.[1] As fate would have it, *Goldfarb* involved a price-fixing scheme by *lawyers*, establishing a minimum charge for title searches relating to real estate. Finding that the activity in question was sufficiently commercial to warrant antitrust regulation, the Court nevertheless cautioned that it would be "unrealistic to view the practice of the professions as interchangeable with other business activities, and automatically to apply to the professions antitrust concepts which originate in other areas. The public service aspect, and other features of the professions, may require that a particular practice, which could properly be viewed as a violation of the [antitrust laws] in another context, be treated differently."[2]

In the few short years since the decision in *Goldfarb*, the courts have been inundated with a variety of lawsuits challenging almost every aspect of medical and hospital practice. Viewed broadly, these cases may be classified in three groupings: (1) disputes between physician and nonphysician providers of health services over matters such as coverage under insurance programs and independent status as hospital providers; (2) disputes between physicians and hospitals or other groups, such as peer review committees or health maintenance organizations (HMOs), over staff privileges, insurance coverage, and forms of practice; and (3) disputes concerning the concentration of hospital ownership in large corporate chains. Although decisions in many of these cases have not reached final conclusion, it has already become evident that the courts are taking an aggressive posture in applying the antitrust laws to medical practices. Probably concerned about what is generally perceived as skyrocketing costs in the health care arena, many courts have eagerly looked to the antitrust laws as a new panacea. In the process, they have frequently ignored the Supreme Court's admonition in *Goldfarb* that the professions should not be too readily analogized to traditional businesses.

This recent proliferation of lawsuits has caused understandable concern among those involved in the health care delivery system. In part, this anxiety may be attributed to the fact that we are still in a "shakedown" period, where the rules of the game have not been clearly established. Although it is unlikely that certainty will ever be achieved in the antitrust area, confusion is sure to be greatest during the transition period, making it difficult to know whether a change in policy is necessary. The heavy penalties that may result if it turns out that a resisted change should have been made creates a strong incentive for modifications that may not ultimately have been required.

It is also true that medical practices have been particularly susceptible to antitrust attack because of the pervasive system of professional self-regulation that has been developed in this field, a system unmatched in any other profession. Ironically, this system was developed to protect consumers against abuses in medical pricing and services at a time when the antitrust laws played no role. Today, it has become a critical element in medicine's legal vulnerability.

Not surprisingly in this climate, medical specialty boards—which are involved in a voluntary credentialing effort designed to establish and certify competence in particular medical specialties or subspecialties—have become concerned. These boards, as well as the medical specialty societies with which they often have formal and/or informal relationships, were subjected to an intensive investigation by the Federal Trade Commission in 1976-77. While no formal action was taken by the FTC, several of its staff members, along with a private consulting organization, published a detailed analysis in 1981 based on the extensive information gathered during the investigation. Entitled *Competition Among Health Practitioners: The Influence of the Medical Profession on the Health Manpower Market*, one of the chapters specifically deals with "Issues in Credentialing Health Professionals" and focuses extensively on the role of the medical specialty boards.

What is perhaps most significant about the report is that, given the recognized pro-enforcement bias of the FTC staff, it is reasonably uncritical of the medical specialty boards. Indeed, in a recent presentation at a seminar sponsored by the National Health Lawyers Association, Arthur Lerner, Assistant Director of the FTC Bureau of Competition, flatly stated, "[T]he FTC has never challenged any medical specialty certification program and absent serious abuse, I can foresee no circumstance where we would." Before breathing too deep a sigh of relief, however, it is worth remembering that government policy is especially fickle in this area; in any event, private parties may seek antitrust redress even when the government does not. Particularly if, as predicted, the supply of physicians increases to the point where there is considerable excess capacity in certain fields, it may well be that the economic significance of board certification will take on increasing significance. If so, the spectre of antitrust attack is likely to loom larger.

Before addressing the details of antitrust analysis in this area, it may be helpful to look at some of the broader philosophical issues. As was suggested earlier, the basic reason the antitrust laws have any significant potential as a threat to specialty certification practices is that the standards and procedures are generally established by members of the profession in question. Those who challenge these practices are quick to assert that these people have a vested interest in protecting entrenched economic interests in a way that benefits those already in positions of authority. According to the FTC staff report referenced above, the specialty boards are a form of "private economic government" in that they "constitute a reticulate system of professional influence over entry into . . . various medical specialties."[3]

Beginning from this cynically phrased premise, antitrust advocates claim that the specialty boards can (or do, depending on the zeal of the advocate) have an anticompetitive effect in two ways: first, they can restrict certification in existing specialties so as to protect certified physicians from legitimate competition by noncertified physicians; and, second, they can prevent the creation of new subspecialties or competing specialties, thereby protecting the turf of existing specialists.

But allegations, as any lawyer is quick to point out, are often not facts. The role played by the specialty boards, even viewed from an antitrust perspective, can be, as the FTC report acknowledges, highly "procompetitive."[4] By providing important information about the qualifications of physicians, who otherwise practice under generic licenses, specialty certification can be helpful to "consumers"—i.e., patients and referring doctors—who must make difficult choices in a complex area. The availability of increased information is generally viewed favorably under antitrust principles, as was made clear in the recent decision prohibiting the American Medical Association's restriction on advertising.[5]

In response to this point, antitrust enthusiasts make two distinct responses, depending on their relative devotion to free-market concepts. The more moderate response is that this information-providing function can be better served by regulatory authorities (such as governmental bodies), who are not dominated or controlled by people who have a direct interest in the economic effects of certification. The more extreme response is that certification may mislead consumers because they tend to rely on it inappropriately. To the extent that consumers need information about the competence of practitioners, the argument proceeds, they can secure it without the presence of any particular "badge of expertise" supposedly conferred by certification.

These responses are unsatisfactory for a number of reasons. The extreme fervor of free-market devotees notwithstanding, the provision of medical care is sufficiently complicated that standardized forms of professional recognition are often a necessary adjunct to informed decision making. Because of the scientific basis of medical knowledge, the special vulnerability of sick people, and the role of third-party reimbursement as a limitation on consumer cost-consciousness, the need for meaningful specialty certification is great. Moreover, the first of these factors, in particular, suggests that professionals themselves should play an important role in establishing the requisite standards and administering the examinations. Aside from concerns generally relating to the bureaucratic inefficiency that often characterizes governmental certifying bodies, it is also important to protect against political considerations that tend to pollute the scientific inquiry necessary to ensure that certification remain a meaningful guidepost for medical consumers.

Despite the temptation to dwell on these interesting philosophical questions, it is necessary to move on to a more particularistic analysis of the activities of the specialty boards, if for no other reason than it is clear that, at least for the foreseeable future, they are certain to remain operative, even in the current atmosphere of aggressive antitrust enforcement. In proceeding, however, it is important to stress that this analysis should be viewed as tentative at best. To date, there have been no antitrust cases squarely dealing with medical specialty boards, and only a relatively few cases raising potentially analogous issues with respect to other professional certifying or accrediting bodies. Even in these latter areas, the decisions provide only limited guidance. The possibility remains, therefore, that the courts, in their wisdom, may someday view these issues differently from the way in which they are analyzed by any lawyer. Unfortunately, there is precedent for such a concern.

This lawyerlike caveat notwithstanding, there are certain principles that can be put forward with the same degree of confidence that is typically conveyed by the wonderful phrase, "reasonable medical certainty." To begin with, it is helpful for analytic purposes to divide the certification process into a "recognition" component and an "enforcement" component. The former deals with the establishment of standards, which are implemented through a testing mechanism such as a written or oral examination. The latter deals with the role of the certifying body in protecting or securing potential or actual economic advantages for those who are certified.

Turning first to the recognition component, it seems fair to say that this process, by itself, should present no substantial antitrust concerns. This would appear to be the case even when certification has significant economic consequences because *others,* in their *independent* judgment, choose to rely on it for such purposes as hospital credentialing or third-party reimbursement. Indeed, one of the consultants to the FTC study discussed above takes the view that certification is an important form of "commercial speech," entitled to constitutional protection under the First Amendment and, therefore, immune (or exempt) from antitrust challenge.[6] The essence of this position is that certification is a form of recognition that provides valuable information to consumers, who are free to assess its relevance in making their decisions about which provider to choose or recommend. If accepted, it would mean that the courts could not even consider antitrust challenges to the recognition aspect of certifying activities.

Even without the commercial speech doctrine—which traditionally has been a rather weak form of constitutional protection—there remains some basis for claiming that the recognition component of certification is exempt from the antitrust laws. In *Marjorie Webster Junior College v. Middle States Association of Colleges and Secondary Schools,*[7] the United States Court of Appeals for the District of Columbia Circuit refused to apply the antitrust laws to an academic accrediting agency that refused to accredit proprietary colleges. Even though the court found that this policy resulted in an "incidental restraint of trade,"[8] it concluded that the essentially noncommercial nature of academic standard setting justified an exemption from antitrust scrutiny.

Although it has been suggested that the exemption in *Marjorie Webster* cannot survive the Supreme Court's later decision in *Goldfarb,* the federal courts in New York recently relied on the *Marjorie Webster* decision to dismiss a challenge to medical school admissions criteria, which were alleged to be arbitrary in a manner that ultimately led to higher prices for medical services by restricting certain categories of potential physicians.[9] Despite these cases, however, it seems unlikely that the recognition component of medical specialty certification will be exempted from the antitrust laws altogether, if for no other reason than because it is likely to be perceived as more "economic" in its impact than college accrediting or medical school admissions decisions.

The fact that a certification process is not exempted from the antitrust laws, however, does not mean that the process runs afoul of those laws. To the contrary, if the certification process operates fairly, it should face no serious problems if challenged. There are several points that merit attention in this regard. First, the eligibility criteria for certification should be reasonable. If whole groups of people are arbitrarily excluded from seeking certification, the courts may become suspicious. This is not to suggest, however, that there cannot be meaningful limitations on eligibility. In the *Marjorie Webster* case, for example, although the court dismissed the antitrust claims, it did proceed to consider the appropriateness of the accrediting body's exclusion of proprietary schools under the "developing doctrines of common law," which essentially involved an analysis that is very similar to the "Rule of Reason" doctrine used in antitrust cases. Concluding that the exclusion was reasonable, the court relied heavily on the expertise of the accrediting body because "professional societies possess a specialized competence in evaluating the qualifications of an individual to engage in professional activities."[10] It would seem that this consideration would also allow for considerable discretion by medical certifying bodies in setting eligibility criteria.

The second potential set of concerns in the recognition area relate to basic fairness in distinguishing among eligible applicants for certification. Although these kinds of considerations are not traditionally deemed relevant by antitrust courts, there has been an increasing tendency to look to structural fairness, as a form of antitrust protection, when private groups regulate their members in a manner that has economic effects. In a particular case, any or all of the following factors might be examined: (1) procedural protection through a meaningful appeals mechanism; (2) lack of undue reliance on "grandfathering" provisions; (3) objective validation of the tests that are used for certification; and (4) "public" participation in policy-making bodies. Because these matters often have significance in areas other than antitrust, they are discussed elsewhere in these proceedings. For present purposes, it is sufficient to note that, with the possible exception of the first requirement, it is unlikely that any will be deemed essential. There are, of course, competing considerations (such as, for example, the need for oral examinations which may not be subject to validation) that justify dispensing with a particular requirement.

The recent decision in *Paralegal Institute, Inc. v. American Bar Association*,[11] which involved a challenge to accreditation standards for paralegal training schools, illustrates a sensible antitrust approach to the recognition component. Although the court did not find the accrediting body's activities to be exempt, it did find them to be lawful. In reaching its result, the court applied what may best be described as a "minimalist" Rule of Reason test, stressing, in particular, the public interest in having quality standards in the field.

In contrast to the approach taken with respect to recognition activities, enforcement activities are generally reviewed carefully by the courts. When a group moves from providing information about competence that consumers may independently choose to consider to attempting to force consumers to rely on certification, the potential for abuse is great. In this regard, it typically does not matter whether the enforcement efforts are undertaken by the certifying body itself, by its certified members acting in concert, or by its parent or sponsoring organizations.

Two recent cases illustrate the kinds of problems that may arise. In *United States Dental Institute v. American Association of Orthodontists*,[12] an unaccredited dental school claimed that two professional associations were attempting to put it out of business by barring members from teaching at unaccredited schools. The result of this effort, according to the unaccredited school, was to prevent dentists from securing training in orthodontial techniques except at the more demanding schools accredited by the professional associations. Similarly, in *Veizaga v. The National Board for Respiratory Therapy*,[13] several noncertified respiratory therapists alleged that two certifying agencies had conspired with several hospitals so that the hospitals would only hire certified therapists. While these cases apparently never resulted in decisions on the merits, in both instances the courts, in preliminary rulings, evidenced significant concern.

In the dentist case, the potentially important consideration is whether the members were acting collectively to boycott the nonaccredited school. If individuals, based on their own decisions, decide not to teach at (or attend) an unaccredited school, that is of no concern to the antitrust laws. But if a group tries to coerce its members to act in a particular fashion— through threatening loss of membership, for example—it is a different matter. Likewise in the respiratory therapist case, the issue of concern would appear to be whether the certifying groups applied unreasonable pressure on the hospitals to adopt their policies. If, for example, these groups attempted to prohibit certified therapists from practicing at a hospital that employed noncertified therapists, it is likely that an antitrust violation would be found.

Although enforcement efforts by certifying bodies tend to be risky, this does not mean that certifying bodies can take no action to promote the worth of certification in the marketplace. First of all, under a well-settled exemption to the antitrust laws, certifying bodies can lobby, in the fullest sense of the word, federal, state, and local governmental bodies, urging them to adopt certification for any purpose, such as licensing and reimbursement. This "collective lobbying" exemption is known as the *Noerr-Pennington* doctrine, which basically protects unrestrained access to governmental authority unless the lobbying effort is shown to be a sham. To the extent that the federal government or a state government (but not necessarily a local government) adopts the certifying body's proposal, that decision would also appear to be protected since such governmental action is not generally covered by the antitrust laws.

Even efforts by certifying bodies to persuade private groups such as hospitals and insurance companies to adopt certification as a standard for certain purposes need not run afoul of the antitrust law. As in the respiratory therapist case discussed above, such efforts may be challenged as a conspiracy, but whether they will be found actionable will depend on the precise activities undertaken by the certifying body. The case law is very limited in this area, but the recent decision by the United States Court of Appeals for the Fourth Circuit in *Virginia Academy of Clinical Psychologists v. Blue Shield of Virginia*,[14] offers some guidance. In that case, clinical psychologists sued Blue Shield and the state chapter of a national medical specialty society alleging that these groups had conspired to give psychiatrists a competitive advantage over psychologists by establishing a restrictive reimbursement policy for the latter. The court found the Blue Shield policy to violate the antitrust laws, but it exonerated the psychiatric society even though the society had specifically made proposals to Blue Shield concerning reimbursement for psychologists. According to the court, "it was not illegal for [the society], as seller of [psychiatric] services, to make recommendations aimed at persuading Blue Shield to adopt its proposal and use its services, absent some form of coercion."[15]

The lesson of *Virginia Academy* for certifying agencies may be that they can provide information about certification to other private entities and even make recommendations, so long as the decision to rely on certification remains an independent decision of the private body. If, on the other hand, the certifying body is in a position to control or dominate the private body—through representation on its board, for example—or to coerce it through economic pressure—by collectively having its members withdraw their services, for example—a conspiracy is likely to be found.

In conclusion, it should be said that, although the antitrust laws have struck fear in the hearts of those engaged in private medical regulatory efforts, the appropriate response is not to overreact. Private medical regulation has had a long, and in large measure, honorable history. It has worked to protect vulnerable patients who must often depend on the competence and goodwill of physicians. The current challenge demands not only a thoughtful look at existing practices, but also a vigilance in protecting that which is good from those who would use the intimidating threat of the antitrust laws to further their own private interests or to restructure social policy to their liking. So long as those responsible for certification activities keep the interests of patients in the forefront, they should have little to fear in the end.

References

1. 421 U.S. 773.
2. 421 U.S. at 788 n.17.
3. Chapter III, page 83.
4. Preface, page 2.
5. *See American Medical Association v. Federal Trade Commission,* 638 F.2d 493 (2d Cir. 1980), *affirmed by an equally divided court,* 50 U.S.L.W. 4313 (1982).
6. See P. Kissam, "Applying Antitrust Law to Medical Credentialing," 7 *Amer. J. of Law & Medicine* 1 (1981).
7. 432 F.2d 650 (1970).
8. 432 F.2d at 654
9. *See Selman v. Harvard Medical School,* 494 F. Supp. 603 (S.D.N.Y. 1980), *summarily affirmed,* 631 F.2d 1204 (2d Cir. 1980).
10. 432 F. 2d at 655.
11. 475 F. Supp. 1123 (S.D.N.Y. 1979), *summarily affirmed,* 422 F.2d 575 (2d Cir. 1980).
12. 396 F. Supp. 565 (N.D. Ill. 1975).
13. 1977-1 CCH Trade Cases ¶ 62,274 (N.D. Ill. 1977).
14. 624 F.2d 476 (1980).
15. 624 F.2d at 483.

Due Process in Certification and Accreditation

Albert J. Feldman, L.L.B.

Introduction

Individuals and organizations who challenge the decisions of private or governmental organizations often assert that the organization did not accord them "due process." Although many private organizations may not, in a technical sense, be required to afford "due process of law" in their decision making, the terminology of constitutional litigation has become so generally known that complaints about the conduct of nongovernmental organizations are frequently characterized in terms of the "denial of due process." Frequently, this characterization is a not inaccurate description of the fundamental nature of the complaint, which is that the organization has made its decision in some fundamentally unfair manner, or that its decision is arbitrary or irrational.

In 1978 the Supreme Court of the United States decided the case of *Board of Curators of the University of Missouri v. Horowitz*,[1] which had presented the issue of the nature of the due process required of a state university medical school in making a decision to refuse to permit an otherwise outstanding student to finish her fourth and last year of schooling on the basis of deficiencies in her clinical competence.

The constitutional "due process" required of the University of Missouri in this situation may well be viewed as the same as the judicially constructed "fairness doctrine" which has been held applicable to private organizations. This paper will describe the development of "due process" concepts applied to private certifying, accrediting, and membership organizations and to similar public or governmental organizations and will explain what the author believes can be viewed as a merger of those requirements of due process applied to both governmental and private organizations.

The elements of due process

The concept of due process in the United States arises from the Fifth and Fourteenth Amendments to the United States Constitution. In criminal law, for example, the Federal Constitutional requirements of due process are generally applicable to state court proceedings, and it is probably fair to say that, in any situation where the actions of a governmental agency of whatever kind may operate to deprive an individual of a "liberty" or a "property" interest, the requirements of due process become applicable.

The elements of due process have been stated by the United States Supreme Court to be "*actor, reus, judex,* [i.e.] regular allegations, opportunity to answer, and a trial according to some settled course of judicial proceedings . . . ."[2] The Supreme court has held that the requirements of due process are flexible and may be varied according to the circumstances and the interests at stake. Obviously in a murder trial, due process would require a rigorous proceeding designed to protect the interests at stake including legal counsel for the accused, a strictly independent tribunal, a trial by jury, if demanded, and so forth. On the other hand, in a high school disciplinary proceeding, some of the requirements might be relaxed or handled more informally.[3] It is probably fair to say, however, that, in any disciplinary proceeding involving some part of the government, an individual must be accorded each of the elements of due process, which are fundamentally notice of the charges, an opportunity to be heard in response, and an adjudication of the matter in dispute by some fair procedure.

Due process applied to governmental organizations: constitutional due process

The requirement of state action. To activate the due process clause of the Fifth and Fourteenth Amendments to the United States Constitution, some government action (called in the case law "state action") must be present. Then the interests at stake must be evaluated to see whether the situation calls for the application of due process rights and, if so, in what form. A two-step analysis is used in this determination.[4] Assuming that the requisite state action exists, it must first be determined whether the aggrieved party's interest rises to the level of a "property" or "liberty" interest and, if so, the competing interests of the individual and state must be weighed to determine what process is constitutionally required.[5] "Due process is flexible and calls for such procedural protections as the particular situation demands."[6]

With respect to the first requirement for the application of constitutional due process, that governmental action be involved, a court in New York has squarely dealt with the issue of whether the activities of a professional association constitute state action under the Fourteenth Amendment. In *Salter v. New York State Psychological Association*,[7] the court held that a professional association, which was the most important association of psychologists within the state, cooperated closely with the state in the formulation of rules governing psychologists, and had members who served on the State Advisory Council, was not a state entity.[8] The court stated that the activities of the association fell "well short" of the *Nixon v. Condon*[9] "test": "whether they (association) are to be classified as representatives of the state to such an extent and in such a sense that the great restraints of the Constitution set limits to their action."[10] The court went on to say that delegation of authority by, or action as agent of, the state must be shown in order to have the activities of the association classified as state action.[11]

There is no question that, under the analysis of the *Salter* case, the activities of the ordinary medical specialty certifying board are not state action. The certification process of such a board does not affect the licensing of physicians to practice medicine within a state, nor is a physician denied the opportunity to practice medicine without certification. Certifying activities are factually very similar to the activities of the New York State Psychological Association and the Middlesex County Medical Society, neither of which was found to constitute state action.[12]

Similarly private accrediting associations have been held not to have the requisite governmental character to render them subject to the due process requirements of either of the Fifth or Fourteenth Amendments. In cases involving school accreditation, schools have attempted to come under the guise of the Fifth or Fourteenth Amendment by claiming that lack of accreditation will deny them the right to obtain federal or state monies for student loans or financial aid. The courts have consistently held that the fact that withholding of accreditation by an accrediting association will deny a private institution access to governmental programs of assistance does not subject the actions of the private association to the constitutional limits applicable to government. See *Parsons College v. North Central Association of Colleges and Secondary Schools.*[13]

Because the courts have rarely found the activities of professional associations to constitute state action, there are few decisions that identify the type of interest an applicant to a professional society has in membership with that organization. One case that does, however, is *Hoberman v. Lock Haven Hospital*,[14] in which the court noted that "*charges* against a person that might seriously damage his standing and association in his community" would come within the concept of "liberty" as defined under the Fourteenth Amendment.[15] *Hoberman* arose after a doctor was charged with unethical behavior by the executive committee of a hospital. While an argument could be made that a denial of certification by a specialty board could activate a liberty interest under the due process clause, even Hoberman does not hold that this fact creates the "state action" necessary to render the requirements of constitutional due process applicable. On the other hand, as is discussed later, the gravity of the interest at stake may well operate to justify judicial intervention on a nonconstitutional theory.

Assuming state action and a constitutionally protected interest, the second level of due process analysis involves a balancing of the interests of the individual against those of the state. The procedures required in any given situation depend upon the outcome of this weighing process.[16] "Due process does not always require a full and formal adversary hearing."[17] It would appear that the more the situation resembles a decision concerning academic qualifications the less formal the requirements of due process are.[18]

Whitfield v. Illinois Board of Law Examiners,[19] presents a factual situation where state action and constitutionally protected interests were at stake in an evaluation of professional qualifications. In *Whitfield*, a failed candidate for admission to the Illinois bar challenged the state's procedures. The court held that the due process clause "requires the state to employ fair procedures in processing applications for admission to the bar and, therefore, that an applicant who has failed the bar examination is entitled to some procedural protections."[20] The court held that the state's procedure for reexamining examinations on request was adequate.[21] Normally, the rational and deliberate procedures utilized by a certifying board would pass this constitutional test.

Disciplinary v. academic criteria for decision making. One of the significant factors that the courts have looked at to determine the procedures required by due process is the nature of the proceeding either as disciplinary or as "evaluative" or as academic. Generally, where the action taken is based upon disciplinary criteria the affected individual is entitled to a "due process" hearing. Action based solely on academic criteria normally has not required such a hearing.[22] This is true of cases involving state action[23] and is also generally true (as discussed in the next section) for cases involving private associations subject to judicial review under the *Falcone* criteria.[24]

One of the difficulties in this area, however, is that it is frequently difficult to determine whether a decision was made for academic reasons or whether it was made for disciplinary reasons. In *Brookins v. Bonnell*,[25] which involved a student who had been dismissed from a state-supported school, the court held that "if the student was actually expelled for reasons other than the quality of his work or if the student failed because of bad faith or arbitrary and capricious action by an instructor, the courts will order the granting of a fair and impartial hearing."[26] The court went on to state that a fair and impartial "due process" hearing is required for those types of issues that adapt themselves readily to a determination by such a hearing.[27]

The reasons cited for not requiring a hearing for decisions based on academic grounds have been that such decisions typically require expert evaluation of cumulative information that is not readily adapted to the procedural tools of judicial or administrative decision making.[28] "Academic evaluations of a student, in contrast to disciplinary determinations, bear little resemblance to the judical and administrative fact-finding proceedings to which we have traditionally attached a full-hearing requirement."[29] The decisions made by a certifying board relating to an applicant's knowledge and skills in the particular field would seem to be academic decisions, not well suited to resolution in a hearing situation, rather than disciplinary decisions.

When decisions are made for disciplinary reasons, the courts have required more stringent procedural mechanisms.[30] Although the precise requirements vary with the individual facts of each case, at a minimum, the applicant is entitled to notice of the reason for the decision, an opportunity to hear the evidence against him, and a chance to present his side of the story before some reasonably fair tribunal.[31] These procedures have been required for dismissals from schools[32] and the refusal to admit an applicant to a professional society.[33] Assuming constitutional due process were applicable, if a certifying board were to refuse to certify an applicant for a reason unrelated to academic qualification, such as bad moral character or misconduct, the board would have to provide notice of the reason for the decision and provide an opportunity for the applicant to be heard in his defense.[34] The more closely the inquiry resembles a judical fact-finding proceeding, the more formal the procedural requirements necessary to meet either "due process" or "fair procedures."

Due process required of academic or certifying governmental organizations. Constitutional due process applies only to governmental organizations or organizations whose operations are so intertwined with those of the government that they can be viewed as the government itself or as its agents. The requirements of due process applicable to a governmental organization making academic or certifying decisions are discussed at greater length later in this paper. However, they may be briefly stated as follows. For strictly academic determinations, fair evaluative procedures are required, but formal hearings are not. For disciplinary determinations, more formal procedural requirements, including a formal hearing, are usually required.

Due process as applied to private organizations

Judicial intervention in private associations. The Fifth and Fourteenth Amendments of the United States Constitution are directed toward the control of governmental conduct. It is a starting point, then, in any analysis of the control of private organizations that such organizations are not ordinarily subject to the requirements of constitutional due process.

As a general rule, membership in a private voluntary association is a privilege that may be granted or withheld by the association at its pleasure, not an enforceable right, and the courts will not interfere to compel admission to membership, no matter how arbitrary or unjust the rejection of the candidate may be.[35] There are, however, situations where the courts will review the procedures used to select the members of private organizations.

A number of theories have been used to justify judical intervention into the membership decisions of private organizations based mostly on public policy concerns. In the leading case in this area, *Falcone v. Middlesex County Medical Society*,[36] the Supreme Court of New Jersey justified intervention into the membership decisions made by a private county medical society on the theory that membership in the society was required in order for a physician to gain hospital staff privileges in that locality. Thus in that geographic area, a physician without county medical society membership was essentially precluded from the ordinary practice of medicine. The court, therefore, viewed membership in the county medical society as an "economic necessity" for the physician and [found] that the association's activities impacted on the vital public interest in the health and welfare of the people.[37] Based on the "economic necessity" and the "public interest" involved, the court held that,

> public policy strongly dictates that the power [to exclude members] should be unbridled but should be viewed judicially as a fiduciary power to be exercised in reasonable and lawful manner for the advancement of the interests of the medical profession and public generally.[38]

The Falcone case has served as a foundation for almost every case dealing with judicial review of membership decisions of private organizations. The courts have used different terminology and in some cases have slightly changed the definition of some of the criteria developed in *Falcone;* however, the basic considerations have been the same.

In *Treister v. Academy of Orthopaedic Surgeons*[39] the court stated that it was balancing the necessity of judicial restraint from interfering with or regulating the affairs of private, voluntary associations against the economic impact on an applicant who is refused admission into the professional association, holding that the court would review the application procedures of a private association when membership in it was an economic necessity. The court took a very narrow view of the meaning of "economic necessity" stating that the test was *not* met where membership in the academy was "a practical necessity [needed] to realize maximum potential achievement and recognition in [a] specialty."[40]

On the other hand, the California courts have taken a much more liberal view as to what constitutes economic necessity. In *Pinsker v. Pacific Coast Society of Orthodontists*[41] the California Supreme Court held that,

> although membership in defendant orthodontic associations could not be said to be 'an economic necessity,' the associations still wielded monopoly power and affected sufficiently significant economic and professional concerns so as to clothe the societies with a 'public interest.'[42]

The California court went on to say that the common law requires not only that fair procedures be used when making membership decisions, but also that those decisions not rest on a rule that is substantively capricious or contrary to public policy.[43] The court refused to make any distinction between cases where initial membership was denied (the so-called exclusion cases) and situations where a member was expelled from an organization. Other courts have made a distinction between the exclusion and explusion cases, providing for a much more detailed judicial reveiw of explusion decisions on the theory that a member of an organization has an important and valuable personal relationship to the organization and the status conferred by the relationship, the loss of which at times may be more harmful than a loss of property or contractual rights.[44]

The *Falcone* analysis has been used to justify judicial review of the membership decisions of a variety of private associations including the refusal of a private accrediting board to grant accreditation to a proprietary college,[45] the decision by a multiple-listing association to refuse to accept a licensed real estate broker into the association,[46] the decisions of private hospitals to refuse to give staff privileges to licensed physicians,[47] the dismissal of a resident from a private teaching hospital,[48] and the refusal of private voluntary medical and dental societies to admit applicants to their associations.[49]

The criteria for whether or not judicial review of the decisions of a professional organization is appropriate was best summed up by Chief Judge Bazelon of the United States Court of Appeals for the District of Columbia when he stated that courts have scrutinized the standards and procedures employed by the associations where "membership in, or certification by, such an association is a virtual prerequisite to the practice of a given profession."[50] The degree of necessity required between membership in the association and the practice of a profession varies among the jurisdictions between the very strict necessity required in *Treister v. Academy of Orthopaedic Surgeons*[51] and the very liberal standard set by *Pinsker v. Pacific Coast Society of Orthodontists.*[52]

What are "fair procedures"? After having determined that the membership decisions of a private organization are of the type subject to judicial review under the criteria discussed above, a court must make a determination as to whether the procedures employed by the organization in making membership or other important decisions are, themselves, fair. The fairness analysis really involves two separate inquiries. "The association's action must be both substantively rational and procedurally fair."[53] Although the California courts are the only courts that have specifically broken the "fair procedures" criteria into two separate lines of analysis, a review of the decisions from other jurisdictions makes it clear that the majority of courts are, in fact, examining both the substance and procedure employed by the association under review.[54] It is important to keep in mind that "fair procedure in a common law sense" is not necessarily equivalent to "constitutional due process."[55]

Substantive fairness. The determination of substantive fairness as based on an examination of the substantive requirements established by the association where the court has first determined that the interests at stake are of the type that require judicial review under the criteria discussed earlier. The courts will examine the membership rules to ensure that they are *not arbitrary*[56] and that they bear some *relationship to the purpose and goals of the association*.

In making such an inquiry, the court must guard against unduly interfering with the Society's autonomy by substituting judicial judgment for that of the Society in an area where the competence of the court does not equal that of the Society. . . . If the society has refused membership . . . through the application of a reasonable standard—one which comports with the legitimate goals of the Society and the rights of the individual and the public—then judicial inquiry should end.[57]

"Only when a society rule is *contrary to public* policy,[58] or is so *'patently arbitrary and unreasonable'* as to be 'beyond the pale of the law'[59] should a court prohibit its enforcement."[60]

One of the legitimate objectives of a professional association may be an attempt to elevate professional standards in order to obtain quality medical and dental care.[61] "The imposition of additional educational requirements above those required for a state license certainly composes one permissible means of attaining such a goal. Moreover, with the continuing advances in medical science, a professional society may well conclude that 'qualification' in a given specialty . . . calls for completion of some courses which concentrate on that specialty."[62] The associations themselves are much *better able to evaluate* these additional educational requirements than are the courts.[63]

Procedural fairness. The other aspect of fairness concerns the *procedures* used by the private organization in making its decisions. All applicants for membership, certification, and so forth, in a professional association which is subject to judicial review under the *Falcone* "procedural fairness" doctrine, are entitled to have their application for membership considered in a fair and reasonable manner.[64] Generally, a fundamental element of fairness is notice of the charges against an applicant, or the reason for his rejection, and some meaningful opportunity for the applicant to be heard in his defense.[65] The courts have not developed hard-and-fast rules as to what specific procedures need be used, nor have they required a trial-type procedure. Instead, it has been left to the associations themselves to develop the methods by which the applicant will be notified of the reason for the denial of his application and the procedures through which he can respond in his defense.[66] The courts have only required that they be reasonable and fair in light of the facts involved.[67]

In *Kronen v. Pacific Coast Society of Orthodontists*,[68] the court approved of the procedures used by an association of orthodontists. In this case, the Pacific Coast Society's rules for membership required that an applicant have five years' associate membership, have successfully completed an orthodontic course of a minimum of 1,500 hours in an approved dental school, be recommended by two current members of the association, and satisfy the membership committee that he possess "the necessary knowledge . . . to ensure competent orthodontic service." The membership committee decided that to satisfy themselves as to the applicant's skill they needed to test his knowledge concerning orthodontics. The applicant in this case failed the examination. He was then given the opportunity to withdraw his application, improve his skill, and reapply. A number of members of the association offered the applicant assistance so that he could qualify for the association. The applicant reapplied but was denied membership because he could not obtain the necessary recommendations. The court concluded that the applicant did not receive arbitrary or improper treatment from the association in considering his application.[69] The examination given to the applicant was fair and was developed and given by a representative and experienced group of orthodontists. The court held that it could reasonably conclude that his failure to obtain membership on his second application was based on an honest professional purpose and on sound and sincere reasons.[70] The court concluded by saying that the qualifying requirements of the association were directed only toward the applicant's professional qualifications and were not themselves arbitrary or unreasonable, nor were they applied in an arbitrary or unreasonable manner.[71]

The courts have taken a similar approach in accreditation cases by reviewing the procedures employed by an accrediting association to ensure that the decision was not arbitrary, capricious, or unreasonable.[72] The courts will examine the decision-making process to assess whether the association followed its own procedures in evaluating an application for accreditation. The association's decision must be supported by some evidence and reasonably related to the legitimate professional purposes of the association.[73] A private institution requesting accreditation is entitled to notice and an opportunity to be heard.[74]

Summary. An analysis of the decisions involving disputes with private certifying and accrediting institutions suggests the following general principles are applicable:

First, the organization must be "fair." This means, first, that the organization must follow some rational, nonarbitrary procedures for the resolution of the controversy. Ordinarily, this means having standards that are logically related to the goals of the organization and having some nonarbitrary manner of their application.

Second, it means that where an organization has established procedures for the resolution of such controversies, they should be substantially followed.

Third, it means that such a private organization must be "substantively fair." That is, it is not entitled to make a decision that is patently or facially wrong or based upon a clearly improper standard.

With respect to the imposition of sanctions or discipline upon an existing member, the requirements of fairness may become somewhat more stringent. An "expulsion" case tends to get more judicial scrutiny than an "application" case. Some notice of what the charges are is ordinarily required and some sort of fair way to present them and afford the individual involved an opportunity to respond is also ordinarily required.

Board of Curators v. Horowitz

Board of Curators v. Horowitz is a case of profound significance to public and private organizations involved in certification and accreditation. In a sense it could be viewed as representing a merger of the requirements of "due process" applicable to both public and private organizations. This is true because the Supreme Court appears to have adopted as the requirement for constitutional procedural due process in making academic decisions, the fairness test that is ordinarily applied to private organizations in making their admission decisions.

The facts of the case were stated by the Supreme Court as follows:

Respondent was admitted with advanced standing to the Medical School in the fall of 1971. During the final years of a student's education at the school, the student is required to pursue in "rotational units" academic and clinical studies pertaining to various medical disciplines such as obstetrics-gynecology, pediatrics, and surgery. Each student's academic performance at the School is evaluated on a periodic basis by the Council on Evaluation, a body composed of both faculty and students, which can recommend various actions including probation and dismissal. The recommendations of the Council are reviewed by the Coordinating Committee, a body composed solely of faculty members, and must ultimately be approved by the Dean. Students are not typically allowed to appear before either the Council or the Coordinating Committee on the occasion of their review of the student's academic performance.

In the spring of respondent's first year of study, several faculty members expressed dissatisfaction with her clinical performance during a pediatrics rotation. The faculty members noted that respondent's "performance was below that of her peers in all clinical patient-oriented settings," that she was erratic in her attendance at clinical sessions, and that she lacked a critical concern for personal hygiene. Upon the recommendation of the Council on Evaluation, respondent was advanced to her second and final year on a probationary basis.

Faculty dissatisfaction with respondent's clinical performance continued during the following year. For example, respondent's docent, or faculty adviser, rated her clinical skills as "unsatisfactory." In the middle of the year, the Council again reviewed respondent's academic progress and concluded that respondent should not be considered for graduation in June of that year; furthermore, the Council recommended that, absent "radical improvement," respondent be dropped from the School.

Respondent was permitted to take a set of oral and practical examinations as an "appeal" of the decision not to permit her to graduate. Pursuant to this "appeal," respondent spent a substantial portion of time with seven practicing physicians in the area who enjoyed a good reputation among their peers. The physicians were asked to recommend whether respondent should be allowed to graduate on schedule and, if not, whether she should be dropped immediately or allowed to remain on probation. Only two of the doctors recommended that respondent be graduated on schedule. Of the other five, two recommended that she be immediately dropped from the school. The remaining three recommended that she not be allowed to graduate in June and be continued on probation pending further reports on her clinical progress. Upon receipt of these recommendations, the Council on Evaluation reaffirmed its prior position.

The Council met again in mid-May to consider whether respondent should be allowed to remain in school beyond June of that year. Noting that the report on respondent's recent surgery rotation rated her performance as "low-satisfactory," the Council unanimously recommended that "barring receipt of any reports that Miss Horowitz has improved radically, [she] not be allowed to re-enroll in the . . . School of Medicine." The Council delayed making its recommendation official until receiving reports on other rotations; when a report on respondent's emergency rotation also turned out to be negative, the Council unanimously reaffirmed its recommendation that respondent be dropped from the School. The Coordinating Committee and the Dean approved the recommendation and notified respondent, who appealed the decision in writing to the University's Provost for Health Sciences. The Provost sustained the School's actions after reviewing the record compiled during the earlier proceedings.[75]

Miss Horowitz argued that due process was applicable to the University of Missouri in making its decision because it had deprived her of a "liberty interest" by substantially impairing her opportunities to continue her medical education or to return to employment in a medical-related field. Without deciding the issue, the Supreme Court assumed that this was true and reviewed the University's actions as if the requirements of constitutional due process were fully applicable to her. The Court then reversed the decision of the Eighth Circuit Court of Appeals, holding that Miss Horowitz had not been entitled to due process. The Court concluded that she had been afforded "at least as much due process as the Fourteenth Amendment requires."[76] The U.S. Supreme Court concluded:

> The school fully informed respondent of the faculty's dissatisfaction with her clinical progress and the danger that this posed to timely graduation and continued enrollment. The ultimate decision to dismiss respondent was careful and deliberate.[77]

The Court distinguished the situation from the suspension of a student from public school for disciplinary reasons stating that the need for flexibility in the application of due process is "well illustrated by the significant difference between the failure of a student to meet academic standards and the violation by a student of valid rules of conduct. This difference calls for far less stringent procedural requirements in the case of an academic dismissal."[78]

The Court explained its reasoning saying:

> Academic evaluations of the student, in contrast to disciplinary determinations, bear little resemblance to the judicial and administrative fact-finding proceedings to which we have traditionally attached a full-hearing requirement. . . .
>
> The decision to dismiss respondent, by comparison, rested on the academic judgment of school officials that she did not have the necessary clinical ability to perform adequately as a medical doctor and was making insufficient progress toward that goal. Such a judgment is by its nature more subjective and evaluative than the typical factual questions presented in the average disciplinary decision. Like the decision of an individual professor as to the proper grade for a student in his course, the determination of whether to dismiss a student for academic reasons requires an expert evaluation of cumulative information and is not readily adapted to the procedural tools of judicial or administrative decision making.
>
> Under such circumstances, we decline to ignore the historic judgment of eduators and thereby formalize the academic dismissal process by requiring a hearing.[79]

The court went on to analyze Miss Horowitz's "substantial due process" claim. This was a claim that, regardless of the procedure followed, her dismissal was clearly arbitrary or capricious. The Supreme Court did not decide if such a claim could be reviewed in the context of an academic decision, but concluded that there was no showing of arbitrariness or capriciousness under the facts of the case.

The Horowitz case says that courts should defer to judgments made in an academic context and that the concept of "due process" applied in such a context requires only that the institution follow a generally fair procedure for evaluating the student, informing him or her of deficiencies and making a rational decision.

The requirements of due process have generally been regarded as more stringent than the fairness requirements applied to private organizations. Viewed in one sense, then, it can be argued that *Horowitz* establishes the most stringent requirements that would be applied to academic decision making, i.e., those requirements applicable to a governmental institution. The requirements applicable to a private organization should be no greater.

Most of the decisions made in connection with certification and accreditation can fairly be viewed as academic or quasi-academic decisions. Specialty boards evaluate the results of the training of physicians, and accrediting organizations evaluate the academic sufficiency of training institutions. These decisions are fundamentally academic ones, and the requirements of due process imposed on the evaluating organizations should be no greater than those announced in *Horowitz*, i.e., communication with the student or candidate about his or her progress and a careful and deliberate decision about the evaluation of that progress.

References

1. 435 U.S. 78, 98 S. Ct. 948, 55 L. Ed. 2d 124 (1978), rev'g Horowitz v. Board of Curators of the University of Missouri, 538 F.2d 1317 (8th Cir. 1976), rev'g 447 F. Supp. 1102 (W.D. Mo. 1975).
2. Cafeteria Workers v. McElroy, 367 U.S. 886, 895, 81 S. Ct. 1743, 1748 (1961) (quoting Murray's Lessee v. Hoboken Land and Improvements Co., 18 How. 272, 280, 15 L. Ed. 372 (1856)).
3. E.g. Goss v. Lopez, 419 U.S. 565, 95 S. Ct. 729, 42 L. Ed. 2d 725 (1975); See Cafeteria Workers v. McElroy, supra, at n.2; Mathews v. Eldridge, 424 U.S. 319, 334, 96 S. Ct. 893, 902, 47 L. Ed. 2d 18 (1976).
4. Board of Regents v. Roth, 408 U.S. 564, 92 S. Ct. 2701, 33 L. Ed. 2d 548 (1978).
5. Stretten v. Wadsworth Veterans Hospital, 537 F. 2d. 361 (9th Cir. 1976).
6. Mathews v. Eldridge, 424 U.S. 319, 334, 96 S. Ct. 893, 902, 47 L. Ed. 2d 18 (1976); n.3, supra.
7. 14 N.Y. 2d 100, 248 N.Y.S. 2d 867 (1964).
8. *Id.* at 871.
9. 286 U.S. 73, 52 S. Ct. 484, 76 L. Ed. 984 (1932).
10. *Id.* at 89.
11. Salter v. New York State Psychological Association, 14 N.Y. 2d 100, 248 N.Y.S. 2d 867 (1964).

12. *Id.;* Falcone v. Middlesex County Medical Society, 34 N.J. 582, 170 A.2d 791, 89 A.L.R. 2d 952 (1961). See also, Pinsker v. Pacific Coast Society of Orthodontists, 12 Cal. 3d 541, 116 Cal. Rptr. 245, 526 P.2d 253 (1974); Note, "Judicially Compelled Admission to Medical Societies: The Falcone Case," 75 Harv. L.R. 1186 (1962), Comment, "Exclusion From Private Associations," 74 Yale L.J. 1313 (1965).
13. 271 F. Supp. 65, 70 (N.D. Ill, 1967); see Marjorie Webster Junior Colleges, Inc. v. Middle States Association of Colleges and Secondary Schools, Inc., 432 F.2d 650, *cert. denied* 400 U.S. 965, 91 S. Ct. 367, 27 L. Ed. 2d 384, (1970); see generally, Comment, "The Legal Status of The Educational Accrediting Agency: Problems in Judicial Supervision and Governmental Regulation," 52 Cornell L.Q. 104 (1966).
14. 377 F. Supp. 1178 (M.D. Pa., 1974).
15. *Id.* at 1185.
16. Ong v. Tovey, 552 F. 2d 305 D(9th Cir. 1977).
17. *Id.* at 307.
18. See Board of Curators v. Horowitz, 435 U.S. 78, 98 S. Ct. 948, 55 L. Ed. 2d 124 (1978); Ong v. Tovey, 552, F.2d 305 (9th Cir. 1977).
19. 504 F.2d 474 (7th Cir. 1974).
20. *Id.* at 478.
21. *Id.*
22. Brookins v. Bonnell, 362 F. Supp. 379 (M.D. Pa., 1973).
23. *Id.*
24. See Pinsker v. Pacific Coast Society of Orthodontists, 12 Cal. 3d 541, 116 Cal. Rptr. 245, 526 P. 2d 253 (1974), where the court required that an applicant who had been denied admission to the defendant "society" be given a chance to defend himself before the Society's membership committee when his rejection was based upon an alleged violation of one of the Society's nonacademic rules. Compare to Salter v. New York State Psychological Association, 14 N.Y. 2d 100, (1964) where the rejection was based solely upon academic criteria and no "hearing" was required.
25. 362 F. Supp. 379 (M.D. Pa., 1973).
26. *Id.* at 382.
27. *Id.* at 383.
28. Board of Curators v. Horowitz, 435 U.S. 78, 98 S. Ct. 948, 55 L. Ed. 2d 124 (1978).
29. *Id.* at 89.
30. *Id.*
31. Goss v. Lopez, 419 U.S. 565, 95 S. Ct. 729, 42 L. Ed. 2d 725 (1975).

32. Id.
33. Pinsker v. Pacific Coast Society of Orthodontists, 12 Cal. 3d. 541, 116 Cal. Rptr. 245, 526 P.2d 253 (1974).
34. Compare Pinsker v. Pacific Coast Society of Orthodontists, 12 Cal. 3d. 541, 116 Cal. Rptr. 245, 526 P. 2d 253 (1974).
35. Kronen v. Pacific Coast Society of Orthodontists, 237 Cal. 2d 289, 46 Cal. Rptr. 808 (1st Dist., 1965), *cert. denied* 384 U.S. 905, 86 S. Ct. 1340 (1966); Grempler v. Multiple Listing Bureau of Harford County, Inc., 266 A.2d 1 (1970).
36. 34 N.J. 582, 170 A.2d 791, 89 A.L.R. 2d 952 (1961).
37. Id.
38. Id.
39. 78 Ill. App. 3d 746, 396 N.E. 2d 1225 (1979).
40. Id. at 755-56.
41. 12 Cal. 3d 541, 116 Cal. Rptr. 245, 526 P.2d 253 (1974).
42. Id. at 552.
43. Id. at 553.
44. Higgins v. American Society of Clinical Pathologists, 51 N.J. 191, 238 A.2d 665 (1968).
45. Marjorie Webster Junior College, Inc. v. Middle State Association of Colleges and Secondary Schools, Inc., 432 F.2d 650, *cert. denied* 91 S. Ct. 367 (D.C. Cir. 1970).
46. Grempler v. Multiple Listing Bureau of Harford County, 266 A.2d 1 (1970); Collins v. Main Line Board of Realtors, 452 Pa. 342, *cert. denied* Main Line Board of Realtors v. Collins 414 U.S. 979, 94 S. Ct. 291 (1973); Hirschfield v. York Board of Realtors, Inc., 59 D&C 2d 243 (1972).
47. Straube v. Emanuel Lutheran Charity Board, 600 P.2d 381 (Or. 1979), *cert. denied* 445 U.S. 966, 100 S. Ct. 1657 (1980).
48. Ezekial v. Winkley, 20 Cal. 3d 267, 142 Cal. Rptr. 418, 572 P.2d 32 (1977).
49. Pinsker v. Pacific Coast Society of Orthodontists, 12 Cal. 3d 541, 116 Cal. Rptr. 245, 526 P. 2d 253 (1974).
50. Marjorie Webster Junior College v. Middle States Association of Colleges and Secondary Schools, 432, F. 2d 650, 655 (1970).
51. 78 Ill. App. 3d 746, 396 N.E. 2d 1225 (1979).
52. 12 Cal. 3d 541, 116 Cal. Rptr. 245, 526 P. 2d 253 (1974).
53. Pinsker v. Pacific Coast Society of Orthodontists, 12 Cal. 3d 541, 550, 116 Cal. Rptr. 245, 526 P.2d 253 (1974).

54. See generally Chafee, The Internal Affairs of Associations Not For Profit, 43 Harv. L. Rev. 933, 1014-1020 (1930).
55. Straube v. Emanuel Lutheran Charity Board, 600 P. 2d 381, 385 (1979), *cert. denied* 445 U.S. 966, 100 S. Ct. 1657 (1980).
56. Falcone v. Middlesex County Medical Society, 34 N.J. 582, 170 A.2d 791, 89 A.L.R. 2d 952 (1961).
57. Blende v. Maricopa County Medical Society, 96 Ariz. 240, 393 P. 2d 926, 930 (1964); See also Pinsker v. Pacific Coast Society of Orthodontists, 12 Cal. 3d 541, 116 Cal. Rptr. 245, 526 P. 2d 253 (1974).
58. Higgins v. American Society of Clinical Pathologists, 51 N.J. 191, 238 A.2d 665 (1968).
59. Falcone v. Middlesex County Medical Society, 34 N.J. 582, 170 A.2d 791, 90 A.L.R. 2d 952 (1961).
60. Pinsker v. Pacific Coast Society of Orthodontists, supra, at 558.
61. *Id.* at 560; Falcone v. Middlesex County Medical Society, 34 N.J. 582, 170 A.2d 791, 89 A.L.R. 2d 952 (1961); Salter v. New York State Psychological Association, 14 N.Y. 2d 100, 248 N.Y.S. 2d 867, 198 N.E. 2d 250 (1964).
62. Pinsker v. Pacific Coast Society of Orthodontists, 12 Cal. 3d 541, 560, 116 Cal. Rptr. 245, 526 P. 2d 253 (1974).
63. *Id.*
64. Pinsker v. Pacific Coast Society of Orthodontists, 1 Cal. 3d 160, 81 Cal. Rptr. 623, 460 P.2d 495 (1969).
65. Pinsker v. Pacific Coast Society of Orthodontists, 12 Cal. 3d 541, 116 Cal. Rptr. 245, 526 P.2d 253 (1974).
66. *Id.*
67. Ezekial v. Winkley, 20 Cal. 3d 267, 142 Cal. Rptr. 418, 572 P.2d 32 (1977).
68. 237 Cal. 2d 289, 46 Cal. Rptr. 808 (1st Dist. 1965), *cert. denied* 384 U.S. 905, 86 S. Ct. 1340 (1966).
69. *Id.* at 307.
70. *Id.*
71. *Id.*
72. Rockland Institute, Division of Amistad Vocational Schools, Inc. v. Association of Independent Colleges and Schools, 412 F. Supp. 1015 (C.D. Cal. 1976).
73. State of North Dakota v. North Central Ass'n of Colleges & Secondary Schools, 99 F.2d 697 (7th Cir. 1938).

74. Marlboro Corp. v. Association of Independent Colleges and Schools, Inc. 556 F.2d. 78 (1st. Cir. 1977).
75. Board of Curators v. Horowitz, 435 U.S. 78, 80-82, 98 S. Ct. 948, 950-951 (8th Cir. 1978).
76. *Id.* at 85, 98 S. Ct. at 952.
77. *Id.*
78. *Id.* at 86, 98 S. Ct. at 953.
79. *Id.* at 89-90, 98 S. Ct. at 955.

The Principle of Reasonableness

Jerald A. Jacobs, J.D.

Introduction

Nearly two hundred years ago, the forefathers believed that the government is best which governs least.[1] Madison, history's ultimate newspaper columnist, argued eloquently and successfully that good and virtuous people require little governance and are even oppressed by what government is necessary to control those who would injure others.[2] A current newspaper columnist, George Will, applies the *Federalist Papers* to today's "big government." He says, "The problem is not bigness, it is unreasonable intrusiveness, which is a function of policy, not size. Besides, inveighing against big government ignores the fact that government is about as small as it will ever be and ignores the fact that government, though big, is often weak."[3] He argues for reasonable balance of competing values, which often requires limits on liberty and resistance to libertarianism—which seeks to maximize freedom for private appetites—to avoid dissolution of public authority, social and religious traditions, and other restraints necessary to prevent license from replacing durable, disciplined liberty.

All this has everything to do with self-regulation, including certification and accreditation, as well as government regulation, since self-regulation—if it is to continue and increase in effectiveness—is essentially quasi-governmental.

This paper examines what are some appropriate roles for private and government regulation, then discusses credentialing, and finally explores the principle of reasonableness in credentialing.

Society requires regulation, but regulation can be effected both through public agencies (federal, state, and local governments) in mandatory mechanisms and through private agencies (professional associations and credentialing boards) in voluntary mechanisms.

There have been many successful voluntary self-regulation mechanisms in addition to professional credentialing, including codes of ethics and product standards and certification. In many ways, these voluntary mechanisms are superior alternatives to enforced government regulation. These voluntary vehicles for self-regulation share certain general advantages, and can best balance competing values, because they are: (1) conventional mechanisms already accepted, understood, and operating effectively; (2) essentially legal and have been endorsed by legislatures, courts, and, perhaps most important of all, federal antitrust agencies; (3) limited, efficient, and benign because they are operated primarily by expert volunteers; (4) involve less delay, red tape, costs, inflexibility, and resistance to innovation than detailed government regulations; and (5) often can take advantage of greater expertise and more comprehensive coverage than is possible with governmental resources.

Self-regulation, however, is not without its drawbacks. The most serious and prevalent danger is the antitrust potential of voluntary mechanisms by which rules and interpretations can be applied to block current and potential competitors. In addition, voluntary mechanisms may sometimes lack the incentive to take account of external societal costs. Thus, the balance struck by self-regulatory bodies between internal profession or industry costs and benefits will often not be the same as the optimum economic and social balance that would be achieved if all relevant costs stemming from a proposed action were internalized.

The real and perceived advantages and shortcomings of government and private sector regulation account in large part for the cyclical nature of American governmental reform. Demands for, and implementation of, increased governmental regulation during the Populist, Progressive, New Deal, and Great Society eras were interspersed with periods of heightened emphasis on the importance of unleashing private-sector forces from excessive governmental restraints. Popular recognition that the private sector had failed to cope adequately with the monopolistic power of robber barons, inadequate food safety, the Great Depression, racial discrimination, and poverty fueled the fires of government regulation. New laws and federal agencies designed to rectify private-sector shortcomings resulted.

Beginning with the Carter Administration's initiatives on deregulation of the airlines, trucking industry, and other areas and continuing on a broader scale with the Reagan Administration, the pendulum has once again swung away from government regulation. "Deregulation" has become the watchword, opening up unique opportunities for the private sector to develop and implement adequate, substitute voluntary methods of dealing with the conditions that gave rise to mandatory regulation.

Deregulatory efforts have focused on achieving reduced or modified government regulation because such regulation has occasionally been considered excessive, inefficient, or oppressive. Although organized and grass-roots sentiment in favor of deregulation is far from unanimous, both major political parties are engaged in close scrutiny of government regulatory agencies for waste, inefficiency, and unnecessary duplication of private-sector initiatives. Leading Democrats and Republicans are actively seeking alternatives to traditional government regulatory activities, providing a receptive environment for innovative approaches to the interaction between government and private regulation.

With this special opportunity come practical and ethical obligations. Practically, should private, voluntary self-regulation efforts fail or even suffer from perceived fundamental inequities, demands for the government to impose its own regulations directly or on voluntary bodies to ensure adequate due process safeguards will begin again. Furthermore, increased societal reliance on self-regulation and decreased governmental scrutiny impose on private associations and boards the ethical responsibilities attendant upon their role as "quasi-governmental" entities. Therefore, both practical and ethical considerations dictate that private self-regulatory bodies impose only impartial, reasonable criteria and follow fair procedures in making decisions with powerful economic effects.

Responsible action by private self-regulatory agencies is a necessary step toward increased use of voluntary self-regulation, but it is not sufficient. Supportive actions by the public and government, the other actors in the tripartite deregulation drama, are also required. Specifically, the public must demonstrate a greater awareness of self-regulation mechanisms that are already in place and must support implementation of their further possibilities.

The required governmental role involves the major deterrent to increased self-regulatory activities: the threat of antitrust lawsuits. Although a blanket exemption is one possible approach to FTC scrutiny of professionals, such an approach is aimed elsewhere than at the potential anticompetitive effects of all self-regulatory activities. Instead, what is needed from government now is further recognition of self-regulation, particularly more precise definitions of what self-regulatory conduct *does not* constitute violations of antitrust laws. Viewed another way, voluntary self-regulatory bodies, including certification and accreditation agencies, need guidance as to what due process and other safeguards they can institute that will absolutely insulate them from antitrust liability. This stops short of seeking futher intrusion of government into the self-regulatory process. The historian Carl Becker noted that no class of Americans has ever objected to any form of government meddling that appeared to benefit that class. Far from government meddling, what self-regulation seems to need most just now is a "night-watchman" approach by government. To achieve this, associations and boards will have to reexamine the reasonableness of their self-regulation criteria and the fairness of their procedures and then will have to *sell* self-regulation to the public and to the government.

Credentialing

A basic purpose of virtually every professional association or board—especially in the medical specialties and other health care professions—is to improve the level of practice by individuals within the profession represented by the association or board. The goal of promoting professional competence is an extremely worthy one. Benefits from achievement of that goal are realized by members of the profession itself as well as by members of the public who deal with the profession.

There are many ways of promoting professional competence. They include presenting informative meetings and education programs, publishing journals of interest to professionals, sponsoring research in areas of concern to a profession, and promulgating and enforcing codes of acceptable conduct.

One further avenue for associations or boards to improve their members' professions is *credentialing*. Credentialing can encompass both certification of individuals who have been tested for proficiency and accreditation of educational institutions that have been approved for certain courses of study. Association or board credentialing programs are usually voluntary. A third kind of credentialing—occupational licensing—is performed by state governments as a legal condition for practicing an occupation rather than as a voluntary endeavor. It is noted, however, that many groups of state-licensed professionals also conduct credentialing programs such as for certification of individuals in specialty fields within their professions or for attainment of achievement levels beyond minimal licensing requirements. This, of course, is true in the medical specialties.

Professional credentialing—both certification and accreditation—has become a very common activity in recent years. The number of entities involved in credentialing was put at 120 in 1965,[4] but today the figure is probably ten times higher. Through credentialing activities, a profession is able to take responsibility itself for prescribing education and experience qualifications for candidates for certification, for prescribing curriculum and faculty qualifications for potential accredited institutions, for administering competitive examinations and conducting assessment visits, and for awarding some hallmark of qualification to the successful. In addition, the profession retains jurisdiction to revoke credentials from an individual or institution that ceases to meet qualifications. Credentialing is therefore the embodiment of *self-regulation* in place of *government regulation*, as discussed earlier.

For the credentialed individual or institution, the hallmark achieved provides prestige, recognition, and earning power for the individual or enrollment power for the institution. Equally important, credentialing enables the public (as well as government and private third-party payers for professional services) to distinguish between those that have attained some qualifying level of competence and those that have not.

In short, professional credentialing programs protect the public, by enabling anyone to identify competent people or adequate schools more readily; and they simultaneously aid the profession, by encouraging and recognizing high professional and institutional achievement.

Legal aspects

The Supreme Court and professional self-regulation. Despite the ubiquitous benefits provided by self-regulation in general and association or board professional credentialing programs in particular, certain aspects of such programs have come under legal attack or possible federal regulation in recent years. The Federal Trade Commission and the Department of Justice have actively pursued alleged illegal self-regulation practices by some professions; some of these challenges have involved credentialing. In addition, private suits continue to arise against association credentialing programs, usually brought by those who have been excluded from qualification by the programs.

The Supreme Court case of *Goldfarb v. Virginia State Bar*[5] opened the way for many of these challenges. In a case concerning a minimum fee schedule for professional legal services, established and enforced by an association of lawyers, the Court held that activities of the "learned professions" are subject to review under the antitrust laws as trade or commerce. The Court rejected arguments on behalf of the association that its minimum fee schedule was actually reasonable under the circumstances because it resulted effectively in setting maximum legal fees for routine services and thereby protected clients from "gouging" by lawyers. However, the Court did reserve some semblance of distinction for professions by saying that "[i]t would be unrealistic to view the practice of professions as interchangeable with other business activities, and automatically to apply to the professions antitrust concepts which originated in other areas."[6] The suggestion of the Court was that it might be inclined to treat a profession differently from the treatment of a business in future cases.

Subsequently, the Supreme Court decision in the case of *National Society of Professional Engineers v. United States*[7] held that an association's ethical ban on competitive bidding was an antitrust violation, regardless of the ban's reasonableness in maintaining the quality of engineering services, and that the apparent distinction drawn in *Goldfarb* between professions and other business activities is not a "broad exemption" from antitrust provisions. An important reference to professional credentialing appears in this decision in a concurring opinion by Justice Blackmun. He states that the Court might be willing to grant some extra margin under the antitrust laws and analyze the reasonableness of, as an example, "[a] medical association's prescription of standards of minimum competence for licensing or certification."[8] Of course, the passing reference by Justice Blackmun to professional credentialing does not carve out any clear precedent for an antitrust exemption for such activities. It only indicates that the Court might not be so harsh and perfunctory in reviewing a challenge to credentialing as it was in reviewing challenges to fee schedules and bidding bans.

The most recent Supreme Court pronouncement on antitrust implications of professional association self-regulation activities is contained in its decision in *Arizona v. Maricopa County Medical Society.*[9] There, an association of physicians agreed among themselves to provide medical services to insured patients under certain insurance programs in accordance with a maximum fee schedule. In effect, the physicians agreed that they would not charge these particular policyholders more than the fee schedule to which they had agreed. They were free to charge less, and they were also free to charge other patients anything they chose. The agreement had a laudable and apparently most reasonable purpose to provide lower cost medical benefits to people who were procuring health services. Notably, the insurance companies involved had encouraged and approved the maximum fee schedule. Nevertheless, the Supreme Court held that this conduct constituted price-fixing in violation of the Sherman Act.

The existing and threatened impact of these three Supreme Court cases on self-regulation programs, including professional credentialing programs, is enormous not only because of the conclusions of the Court in the cases but even more because of the methodology the Court used in reaching those conclusions. In all three cases a *per se* test of antitrust liability was used in the Court's analyses as opposed to the broader *reasonableness* test. The difference is extraordinarily important and merits some explanation.

Section 1 of the Sherman Act condemns in broad language concerted conduct that restrains trade.[10] In enacting the Sherman Act, Congress left to the courts the task of defining the scope of this mandate. The statute cannot mean what it literally says, for if it did the Sherman Act would outlaw the entire body of private contract law. All contracts restrain trade. The contractual relationship binds parties to a particular course and by so doing limits the commercial opportunities of others who might have made the sale or purchase.[11] As Justice Brandeis said in 1918, "[T]he legality of an agreement or regulation cannot be determined by so simple a test, as whether it restrains competition. Every agreement concerning trade, every regulation of trade, restrains. To bind, to restrain, is of their very essence."[12]

So the Supreme Court, relying on what guidance it could find in the common law, fashioned a workable test. Under it, courts look to see whether the restraint on trade is undue or unreasonable. Over the years, they have employed two distinct methods of analysis—the *per se* test and the *reasonableness* test.

The *per se* doctrine invalidates without further inquiry arrangements that directly stifle competition. The theory of the *per se* test is that certain kinds of restraints are so grievous as to demand summary determinations of their illegality without wasting judicial time on review of the purpose or effect of the restraints. As yet, only price-fixing or fee-setting cases have employed consistently the *per se* test, although there are some indications that the test might be employed in other kinds of antitrust cases, such as boycotts or market allocations.[13] As to professional association antitrust cases, the *per se* test was applied by the Supreme Court in *Goldfarb*, in *Professional Engineers*, and in *Maricopa*, all of which involved professional fees. The effect of a court's application of a *per se* test is to prohibit any justification for an activity proscribed by the Sherman Act once it is shown merely that the activity has been conducted.

Where an arrangement does not obviously stifle competition, but may adversely affect it, courts will analyze the arrangement to determine its purpose and effect. If either is anticompetitive, it will be struck down. Under the *reasonableness* test, again in the words of Justice Brandeis, "The true test of legality is whether the restraint imposed is such as merely regulates and perhaps thereby promotes competition or whether it is such as may suppress or even destroy competition."[14]

Whether a court chooses to employ the *per se* test or the *reasonableness* test in analyzing an association or board self-regulation program could well be the difference between a finding of legality and a finding of illegality. In the *National Society of Professional Engineers* case especially, the Supreme Court has refused to move from the inflexible position that promotion of competition is the only valid goal of self-regulation activities, and any other social or economic goal cannot be considered more important than, or even as important as, the promotion of competition.

As yet, neither the Supreme Court nor any other court has applied the most rigorous *per se* antitrust test to professional association or board self-regulatory activities that do not entail fees. It appears most likely that a credentialing program would be analyzed as to the *reasonableness* of any restraint imposed in the program (such as the denial to certain individuals or institutions or the certification or accreditation offered in the program). Nevertheless, the harshness of the rationale used in the Supreme Court's *Goldfarb, Professional Engineers,* and *Maricopa* decisions has been well-publicized. In applying a *per se* antitrust analysis to self-regulation activities where the promoters of those activities seemed to be at least honorably motivated but were precluded from having their motivation even considered by the Court, anxieties have been raised for associations or boards that conduct any kind of self-regulation programs, even, as with credentialing, where a *per se* analysis is most unlikely to be employed.

Another case, not involving the distinction between the *per se* test and the *reasonableness* test, demonstrates another line of possible antitrust challenge to voluntary credentialing. It is the Federal Trade Commission's holding that provisions in the code of ethics of the American Medical Association were illegal under the FTC Act.[15]

In *AMA*, ethical canons allegedly prohibiting physicians from advertising and solicitation were challenged under Section 5 of the Federal Trade Commission Act.[16] The Association defended its ethical canons on the grounds that no effect on price had been shown by the Commission and that the restraints were necessary to prevent deception of patients. The FTC found the purpose and effect of the canons to be anticompetitive and ordered them withdrawn. In a federal appellate court challenge, AMA argued not only that the commission was substantively wrong in its decision, but also that FTC has no authority over the association because it is a nonprofit organization. The appellate court also decided against AMA, both substantively and on the jurisdiction issue.[17] But the court did modify the commission order to emphasize the right and ability of AMA to engage in its self-regulation by prohibiting false or deceptive advertising or solicitation. The United States Supreme Court affirmed the appellate court decision against AMA without issuing an opinion and in a four-to-four decision.[18] Vigorous attempts by AMA and others to obtain legislative clarification of the Federal Trade Commission's authority over the professions have so far proved unsuccessful.

The AMA's experience with FTC demonstrates that commission challenges to the reasonableness of professional credentialing pose an additional antitrust threat. It should be noted, however, that many professional credentialing programs are conducted through certification or accreditation boards that are often independent from the professional associations which may have established the boards originally. The commission's legal authority over such boards is far more questionable than it was in the AMA circumstances, although this has not prevented FTC from attempting to exercise authority over such independent professional credentialing boards from time to time.

Finally, a fifth Supreme Court antitrust case bears consideration because it provides yet another dimension to the threat of antitrust challenges to professional credentialing programs.

In May 1982, the Supreme Court issued a decision that significantly broadens the potential antitrust liability of all professional associations or boards, particularly those engaging in self-regulation. In *American Society of Mechanical Engineers, Inc. v. Hydrolevel Corp.*,[19] the Court held that a professional association that set product standards was liable under the antitrust laws for acts of its agents because the acts were committed with the "apparent authority" of the association, even though the association's directors and staff did not ratify the acts, and even though the acts did not benefit the association. In borrowing a longstanding "apparent authority" concept from basic contract law and applying it to antitrust law for the first time, the Court stated that a rule that imposes liability on a nonprofit standard-setting organization is consistent with the legislative intent that private rights of action under the antitrust laws be used effectively to deter antitrust violations. The Court found that an association is responsible for preventing antitrust violations through the misuse of its reputation by its agents, including those who are merely unpaid volunteers.

In *Hydrolevel*, a professional association of mechanical engineers that issued product standards for boiler safety cut-off valves had given authority over the subcommittee responsible for that standard to a volunteer chairman employed by the major manufacturer of those valves. When an innovative competitive product appeared on the market, the subcommittee chairman contrived to have an interpretation issued declaring that the new product did not meet the accepted standard. The association's board of directors, officers, and senior staff apparently were unaware of the interpretation. As a result of it, the competing manufacturer could not sell its product and went out of business. It brought an antitrust challenge against the association in which a lower court awarded 7.5 million dollars in damages; later an appellate court affirmed the decision but ordered reconsideration of the damages.

In affirming the decision, the Supreme Court said it sought to "ensure that standard-setting organizations will act with care when they permit their agents to speak for them."[20] The Court repeatedly referred to the power that trade and professional associations have in affecting the entire economy of the country and noted that the mechanical engineers organization was virtually "an extra-governmental agency, which prescribes rules for the regulation and restraint of interstate commerce."[21] Justice Blackmun pointed out that associations are "rife with opportunities" to violate the antitrust laws.[22] The Court's principal concern was that the association had failed to implement any meaningful safeguards that would prevent its reputation from being used to hinder competition in the marketplace. Three dissenters argued that the Court's holding adopts an "unprecedented theory of antitrust liability . . . with undefined boundaries. . . ."[23] Nevertheless, the message to associations and boards, particularly those engaging in any form of self-regulation activities, is clear: they are strictly liable for ensuring that both volunteer and employed "agents" do not violate the antitrust rules through their participation in those association or board activities.

It is clear, then, that the legal climate for self regulation programs initiated and conducted by professional associations and boards has become chilled as a result of these five Supreme Court cases that have been decided and well-publicized in the past eight years, three of them in 1982 alone. In *Goldfarb, Professional Engineers,* and *Maricopa,* the Court has imposed the most restrictive antitrust analysis upon self-regulation programs, holding such programs *per se* anticompetitive and illegal without consideration of any justification for the programs (admittedly, all involved professional fees, which is not a factor in credentialing programs). In *AMA*, the Court has effectively affirmed, but has not explained, a decision that the Federal Trade Commission has authority over a major professional association; and legislative attempts to change that situation have not been successful. In *Hydrolevel*, the Court fashioned a sweeping new theory of antitrust liability, that of apparent authority, in the context of a professional association's product standards program which may well be adaptable to professional credentialing programs also.

Legal challenges to credentialing. Looking beyond the major Supreme Court cases, the legal "history" and current status of professional credentialing are revealed more specifically in informal federal antitrust enforcement agency pronouncements and in lower-court litigation that actually has involved credentialing issues. No extensive direction concerning professional credentialing, either involving certification and accreditation, has been provided by the two federal antitrust enforcement agencies. The Department of Justice rarely has challenged credentialing programs directly, although some years ago the department charged an association of pathologists with violations that involved accreditation of laboratories. In a settlement of the charges, the College of American Pathologists specifically was allowed to maintain "lawful, reasonable and nondiscriminatory technical and performance standards for the operation or accreditation of laboratories."[24]

More recently, the Department of Justice gave its advice to an association on a proposed professional certification program under the department's business review procedure, in which the government analyzes a proposed activity and indicates if the activity might be challenged on antitrust grounds. The National Audio-Visual Association, Inc., proposed to confer the title of "Certified Media Specialists" on qualifying individual professionals. In its advice to the association, indicating there would be no antitrust challenge, the Department of Justice relied on several aspects of the proposed program: Initial certification would be granted without examinations on the basis of successful completion of certain association-sponsored courses or on the basis of nine years of professional experience; recertification and courses would be open to members and nonmembers alike (although fees for nonmembers could be higher to reflect members' support of the activities through payment of dues); decertification would result only from failure to maintain certified status, not for ethical reasons;

the association would not discourage anyone from dealing with uncertified individuals and would not recommend individuals to customers or suppliers.[25]

The Federal Trade Commission has never challenged directly a voluntary professional credentialing program, but it has issued various advisories establishing principles that FTC would no doubt adhere to in professional credentialing cases.

Two years ago FTC refused to issue an advisory opinion (similar to the Department of Justice business review procedure) approving a proposed plan by the National Institute of Moving Consultants to certify professional "moving consultants," who were described as estimators and salesmen for moving services. FTC claimed that the purposes of the programs were too closely related to pricing of moving services, that standards for refusing or revoking certification were too vague, and that there were sufficient, less restrictive alternative methods for obtaining certification already available.[26]

The FTC has refused to issue an advisory opinion approving a proposed plan by the Board for Certification in Pedorthics for similar reasons. Although noting that "certification programs can be helpful to consumers by informing them that practitioners (and establishments) meet meaningful levels of occupational competency," the commission cited what it considered several failings in the proposed plan: first, required qualifications for applicants were too indefinite; second, there was no process for appealing adverse decisions to a body other than the credentialing group itself; and, third, certified professionals would be subject to "unreasonable" ethical restrictions such as a tacit ban on advertising.[27]

In the area of institutional accreditation, FTC has commented adversely to the Department of Education (which recognizes accrediting bodies in higher education) about the Liaison Committee for Medical Education (which accredits medical schools). In its statements in March 1977 and December 1978 to DOE, the FTC staff informally noted what it considered "major defects" in the medical school accrediting program of the Liaison Committee. FTC highlighted the perceived lack of "autonomy" of the Committee because of its various ties to the American Medical Association and the Association of American Medical Colleges. These ties include appointment of most committee members from AMA and AAMC, administration of the committee by those associations, lack of a separate office for the committee, and AMA and AAMC veto power over committee decisions.[28]

Again, it must be emphasized that neither the Department of Justice nor the FTC has yet spoken definitively on professional credentialing by associations or boards in cases brought by them and reviewed by courts. The agency views cited above have been expressed only in various informal pronouncements.

For the time being, the legal precedents for the adequacy of policies and procedures of professional credentialing programs must be found in lower-court nongovernmental cases, usually brought against an association or board by some individual or institution denied or excluded from credentialing.

One important federal appellate court accreditation case, for example, held that an educational credentialing body was justified in denying accreditation to a women's junior college on the basis that the college was a proprietary rather than a nonprofit institution. The court found no antitrust violation as alleged by the college in its lawsuit.[29]

Two interesting state court cases are also important because they extensively discuss issues of denial of individual certification to health care professionals.[30] In one case the denial was upheld; in the other it was overturned. In the case upholding denial, admission to a defendant psychological association (which was effectively a certification process) was not a prerequisite for employment as a professional psychologist because there already existed a separate state occupation licensing program. In the case overturning a denial, admission to a defendant medical society (again effectively a certification process) was a prerequisite for employment as a physician because, without admission, a physician could not use local hospital facilities.

The lesson is that court will likely look more closely and overturn more readily any certification decision by a professional entity where the certification is a prerequisite for employment as a professional.

A federal antitrust case is instructive as to the type and level of review of professional credentialing that courts will undertake. In *Veizaga v. National Board for Respiratory Therapy*,[31] several plaintiffs brought an action against a national association, its certifying board, and an outside contract firm that administered certification examinations for the board. The plaintiffs alleged that the three bodies improperly engaged in certification and registration of individuals as qualified to perform respiratory therapy. They also sued several hospitals that used the certification and registration criteria as the basis for hiring respiratory therapy professionals. The allegations of the plaintiffs also included racial discrimination charges and antitrust charges of group boycott and monopolization by the certifying groups.

The court never reached the merits of the complaint (which turned on the issue of whether the challenged credential is a *valid measure* of competence), but it carefully considered whether a certifying board, its related association or its contract testing service could benefit from any professional exemption from the antitrust laws, and whether the group boycott allegations must be considered *per se* illegal or subject to an analysis of the *reasonableness* to determine if they are illegal. The court set up a two-step process whereby the commerical and noncommercial aspects of the alleged certification restrictions were to be analyzed separately, with only the noncommerical aspects subject to an assessment of their reasonableness. The court dismissed out of hand the allegations that certification of respiratory therapists by the plaintiff group effected monopolization of that profession.

The most recent important lower-court decision affecting professional credentialing is *Marrese v. American Academy of Orthopaedic Surgeons*.[32] Here two surgeons were refused membership in a national medical specialty association (the requirements for which effectively involved a certification procedure) "without a hearing or a statement of reasons." They were unsuccessful in a state court challenge because the court found that membership was not "an economic necessity." In a subsequent federal court challenge, the association refused, as requested by the surgeons and then ordered by the court, to produce records relating to the membership denials. In an extremely limited review of only the procedural timing of the lower court's order against the association to produce the records, a federal court of appeals reversed that order and then opined at length (and without any precedent-setting implications) that the association's membership denial should be reviewed using the *reasonableness* test rather than the *per se* test and that, using such a test, only if the denial had a demonstratable "anticompetitive market effect" should it be considered illegal.

The facts in the *Marrese* case emphasized a dual analysis that is likely to be conducted in any challenge to a voluntary professional credentialing program. On one hand, a court will ordinarily review the reasonableness of the substantive criteria on which a credentialing decision has been based, as occurred in many of the cases discussed in this paper. Equally important, however, a court will obviously also review the fairness of the procedures employed by the credentialing organization in reaching its determination. Indeed, since court cases are themselves conducted according to extensive procedural requirements, it may be said that courts reviewing association or board professional credentialing determinations are perhaps more likely to focus on a review of the fairness of credentialing procedures (with which courts are familiar) than on review of the reasonableness of credentialing criteria (with which courts are likely to be less familiar, especially in highly technical or scientific professions).[33]

Federal involvement in credentialing. Direct involvement by the federal government in voluntary professional credentialing programs conducted by associations or boards has been very limited and has occurred only in certain federal activities related to accreditation in higher education or to certification of health care personnel.

As referred to earlier, the Department of Education currently "recognizes" private associations or boards that accredit education and training programs for higher education.[34] Recognition is provided to those accrediting entities that meet DOE-established criteria; accreditation by a recognized entity is often important or essential for education and training programs to receive certain federal grants.

In another area, the federal Consumer-Patient Radiation Health and Safety Act of 1981 was passed that year as part of the massive Omnibus Reconciliation Act.[35] The new law mandates that states ensure certification of individuals and accreditation of education for those individuals whose professional responsibilities include exposing patients to x-rays. The federal government is to establish guidelines and model state legislation to effect this certification and accreditation. Notably, the act specifies use by the states of existing private voluntary certification and accreditation programs, such as those conducted by associations or boards, as preferable to the establishment of government programs. This law represents the first direct federal endorsement and encouragement of professional credentialing, albeit in the very defined area of nonphysician and nondentist health care personnel who expose patients to x-rays.

Practical guidelines on "reasonableness." For this analysis of the antitrust context of the *reasonableness* criteria for certification and accreditation, and from an analysis of the specific agency and court actions regarding the challenged *reasonableness* of specific credentialing programs, one can loosely fashion some guidelines to help avoid a finding of unreasonableness when a certification or accreditation decision is challenged. The guidelines are, of course, not strict rules applicable in every case; but they do evolve from pronouncements by those in authority—particularly the federal antitrust enforcers.

First, the required qualifications criteria at the heart of every credentialing program must be *reasonable*. The following guidelines should be considered:

1. Criteria should be no more stringent than necessary to ensure minimum qualifications, especially where credentialing is of significant economic value. This would not, of course, prevent a certification or accreditation program from targeting its criteria to a higher level than minimum competence, such as for expertise or achievement, if the credentialing criteria are appropriate.
2. Criteria must not have the purpose or effect of unreasonably restricting or boycotting competitors. Ultimately, credentialing programs, to satisfy a reasonableness test, may have to demonstrate that they promote competition and are not merely neutral to it.
3. Criteria should be established only after reasonable notice and opportunity to participate is afforded to all those who may be affected by credentialing requirements, including potential candidates and users of their services. The more sun that shines on the process, the less likely are potential challenges.

In addition to reasonable criteria, credentialing programs must follow reasonable, objective, and impartial procedures. The following guidelines might be considered:

1. Participation should ordinarily be voluntary and open to those who are not members of the association or board.
2. All candidates should be treated equally; it may not be considered fair to exempt current credentialed individuals or institutions from new credentialing requirements.
3. Although general promotion of a credentialing program is not a problem, associations and boards should not promote credentialed individuals by name or disparage the noncredentialed.
4. Credentialing should not be used to "blackball" or limit the number of competitors arbitrarily.
5. Denial of credentialing should be made by written notice giving the reasons and offering the opportunity for an appeal in writing or at a hearing to be decided by a body other than the one that made the initial decision.
6. Decisions on applications should be made by an objective body not composed exclusively of credentialed individuals who might stand to gain financially from a decision affecting competitors.

The emerging law in this area points clearly to this rule—as voluntary professional credentialing programs become more accepted and thus useful for basing decisions on employment, advancement, assignment of tasks and reimbursement, those associations or boards responsible for the programs will be held to increasingly detailed governmental scrutiny of the substantive reasonableness and procedural fairness of the programs. Properly conducted professional credentialing programs based on the principle that credentialing exists primarily to benefit and protect the public offer perhaps the best methods of self-regulation of professional services as an alternative to government regulation. Ultimately, perhaps the most "reasonable" program of certification or accreditation is the one that best protects the public.

Conclusion

In conclusion, it seems evident that the current political climate is uniquely favorable to encouragement and advancement of self-regulatory programs, including those involving reasonable certification and accreditation. But to be successful, the programs must be enlightened with responsibility to society and regard for legal hazards. In a *Sports Illustrated* profile of the famous Amos Alonzo Stagg some years ago, it was described how the retired football coach would mow his lawn by hand: "He mowed it to death," his widow later said. One day a neighbor reported the neighborhood boys had been playing on it and ripping it up daily. "You'll never raise grass that way," the neighbor said. "Sir," answered Stagg, "I'm not raising grass; I'm raising boys."

Certification and self-regulation programs must not just foster *rules*. They can foster quality, competence, morality—*virtue*. When and if they do, and do so reasonably, they will grow and prosper like Stagg's boys.

References

1. H. Thoreau, *Civil Disobedience*.
2. Federalist Papers 10 and 51.
3. Will, *The Pursuit of Happiness and Other Virtues*, 45.
4. Bradley, The Role of Trade Associations and Professional Business Societies in America, 95–96 (1965).
5. 421 U.S. 733 (1975).
6. 421 U.S. at 778, 788 note 17.
7. 435 U.S. 679 (1978).
8. 435 U.S. at 700 (joined by Justice Rehnquist).
9. 73 L. Ed. 2d 48, 102 S. Ct. 2466 (1982).
10. 15 U.S.C. Section 1 (1976).

11. *See* L. Sullivan, Law of Antitrust, 165–166 (1977).
12. *Chicago Board of Trade v. United States*, 246 U.S. 231, 238 (1918).
13. See Taylor, Rule of Reason Cases Since NSPE, 51 Antitrust L.J. 185 (1982).
14. 246 U.S. 231, 238.
15. *American Medical Assn.*, FTC Docket No. 9064 (Oct. 12, 1979); 94 F.T.C. 701.
16. 15 U.S.C. Section 45(a)(1)(1976).
17. 638 F.2d 443 (2d Cir. 1980).
18. 102 S. Ct. 1744 (1982) (Justice Blackmun took no part in the consideration or decision of the case).
19. 72 L.Ed. 2d 330, 102 S. Ct. 1935 (1982).
20. 72 L.Ed. 2d at 347.
21. 72 L.Ed. 2d at 342.
22. 72 L.Ed. 2d at 343.
23. 72 L.Ed. 2d at 348 (dissenting opinion of Justices Powell, White and Rehnquist).
24. *United States v. College of American Pathologists*, 1969 CCH Trade. Cas. ¶72,825 (D.C. Ill. 1969).
25. U.S. Department of Justice Press Releases of October 31, 1978 with attached letter of John H. Shenefield, Assistant Attorney General, Antitrust Division.
26. FTC Advisory Opinion to National Institute of Moving Consultants, 89 F.T.C. 668 April 15, 1977.
27. FTC Advisory Opinion to Board for Certification in Pedorthics, 91 F.T.C. 1204 June 15, 1978.
28. FTC Press Release of December 11, 1978 with attached letter of Alan K. Palmer, Deputy Director, Bureau of Competition and statement of Daniel C. Schwartz, Acting Director, Bureau of Competition of March 24, 1977.
29. *Marjorie Webster Junior College v. Middle States Association of Colleges and Secondary Schools*, 432 F.2d 650 (D.C. Cir.), *cert. denied* 400 U.S. 965 (1970).
30. *Salter v. New York State Psychological Association*, 14 N.Y.S. 2d 100, 248 N.Y. 2d 867 (Ct. App. N.Y. 1964); *Falcone v. Middlesex County Medical Society*, 34 N.J. 582, 170 A.2d 791 (1961); see also *Bogus v. American Speech and Hearing Association*, 582 F.2d 277 (3d Cir. 1978).
31. 1977–1 CCH Trade Cases 61,274 (N.D. Ill. 1977).
32. 692 F.2d 1083 (7th Cir. 1982).

33. In *Silver v. New York Stock Exchange*, 373 U.S. 341 (1963), the U.S. Supreme Court invalidated the self-regulation activity of the New York Stock Exchange in denying telephone line access to two Texas securities dealers primarily because the NYSE used inadequate "due process" in its self-regulatory activity; in *Gibson v. Berryhill*, 411 U.S. 564 (1973), the U.S. Supreme Court addressed the licensing and ethical restraint activities of the Alabama Board of Optometrists and invalidated those activities in part because adequate procedures had not been used to minimize economic interest and professional bias; in *Falcone v. Middlesex County Medical Society*, 34 N.J. 582, 170 A.2d 791 (1961), a county medical society's decision to exclude a physician—and thereby deny hospital privileges—was overturned primarily on substantive grounds but the court also took issue with the fact that the decision was based upon an "unwritten rule" of the society; likewise in *Pinsker v. Pacific Coast Society of Orthodontists*, 12 C.3d 541, 526 P.2d 253 (1974), the court noted that exclusionary practices were unreasonable and because, "in applying a given rule in a particular case, the society acted in an unfair manner"; in *McCreery Angus Farms v. American Angus Association*, 379 F.Supp. 1008, 1010 (S.D. Ill. 1974), a case involving association rules for purebred livestock, the court specifically noted that private regulation must not be based upon "[o]ld, ad hoc, informal and pro forma committee procedures bordering upon the arbitrary"; finally, in *Blalock v. Ladies Professional Golf Association*, 359 F.Supp. 126, 1268 (N.D. Ga. 1973), a federal court overturned disciplinary action against a professional golfer (accused of moving up her ball in a tournament) because the application of ethical standards was based upon "a completely unfettered, subjective and discretionary determination of an exclusionary sanction by a tribunal wholly composed of competitors."
34. *See* Higher Education Act, 20 U.S.C. Section 1001, 1201 (1980).
35. 42 U.S.C. Section 1001 (1981).

Validity and Reasonableness

John S. Lloyd, Ph.D.

Introduction

Recently, law has encountered psychology in a number of ways. One of these encounter points has been in cases involving psychological testing and assessment procedures. I will review two areas in which the courts have encountered psychological tests: employment and educational testing. I will look at particular cases in these two areas to illustrate how courts have dealt with the concept of validity. By so doing, I intend to suggest that those who certify and accredit, although not yet involved in such court cases, might learn the rules of this game should the need to play it ever arise. To win in the adversarial legal arena—if you will pardon a mixed metaphor—the best offense may be a pound of prevention. I will begin with some definitions, then review pertinent cases first in employment testing and second in educational testing, and end with conclusions and recommendations.

Definitions

Certification and *Accreditation* are both methods of quality control through voluntary, professional peer review. They both are methods of evaluation. As such they involve comparing a measure of the present state (what is) with an agreed-upon standard (what ought to be). Certification entails an evaluation of individuals, accreditation the evaluation of programs or institutions. Both award peer recognition to those meeting or exceeding the standard and withhold it from those who do not. By definition, then, both certification and accreditation involve discrimination and exclusion. In doing so they run the risk of violating constitutional, statutory, and regulatory prohibitions against such acts. One way they could be found in violation of these prohibitions is if they were found to be unfair. The determination of whether such acts are unfair ultimately is up to our legal system to decide.

Certification and accreditation entail considerable professional expertise and judgment; first, in determining the standards, and second, in determining whether these standards have been met. Courts traditionally have been reluctant to become involved in areas of others' expertise and judgment, particularly those cases requiring expertise and judgment in another profession. Also, certification and accreditation have occupied a somewhat ambiguous legal position: e.g., are they private agencies or do they fulfill a quasi-governmental role? Are they trade associations or associations of learned professionals? Are they truly voluntary or are they really mandatory? Whether for these or other reasons, certification and accreditation have rarely been tested in court. Were they to be tried in court, it is likely that they would be themselves judged by two legal standards: validity and reasonableness.

When used in ordinary conversation, the words "validity" and "reasonableness" are readily understood. Like so many words in our language, they have more than one definition, and their meaning depends on the context in which they are used. Within the context of this conference, these words take on special meaning.

Our Anglo-American judicial system is founded on the principle of *reasonableness*. Judges and juries are supposed to be guided by reason and reasonableness in arriving at verdicts. Guilt or negligence must be proved "beyond a reasonable doubt." There must be reasonable cause for determination. To be reasonable is to be just, fair, or equitable; not immoderate or excessive; not arbitrary or capricious—in a word, prudent. The invisible hand of the "reasonable man (or woman)" is ubiquitous.

Validity, too, is a word frequently used in our legal system. It means to be binding or to have legal strength or force. We speak of the validity of contracts, convictions, obligations, oaths, passports, trademarks. In recent years, courts have relied increasingly on scientific evidence in their proceedings (e.g., Imwinkelried, 1981; Suggs, 1979). In this context, validity has a slightly different meaning; here it refers to the accuracy of a measurement. When applied to psychological tests or other evaluation procedures, validity means the degree to which the test or procedure actually measures what it is intended to measure.

If certification and accreditation were charged with violating the Sherman Antitrust Act, their procedures and their criteria might be subjected to a reasonableness test by the judiciary. However, the validity of their evaluation procedures might not be questioned. Since the antitrust implications of certification and accreditation are covered substantially elsewhere in this conference, I would like to direct your attention to two other arenas where courts have been setting precedents, using the "standards" of validity and reasonableness, which may have implications at least for certification. This is because specialty boards use written and, in most cases, oral examinations in their certifying process. These cases are in the areas of employment and educational testing and involve alleged violations of constitutional and civil rights.

Employment testing

The Civil Rights Act of 1964 prohibits discrimination on the basis of race, color, religion, sex, or national origin. Title VI of the act applies to education; Title VII applies to employment. Shortly after the enactment of the Civil Rights Act, the federal government established an Equal Employment Opportunity Commission (EEOC) to enforce Title VII. By 1966, EEOC had published a set of *Guidelines on Employment Testing Procedures;* these were revised in 1970. When the act was amended in 1972 to include government at well as private employees, there was already in existence at least one other set of regulations governing employment discrimination among federal agencies. It was not until 1978 that these different sets of regulations were combined into the *Uniform Guidelines on Employee Selection Procedures.*

Although educational discrimination cases might seem more relevant to certification and accreditation, employment discrimination cases have reached the Supreme Court and thus involve more precedent-setting decisions. Also, licensure and certification are covered by the *Uniform Guidelines* "to the extent that they may be covered by federal law." However, "Voluntary certification boards, where certification is not required by law, . . . are not subject to these guidelines." Since ABMS was involved in and at least partially responsible for getting that exemption, I will discuss employment testing cases first.

Basically, the *Uniform Guidelines* say that if an employer's policies and practices result in "adverse impact" on the employment opportunities of any protected minority group, the employer must demonstrate the validity of the practices or procedures by showing that such are related to job performance. (Conversely, the validity of selection procedures is not questioned if the procedures do not result in adverse impact!) This principle had been enunciated by the earlier version of the EEOC *Guidelines*. In addition to validating tests or other evaluation instruments used in selection, employers are required to consider alternative methods that might produce less adverse impact. The *Uniform Guidelines* not only apply to hiring decisions but also to promotion/demotion, retention, and the like. Although there are a number of controversial issues surrounding the *Uniform Guidelines* (e.g., what constitutes "adverse impact"), I will concentrate my attention on one issue, namely the definition of validity and job relatedness.

The *Uniform Guidelines* adopted minimum technical standards for validity studies. They were designed to conform (as were the earlier EEOC *Guidelines*) with another set of standards for educational and psychological tests that had been developed by the American Psychological Association in cooperation with the American Educational Research Association and the National Council on Measurement in Education. These standards were published in a document entitled *Standards for Educational and Psychological Tests* in 1974. They originally had been developed as "technical recommendations" for tests in 1954 and revised in 1966 and revised again in 1974. (The 1974 version of the *Standards* is currently being revised once again.) That these technical recommendations were never intended for use as legal standards can be seen from the following statement from the introduction to the 1974 *Standards:*

A final caveat is necessary in view of the prominence of testing issues in litigation. This document is prepared as a technical guide for those within the sponsoring professions; it is *not* written as law. What is intended is a set of standards to be used in part for self-evaluation by test developers and test users. (p. 8) (Emphasis in original.)

Yet these *Standards*, "written to promote excellence" (p. 7), were adopted as "minimum standards" in the *Uniform Guidelines*, and, as will become apparent later, eventually were adopted as legal standards by the Supreme Court.

Since the 1954 version of the *Standards*, validity has been held as of utmost importance in determining the adequacy of tests and other measuring devices. Here is what the 1974 *Standards* say about validity:

Questions of validity are questions of what may properly be inferred from a test score; validity refers to the appropriateness of inferences from test scores or other forms of assessment. The many types of validity questions can, for convenience, be reduced to two: (a) What can be inferred about what is being measured by the test? (b) What can be inferred about other behavior?

The first question inquires into the intrinsic nature of the measurement itself. . . .

The second question inquires into the usefulness of the measurement as an indicator of some other . . . behavior. In this context, the essential problem is to reach some conclusion about how well scores on the test are related to some other performance, and it is appropriate to speak of the closeness of the relationship. (p. 25)

Thus, validity can be logical or rational (the first question) and it can be empirical (the second question). It can be determined by reason alone as well as by scientific data (validity studies).

To continue to quote from the 1974 *Standards:*

There are various methods of validation, and all, in a fundamental sense, require a definition of what is to be inferred from the scores and data to show that there is an acceptable basis for such inferences.

It is important to note that validity is itself inferred, not measured. . . . It is . . . something that is *judged* as adequate, or marginal, or unsatisfactory. (p. 25) (Emphasis in original.)

Thus, while empirical evidence may be presented, the ultimate determination of validity rests on a reasoned judgment.

The *Standards* divide validity into three types—and these will be familiar to those of you in the audience who have attended our previous conferences—content, criterion-related, and construct validity. Which type of validity is most appropriate depends on the kinds of inferences one might wish to draw from test scores. The three types of validity are discussed independently for convenience; in reality they are interdependent. "A thorough study of a test may often involve information about all (three) types of validity." (p. 26)

Content validity is most commonly used for tests of knowledge or skill. "To demonstrate the content validity of . . . test scores, one must show that the behaviors demonstrated in testing constitute a representative sample of behaviors . . . (within) a desired performance domain." (p. 28) In an educational setting, the performance domain would be defined by the instructional objectives to be achieved. In an employment setting, the performance domain would be defined by a job analysis. In both cases, the performance domain must be explicit and specific so that the content of the test (the sample) can be checked against the content of the universe of tasks in the performance domain. Thus, content validity is determined by how representative the sample is of the universe—this is usually done by simple observation or comparison but it could involve statistical methods.

Although content validity usually does not require empirical evidence—it is primarily a rational judgment—the *Standards* are quick to point out the distinction between content validity and something called "face validity."

> It should be clear that content validity is quite different from face validity. Content validity is determined by a set of operations, and one evaluates content validity by the thoroughness and care with which these operations have been conducted. In contrast, face validity is a judgment that the requirements of a test merely *appear* to be relevant. (p. 29) (Emphasis in original.)

Yet to the reasonable judge, in making a determination about the validity of a selection procedure, the above distinction may appear academic.

According to the *Uniform Guidelines*, "Evidence of the validity of a test or other selection procedure by a content validity study should consist of data showing that the content of the selection procedure is representative of important aspects of performance on the job for which the candidates are to be evaluated." (Sec 5.B) "A selection procedure can be supported by a content validity strategy to the extent that it is a representative sample of the content of the job." (Sec 14.C.1) "There should be a job analysis which includes an analysis of the important work behavior(s) required for successful performance and their relative importance and, if the behavior results in work product(s), an analysis of the work product(s)." (Sec 14.C.2) "To demonstrate the content validity of a selection procedure, a user should show that the behavior(s) demonstrated in the selection procedure are a representative sample of the behavior(s) of the job in question or that the selection procedure provides a representative sample of the work product of the job." (Sec 14.C.4)

Criterion-related validity, according to the 1974 *Standards*, can be further divided into two subtypes: concurrent and predictive. One or both of these types of validity should be used "when one wishes to infer from a test score an individual's most probable standing on some other variable called a criterion." (p. 26) *Predictive validity* refers to performance on a criterion measured at some point in the future; *concurrent validity* refers to performance on a present criterion. In criterion-related validity studies, the correlation between performance on the test or other measurement and performance on the criterion is determined statistically (empirically). This correlation is known as a validity coefficient. Very simply, a judgment is made about the validity based on the relative magnitude of the validity coefficient.

According to the *Uniform Guidelines*, "Evidence of the validity of a test or other selection procedure by a criterion-related validity study should consist of empirical data demonstrating that the selection procedure is predictive of or significantly correlated with important elements of job performance." (Sec 5.B) In criterion-related validity studies, not only must a job analysis be performed, but measures of job performance must also be developed as a criterion.

The degree of relationship between selection procedure scores and criterion measures should be examined and computed, using professionally acceptable statistical procedures. Generally, a selection procedure is considered related to the criterion, for the purposes of these guidelines, when the relationship between performance on the procedure and performance on the criterion measure is statistically significant at the 0.05 level of significance, which means that it is sufficiently high as to have a probability of no more than one in twenty to have occurred by chance. (Sec 14.A.5)

Thus, the *Uniform Guidelines* set an objective standard for validity coefficients, while the test *Standards* do not.

Construct validity is the most difficult of the three types of validity to measure—and to define. According to the 1974 *Standards:*

Judgments of construct validity are useful in efforts to improve measures for scientific study of a (psychological) construct. . . . (Or) to learn more about the psychological qualities being measured by a test. . . .

Evidence of construct validity is not found in a single (criterion-related) study; rather, judgments of construct validity are based upon an accumulation of research results. . . . (pp. 29–30)

Correspondingly, the *Uniform Guidelines* say that "Evidence of the validity of a test or other selection procedure through a construct validity study should consist of data showing that the procedure measures the degree to which candidates have identifiable characteristics which have been determined to be important in successful performance in the job for which the candidates are to be evaluated." (Sec 5.B)

Construct validity is a more complex strategy than either criterion-related or content validity. . . . The user should be aware that the effort to obtain sufficient empirical support for construct validity is both an extensive and arduous effort involving a series of research studies, which include criterion-related validity studies and which may include content validity studies. . . . There should be a job analysis (for construct validity studies). This job analysis should show the work behavior(s) required for successful performance of the job, or the groups of jobs being studied, the critical or important work behavior(s) in the job or group of jobs being studied, and an identification of the construct(s) believed to underlie successful performance of these critical or important work behaviors in the job or jobs in question. . . . The user should show by empirical evidence that the selection procedure is validly related to the construct and that the construct is validly related to the performance of critical or important work behavior(s). (Sec 14.D.1–3)

I have spent considerable time on these definitions to the point of actually quoting from the 1974 *Standards* and the 1978 *Uniform Guidelines* because they serve as a background for the court interpretations of validity in the studies to be cited below.

The use of tests in employee selection in this country dates back to the latter part of the nineteenth century. It was not until the First World War, however, that the use of standardized paper-and-pencil tests for selection really caught on. By the 1950s, testing had already become a "big business." Prior to the 1960s, few questioned the validity of "professionally developed" tests for employment or any other use. The fact that minority groups generally performed poorly on these tests only served as "proof" that the tests were valid, because these results conformed to conventional wisdom—they seemed reasonable. But beginning in the late 1950s and continuing throughout the 1960s, and even the 1970s, the winds of public opinion shifted from blaming the discrepant results on the test takers to blaming the results on test developers and test users. This shift has resulted in the validity as well as the reasonableness of employment tests to come under judicial scrutiny.

Griggs v. Duke Power Co. (1971) was the first major challenge to employment testing to reach the Supreme Court on grounds of violating Title VII of the Civil Rights Act. In *Griggs*, a unanimous Supreme Court ruled that "great deference" should be paid the EEOC *Guidelines* in deciding such cases—and, indeed, it did so. In so doing, the Court overruled a district court decision, which had been concurred in by a court of appeals panel, that the EEOC *Guidelines* should not apply. The EEOC *Guidelines* had established a two-step process for employment testing litigation: First the plaintiff must establish a prima facie case of discrimination against protected minorities; then the burden of proof shifts to the defendant-employer to demonstrate that the test or other selection procedure is a "reasonable measure of job performance." (*Griggs*, p. 436) The Supreme Court also ruled in *Griggs* that discrimination could be proved regardless of intent.

Although the Supreme Court introduced the concept of job-relatedness into employment testing law in the *Griggs* case, it did little to clarify what the term meant. Thirteen black employees who were working in the lowest-paying jobs in the defendant company charged in a class-action suit that they had been placed in those jobs and were kept from advancing to higher-level jobs as a result of the company's selection procedures, which were discriminatory. Among the selection procedures used were two standardized general ability tests—Wonderlic Personnel Test (a measure of general intelligence) and the Bennett Mechanical Comprehension Test. The Court overruled the company's assertion that these tests were valid selection devices because they were professionally developed and standardized. The company had not conducted a job analysis nor attempted any validity studies; it had employed the tests in an attempt to upgrade the quality of the work force. The Court found that the tests were too "broad and general" to reasonably be predictive of performance in the unskilled jobs for which the plaintiffs had been hired. Thus, it appeared as if the Court had determined the validity of the tests on the basis of reasonableness (face validity), while calling for future employers to provide empirical evidence of job-relatedness.

In a case decided four years later (1975), the Supreme Court dealt with a similar set of issues. In *Albemarle Paper Co. v. Moody*, the Court maintained (but not unanimously) job-relatedness as a requirement for validity, and it again referred to the EEOC *Guidelines* as well as the testing *Standards*. The Court ruled that a test was job-related if it correlated significantly with important elements of work behavior. Job-relatedness must be demonstrated; it cannot be proved through "hearsay." Although the defendant-employer had conducted a last-minute concurrent validity study, the evidence for validity of the two standardized ability tests used (Revised Beta Exam [nonverbal intelligence] and Wonderlic Personnel Test) was criticized because of its reliance on subjective supervisors' judgments as a criterion measure and because of the absence of careful job analysis for all jobs for which the tests were used. In *Albemarle*, the Court even found criterion-related validity wanting when the EEOC *Guidelines* were used as a standard of comparison. According to one observer:

Both *Griggs* and *Albemarle* appeared to establish clear trends in the Court's application of Title VII to employment tests that had a disparate impact on minorities. They represented increasingly explicit endorsements of the EEOC guidelines interpreting the Civil Rights Act of 1964. Both opinions embodied rigorous standards of test validation and seemed to signal the Court's intention to require increasingly careful study of the relationship between an employment test and the job for which it was used. These decisions also seemed to put a large number of issues from a relatively specialized area—psychological test theory—squarely before the courts. Employers and their psychologists were given notice that "professionally developed" tests were not enough: the courts would actually examine the manner in which these professionals developed and used their tests. Indeed, the Supreme Court appeared willing—and able—to hold the practitioners of psychological testing to the highest standards of their profession. (*Haney*, 1982, p. 19)

That all seemed to turn about a year later when the Supreme Court decided *Washington v. Davis* (1976). The case was litigated under the Equal Protection Clause of the Constitution rather than under Title VII, which had been used in *Griggs* and *Albemarle*. *Davis* differed from *Griggs* and *Albemarle* in other important respects as well (e.g., plaintiffs in *Davis* were not employees but unsuccessful applicants; the jobs involved differed in terms of skill complexity). The Court decided in *Davis* that employment tests did not have to be related to job performance as was the case under Title VII, but merely had to show a reasonable basis for the tests in use. The Court agreed with a lower-court ruling that a test shown to be related to performance in an entry-level job training program was sufficient to satisfy the job-relatedness requirement—regardless of its relationship to subsequent job performance. Thus, the court seemed to draw a distinction between the validation requirements for cases brought under Title VII and those brought under the Constitution.

In a nontesting case the same year (*General Electric v. Gilbert* [1976]), which did involve Title VII, the Supreme Court held that while the *EEOC Guidelines* "constitute a body of experience and informed judgment to which courts and litigants may properly resort for guidance" (pp. 141-142), they do not have the power to control, only to persuade. In at least two post-*Albemarle* decisions, the Supreme Court has been less dogmatic about the methods to be used in proving job validity. Whether content validity or criterion-related validity will satisfy the Court remains a question.

A look at lower-court decisions regarding employment testing and Title VII does not shed much light on the answer. Most court decisions have ruled against the employment tests involved. Thus there is some guidance about what evidence will *not* suffice but little guidance regarding what will. Among the deficiencies cited by the lower courts have been inadequate job analysis, use of unvalidated cutoff scores, absence of significant statistical correlation, the use of weak or inappropriate criteria, weaknesses of correspondence between skills tested and domain of job skills, and inadequate attempt to identify an alternative with less adverse impact. (*Wigdor*, 1981, pp. 63-64)

Wittingly or not, these employment testing decisions have led to (or confirmed) the now widely held belief that no test, no matter how well developed and validated, can pass muster in court when held up to the "minimum standards" promulgated in the *Uniform Guidelines*. As a consequence, many employers appear to be discontinuing the use of tests in the employee selection process in favor of less costly alternatives—either voluntarily or by fiat. A case in point is the Professional and Administrative Career Examination (PACE) used by the federal government to select employees from among college graduates. In 1979, a class-action Title VII suit was brought against the government's Office of Personnel Management (OPM) by four minority plaintiffs (*Luevano v. Campbell* [1981]). PACE had been in use since 1976, and numerous studies of the exam had been conducted so that there was considerable evidence in favor of its content, construct, and criterion-related validity. Yet the foundation for the *Luevano* suit was that PACE was not validated in accordance with the *Uniform Guidelines*. Specifically, although all 118 jobs for which PACE was used had been analyzed prior to validation, only 27 of the jobs had been selected for more intensive job analysis; only four jobs had been included in empirical validity studies; only concurrent validity studies had been conducted, when predictive validity studies would have been preferred; and no alternative selection devices had been considered (*Olian & Wilcox*, 1982, p. 665). In November 1981, a consent decree was agreed to which called for the phasing out of PACE over the next three years and the search for alternatives which do not create (or create less) adverse impact, as PACE had done. In exchange, OPM denied guilt in using PACE in violation of Title VII. Even though the case was settled out of court and theoretically sets no legal precedent, its long-range implications on employment testing remain to be seen. Would OPM have been able to demonstrate the validity of PACE had the case gone to trial? Can alternatives to tests like PACE be found? At what cost? How valid will they be compared to paper-and-pencil instruments like PACE? Will less-valid alternatives be preferred because they create less adverse impact? What about reverse discrimination?

Thus, in deciding employment testing cases since the early 1970s, the courts, including the Supreme Court, have been inconsistent in their judgments about validity. Although the need for job-relatedness seems to have been a constant in these cases, courts' judgments about whether rational or empirical validity studies will suffice seems to depend on the particular case. For example, recently the Supreme Court refused to review two appellate court decisions involving validation of employment tests.

In the first case (*Firefighters Institute for Racial Equality v. City of St. Louis* [1981]), the appellate court required the defendant to provide empirical evidence of validity when the former had argued that the paper-and-pencil and simulation selection devices had rational validity. In the second case (*Guardians Association of New York City v. Civil Service Commission* [1981]), the appellate court found that, even though a criterion-related validity study was feasible, appropriate content validity evidence would have been satisfactory.

What does all this have to do with certification and accreditation in medicine? After all, don't the *Uniform Guidelines* specifically exclude "voluntary certification boards" from their definition of "test users" who are responsible for conforming? But employers who use certification in making employment decisions are not exempt. An employer has been found by a Maryland District Court to be anyone "who significantly affects access of any individual to employment opportunities, regardless of whether that party be technically described as an 'employer' of an aggrieved individual as that term has generally been defined at common law." (*Vanguard Justice Society v. Hughes* [1979]). And, as has been seen, the *Veizaga v. National Board of Respiratory Therapy* suit was brought against a voluntary certifying agency not only on antitrust grounds, but also on employment discrimination (Title VII) grounds. Also named as co-defendants in this suit were nine Chicago hospitals, a test service agency which assisted the board, and the associated membership society. Plaintiffs charged that the defendant board's "examinations discriminated against minorities and had the effect of excluding such persons from consideration in employment and promotion decisions by hospitals. . . . Plaintiffs submitted numerous job advertisements placed by the hospitals in Chicago newspapers for positions requiring 'registered, certified, or eligible' practitioners." (*Bryant*, 1981, pp. 144–145) Fortunately, or unfortunately, this suit was settled out of court and never brought to trial—thus, no legal precedent was set. Neither was guidance given on the issue of whether certification and accreditation agencies are subject to the same fate as employers under the *Uniform Guidelines*. Who is responsible for validating certification evaluation procedures? Would job relatedness be an issue in a Title VII suit against a certifying board? If so, how would a job analysis be done? What type of validity study—rational or empirical—would be required by the court? Could an accrediting agency whose standards involve the employment of board certified personnel as program directors be implicated in a suit against certifying boards?

Educational testing

The other area that bears watching by certification and accreditation agencies is related to educational testing cases. Tests and other methods of assessment permeate our educational system—both standardized and nonstandardized (teacher-made)—for purposes of determining achievement of past learning and aptitude for future learning, for both formative and summative evaluations.

The classification of students by the use of standardized testing has been widespread. It was originally accepted as a more objective, scientific means of grouping students and an improvement in practice over former reliance on the subjective evaluations of teachers and administrators. . . .

Beginning in the 1960s, however, a series of legal challenges indicated that the balance of public opinion had begun to shift away from this generally positive view of standardized testing. . . .

By the end of the 1970s, many uses of standardized testing had been linked, whether rightly or wrongly, with the notion of unfair treatment in the educational setting. In this atmosphere of ever-increasing heavy judicial scrutiny, the survival of testing as a factor in educational decision making has come to depend on its compliance with an extremely complex body of law being adjudicated in courts throughout the country. (Hollander, 1982, pp. 196–197)

As in employment testing, constitutional, statutory, and regulatory requirements exist that protect educational test takers. Two types of cases have involved educational testing and validity: those in which tests were used to place students in classes for the educable mentally retarded (EMR) and minimum competency testing for (MCT) high school graduation. Landmark cases of both types have gone to trial on grounds of alleged violations of the Fourteenth Amendment and Title VI. Although none of these cases has yet reached the Supreme Court, it is instructive to examine them more closely, particularly as they involved the question of test validity—and I shall do so next.

With regard to cases involving placement of students in EMR classes, two recent decisions stand out. Both cases were decided during the 1979–80 school year by federal district courts in California and Illinois. Both relied on an earlier decision in the District of Columbia (*Hobson v. Hansen* [1967]) which involved a charge that the use of a standardized group intelligence (IQ) test resulted in a disproportionate number of minority students being placed in special handling classes.

In the first of the two landmark EMR cases (*Larry P. v. Riles* [1979]), the court found in favor of the plaintiffs and against the California State

Department of Education on a number of grounds. The one relevant to this presentation had to do with the validity of using a standardized, individually administered IQ test (Wechsler Intelligence Scale for Children) for placing students in EMR classes. In *Larry P.* the judge heard the testimony of expert witnesses for both sides on the validity of the test in question and decided that the defendant had not provided sufficient evidence that the test had been validated for the purpose for which it was being used. The defendant was unable to counter the plaintiff's arguments (bolstered with data) that the only empirical evidence for the validity of the IQ test used was based on an inappropriate criterion—achievement test scores. The only appropriate criterion, the plaintiff argued, was classroom grades—and proceeded to introduce results from one study conducted within the state that showed a nonsignificant correlation between the test and that criterion. Because the defendant could not muster sufficient empirical evidence to the contrary, either through studies done within the state or through published studies cited by expert witnesses, the court found in favor of the plaintiff.

In addition, the judge found the test to be culturally biased against black students. Cultural bias was inferred from the fact that the test was never designed to eliminate it. Although the test norms had been standardized on a population of white middle-class children and later re-standardized on a mixed-race population, it had never been standardized on all black children. Bias also was inferred from lower validity coefficients for black students in the studies cited above.

In stark contrast to the California case, the judge in the other landmark EMR case in Illinois found that the same IQ (WISC/WISC-R) test used for a similar purpose was *not* culturally biased against black students. In this case (*Parents in Action on Special Education [PASE] v. Hannon*, [1980]), instead of relying almost solely on the testimony of expert witnesses and arguments by attorneys (as was done in the California case), the judge examined two standardized, individually administered IQ tests (WISC/WISC-R and Stanford-Binet Intelligence Scale) item by item and on the basis of his subjective judgment ruled them biased or not. In the process, he read every item (400+) from these two widely used IQ tests along with their answers into the court record! This may have the effect of invalidating these two IQ tests as they are currently used. In the end, the judge ruled that only eight items on one test and one item on the second test were suspect; therefore, the IQ tests were not discriminatory. He did not rule on the validity of the test for placement in EMR classes; therefore, no judicial standard was employed.

These two EMR cases demonstrate that different judges may use different means to evaluate the merits of the same educational test and come to different conclusions—both of which seem reasonable under the circumstances.

Perhaps MCT cases are more relevant for certification. MCT or basic skills testing programs have been initiated in three fourths of the states to determine who shall be awarded high school diplomas. The landmark case in this arena was *Debra P. v. Turlington* (1979). This was a class-action lawsuit brought by ten black twelfth-grade public school students in Florida challenging the state's functional literacy exam which they had failed and thereby would not receive a diploma—i.e., not be certified as functionally literate. In distinction to the EMR cases, the test in this case was a paper-and-pencil, group-administered exam recently constructed for the state with the assistance of a test service agency (ETS) especially for this purpose.

Regarding the validity of the test, the court relied on expert testimony. The court attempted to determine whether the test could reasonably be used to evaluate the skill objectives established by the state board of education. The court was persuaded that the objectives were adequately covered by the test and that the test had adequate content validity. The plaintiffs also charged that the test was culturally biased against black students, but the court found the preponderance of evidence to the contrary.

The trial court reached its verdict in the summer of 1979, declaring the test to be both fair and valid but placing a four-year moratorium on its use as a diploma requirement on the grounds that the MCT had been put into place too quickly and thereby "caught" some students who had been educated under previous disadvantaged (segregated) conditions. Both sides in the case appealed the verdict. Two years later (1981), a three-judge appellate court, in reviewing the same evidence and testimony as the trial court, found in favor of the plaintiffs and sent the case back to the trial court for a new hearing at which the defendant (state) must demonstrate that the content measured by the test was not only specified by the state objectives but also was the content *actually taught* in the schools. This is clearly a new definition of content validity.

At about the same time as the *Debra P.* case was being reviewed by the appeals court, a similar case was being tried in a neighboring state (*Anderson v. Banks* [1981]). Here an MCT program in a Georgia county school system was being challenged as unconstitutional. No civil rights violations were alleged. The judge ruled in favor of the plaintiffs. On the question of the validity of the competency test, the judge, noting the *Debra*

P. appeals court decision just six weeks earlier, decided that the defendant was unable to show proof that the test measured what was actually taught, i.e., possessed "instructional validity."

The full implications of these decisions on other MCT programs as well as other courts' definitions of content validity in educational testing cases remain to be seen. How does one determine what is actually taught? What is to prevent teaching to the test? Is content validity the same as or different than instructional validity? Can instructional validity be determined for a group of students, or must it be done for each individual student?

Thus, in the educational testing arena, there have been fewer cases involving the validity question and, because they have been tried in the lower courts and not (yet) beyond, have involved less precedent-setting decisions than those cases involving employment testing. The former cases also appear to be more benign in their requirements with regard to validity, relying more on rational, content-validity approaches instead of insisting on empirical, criterion-related validity studies. They have not had regulations such as the *Uniform Guidelines* to "assist" them in their judgments, but the 1974 *Standards* have been available. There has not been a consistent issue like job-relatedness to contend with. Although the question whether instructional validity is a part of content validity or a separate type of validity has been raised, it remains to be seen whether all educational competency tests will have to be validated against not only the educational objectives but also the content of what is actually taught. In any event, the courts seem to have favored reasonableness in their judgments of test validity in educational testing cases.

Conclusions and recommendations

Validity appears to have recently taken its place, second only to, if not alongside, reasonableness as a judicial standard in cases involving tests and other evaluation instruments. Validity and reasonableness are both judgments based on the facts and circumstances brought forth in a court of law. As such, they are no more or less fallible than other human decisions made under conditions of uncertainty.

Abundant evidence from psychological research . . . suggests that in many contexts decision makers' intuitive, common-sense judgments depart markedly and lawfully (in the scientific sense) from the actual probabilities. People use a number of simplifying (cognitive processing) operations, called "heuristics," to reduce the complexity of information which must be integrated to yield a decision. These simplifying strategies often lead to errors in judgment. . . .

On other occasions decision heuristics may facilitate proper and efficient decision making. The accuracy of the judgments produced by heuristic processes depends to a great extent on the nature of the question at hand. . . .

One fact, however, can be unambiguously derived from the extensive literature on the psychology of decision making. People tend to be overconfident in their judgments. Not only do individuals tend to overestimate how much they already know (citation omitted), but they also tend to underestimate what they have just learned from facts presented in a particular context. Once they do know an outcome, people fail to appreciate how uncertain they were before learning of it. . . .

These findings have strong implications for the legal process. (*Saks & Kidd*, 1980-81, pp. 127-144)

In their quest for certain justice, judges may overlook or deny their heuristic biases. One conclusion I reach from the above cursory review of testing cases is that there exists tremendous potential for such biases when judgments about validity and reasonableness are involved. Whether and what errors in judgment were involved in the testing cases reviewed will never be known. What seems clear is that the decisions about the validity of the tests—even when the same tests were involved in different cases—were inconsistent. The problem with this inconsistency is that it makes predicting future judicial behavior difficult.

There are a number of reasons for such inconsistency beyond judgmental bias. First, the facts and circumstances of each case differed. Second, the involvement of testing and test validity in the legal system is a relatively recent phenomenon, and, therefore, there exist few precedents on which to rely for guidance in making judgments. In the absence of such precedents, the courts have relied on professional standards regarding validity—standards that were never intended for that purpose. Even though validity is a central concept in the 1974 *Standards* (as it had been in earlier versions), there still is considerable disagreement among professionals within the fields of psychology and education regarding the meaning of the concept. For example, there is a growing doubt that distinguishing between three (or more) types of validity has served a useful purpose. Even though construct validity has been difficult to conceptualize and operationalize, the opinion is being expressed that all validity is in the final analysis construct validity. Content validity has received considerable criticism of late because of its multiple meanings (to wit *Debra P.*), and there is growing pressure for discarding it as a form of validity. Regarding criterion-related validity, disagreement exists regarding the practical (as opposed to statistical) significance of a validity coefficient. Can the results of validity studies carried out in one setting be generalized to others? Given the degree of disagreement about validity among those outside the legal system who created it, is it any wonder that judges are inconsistent?

Even though certification and accreditation agencies have been relatively immune from court battles at least in the recent past, these agencies should take note of what has happened in court cases in analogous arenas. If they were to have to go to court in the future, would they be able to defend their evaluation procedures against these two standards? If accreditation were involved, would the validity as well as the reasonableness of their evaluation procedures be scrutinized? Would validity be judged on rational or empirical grounds? Would certification be judged on the basis of its ability to evaluate past educational objectives (content validity) or on the basis of its ability to predict future job performance (predictive validity)? If the former, would instructional validity be involved—i.e., would certification have to consist of an evaluation of what was actually taught, as well as what was supposed to be taught? If criterion-related validity were required, what would constitute an adequate job analysis and criterion measure of job performance?

If my analysis of court cases involving employment and educational testing is correct and applicable, any one of the above may be possible depending on the circumstances of the case. If charged with violating the Fourteenth Amendment, a purely rational approach to demonstrating validity may be necessary. If charged with violating the Civil Rights Act, discrimination will have to be proved by the plaintiff(s). If the plaintiff(s) is (are) successful, a rational approach to demonstrating validity will be most likely. However, if discrimination is charged under Title VII, rational and empirical evidence of validity may be required. In any event, the standard of reasonableness will be applied—and, it is to be hoped, prevail.

What should certification and accreditation agencies do? First, continue to stay out of trouble. Second, certification agencies should begin (or continue) to gather evidence of the validity of their evaluation procedures— first rational evidence (content validity), then empirical evidence (criterion-related validity). In addition to ensuring their reasonableness, accreditation agencies should begin to examine the validity of their evaluation procedures. Are accredited programs or institutions better than those that are not accredited? If so, in what ways? If not, should they be?

Finally, how much evidence of validity is enough? Be reasonable!

Summary

If they are not already doing so, accreditation and certification agencies, especially the latter, should watch what happens in two arenas in which testing has been on trial in recent years—employment testing cases and educational testing cases. In decision making about cases in these two arenas, validation as well as reasonableness has been used as a judicial standard. Both validation and reasonableness are easy to define in the abstract, but, in their application to concrete circumstances, their meaning becomes mercurial. As one looks across a number of testing cases, the courts have been inconsistent in their application of these standards. They have been inconsistent because both standards rely on fallible human judgment. In the future, trials involving tests and other evaluation procedures will more than likely continue to be scrutinized by these same two standards of validity and reasonableness. What remains uncertain is what type of validation evidence—rational or rational and empirical—will be required by the courts, and how much evidence of validity will be enough?

Certifying boards should continue to amass evidence of the validity and reasonableness of their evaluation procedures—both rational and empirical evidence. With regard to the former, certifying boards should explicitly define and update the domain of competence in their respective specialties. Then their certifying examinations should be developed as representative samples from that domain. Many boards have begun to do so. With regard to empirical evidence, certifying boards should conduct validity studies regarding the relationship of their certifying examinations to other measures of competence and performance during training and during practice. Several boards have begun to do so. Accrediting agencies should also look to the validity as well as the reasonableness of their procedures. Are the products of accredited programs or institutions better than the products of nonaccredited programs or institutions? As for the courts, I would counsel reasonableness in their expectations with regard to the validity of tests and other evaluation procedures, especially regarding empirical validity. Validity studies are extremely difficult and costly to conduct. They generally lead to equivocal results for reasons that are numerous and not yet entirely clear.

References

American Psychological Association, American Educational Research Association, National Council on Measurement in Education. *Standards for Educational and Psychological Tests.* American Psychological Association, Washington, D.C., 1974.

Bryant, S. K. "Voluntary Certification and the Uniform Guidelines on Selection Procedures: A Potential Problem for Personnel Managers."

Health Policy & Education, 2:135–152, 1981.

Equal Employment Opportunity Commission, Civil Service Commission, Department of Labor, Department of Justice. *Uniform Guidelines on Employee Selection Procedures.* Federal Register, August 25, 1978, 43(166), 38290–38315.

Hallander, P. "Legal Context of Educational Testing." In Wigdor, A., Graner, W. R. (Eds.) *Ability Testing: Uses, Consequences, and Controversies.* Part II. Washington, D.C.: National Academy Press, 1982.

Haney, C. "Employment Tests and Employment Discrimination: A Dissenting Psychological Opinion." *Industrial Relations Law Journal*, 5:1–86, 1982.

Imwinkelried, E. J. "A New Era in the Evolution of Scientific Evidence—A Primer on Evaluating the Weight of Scientific Evidence." *William & Mary Law Review*, 23:261–290, 1981.

Olian, J. D., Wilcox, J. C. "The Controversy over PACE: An Examination of the Evidence and Implications of the Luevano Consent Decree for Employment Testing." *Personnel Psychology*, 35:659–676, 1982.

Saks, M. J., Kidd, R. F. "Human Information Processing and Adjudication: Trial By Heuristics." *Law & Society Review*, 15:123–160, 1980–81.

Suggs, D. L. "The Use of Psychological Research by the Judiciary: Do the Courts Adequately Assess the Validity of the Research?" *Law & Human Behavior*, 3:135–148, 1979.

Wigdor, A. "Psychological Testing and the Law of Employment Discrimination." In Wigdor, A., Garner, W. R. (Eds.) *Ability Testing: Uses, Consequences, and Controversies.* Part II. Washington, D.C.: National Academy Press, 1982.

Cases cited

Albemarle Paper Co. v. Moody, 422 U.S. 405 (1975).

Anderson v. Banks, 520 F. Supp. 472 (1981).

Debra P. v. Turlington, 474 F. Supp. 244 (1979).

Firefighters Institute for Racial Equality v. City of St. Louis, 616 F. 2d 350 (1980).

General Electric v. Gilbert, 429 U.S. 125 (1976).

Griggs v. Duke Power Co., 401 U.S. 424 (1971).

Guardians Association of New York City v. Civil Service Commission, 630 F. 2d 79 (1980).

Hobson v. Hansen, 269 F. Supp. 401 (1967).

Larry P. v. Riles, 495 F. Supp. 926 (1979).

Luevano v. Campbell, D.C. District Court #79-0271 (February 24, 1981).

Parents in Action on Special Education v. Hannon, 506, F. Supp. 831 (1980).

Vanguard Justice Society v. Hughes, 471 F. Supp. 670 (1979).

Washington v. Davis, 426 U.S. 229 (1976).

Standards Affecting Training Programs

Joseph Neff Ewing, Jr., J.D.

Introduction

This paper will briefly summarize some of the important aspects of the standards for the organization and conduct of medical residency training programs. There are many rules and regulations under both state and federal law covering matters such as the registration of residents and of training programs and reimbursement for the patient care rendered by residents and for the cost of their training. Those rules and regulations, however, do not have a direct impact on the way in which a residency program is operated, and this paper will not refer to them, except incidentally. The standards for the operation of such a program are found principally in the *Essentials of Accredited Residencies in Graduate Medical Education* adopted by the Accreditation Council for Graduate Medical Education.

The "residency" is a product of the age of specialization in medicine and is an outgrowth of the need for further education and training in the various specialized fields of medicine after graduation from medical school. Because completion of an approved residency is a condition of eligibility for a physician to sit for one of the 23 specialty board examinations, the bodies involved in the development and approval of residency programs have a considerable impact on the health care market place. In the case of a hospital, for example, receipt of certain types of federal funds and research grants is conditioned on having an approved residency program. In addition, hospitals with approved programs benefit financially, since residents provide a relatively inexpensive source of medical manpower whose services rendered in conjunction with an approved program are reimbursable.

Residency program approval, therefore, is a matter of considerable import, not only to hospitals but also to physicians to whom specialty board certification is of increasing significance. Also, the number of programs approved in particular specialties and their location can affect the market for medical services, as they can effectively determine the number, type, and distribution of specialists in practice.

Accreditation council for graduate medical education

The development of residency training programs is relatively recent in the long history of the practice of medicine, and the approval, or "accreditation," of such programs is even more recent. Some of the principal events in this connection are:

1914 — First list of hospitals with approved internships published by the Council on Medical Education of the AMA.

1919 — *The Essentials Of An Approved Internship* first published.

1920 — The Council on Medical Education of the AMA created 15 committees to recommend the training necessary for expertness in various specialties.

1923 — *Principles Regarding Graduate Medical Education* published.

1927 — First listing of residency training programs published by AMA.

1928 — The House of Delegates of the AMA approved the first *Essentials of Approved Residencies and Fellowships*.

1937 — The American College of Surgeons began a program to set standards for surgical education.

1940 — The Council on Medical Education of the AMA was developing cooperative arrangements with ten of the certifying boards for reviewing residency programs.

1952 — A proposal was made to the Council on Medical Education of the AMA that committees be developed in cooperation with the certifying boards to act for both groups in approval of hospitals for residency training. This led to the residency review committees.

1972 — The Liaison Committee on Graduate Medical Education was formed by the AMA and four other organizations.

1975 — The accreditation of residency training programs came under the umbrella of The Liaison Committee on Graduate Medical Education.

The approval, or "accreditation" of residency training programs is now under the aegis of the Accreditation Council for Graduate Medical Education (ACGME) and its Residency Review Committees. The ACGME is made up of five sponsors: the American Board of Medical Specialties, the American Medical Association, the American Hospital Association, the Association of American Medical Colleges, and The Council of Medical Specialty Societies along with one representative from the Resident Physicians Section of the AMA, one public member, and one nonvoting federal member.

There is a residency review committee for each of the specialties, and each such committee consists of representatives appointed by the Council on Medical Education of the AMA, by the specialty board concerned, and, in most cases, by a national professional association of the specialty field involved. ACGME accreditation is granted for training programs only in specialty fields in which the 23 recognized specialty boards grant certificates.

Although the number of approved residency *programs* has decreased in recent years (there were 4,573 such programs as of September 1, 1982), the number of residency *positions* has increased from 5,118 in 1940 to 73,094 offered for the 1983–84 year. In a survey conducted by the Association of American Medical Colleges in 1979, 93 percent of the graduating seniors who responded indicated that they intended to complete a residency program and meet the requirements to be certified.

Accreditation and review procedures

The process for accreditation and review of residency training programs is set forth in detail in the Directory of Residency Training Programs published each year by the American Medical Association and popularly known as the "Green Book." Accreditation of a residency program indicates that it meets the general requirements and the special requirements of the *Essentials of Accredited Residencies,* which are also set forth in the Green Book.

On receipt of an application for accreditation of a new program, or at the time for the periodic review of one or more ongoing programs at a given hospital, a member of the ACGME staff visits the hospital to make a survey of the institution and of the programs under review. He submits a report and the other information furnished by the program directors to the appropriate residency review committees, which then make recommendations to the ACGME for denial of accreditation, for provisional accreditation, or for full accreditation or take the final action themselves if accreditation authority has been granted to those residency review committees by the ACGME.

Many state regulatory boards become involved at the review stage. In Pennsylvania, for instance, the regulations provide that the state Board of Medical Education and Licensure works cooperatively with the Council on Medical Education of the AMA in evaluating and approving training programs in the state (49 Pa. Code § 17.63). The state board may send a representative to be present during formal review sessions by any Residency Review Committee (49 Pa. Code § 17.65), and each hospital has the affirmative duty to inform the board when a residency program has been approved, probationed, or disapproved and must furnish a report to the board annually giving the names of its residents and other enumerated information regarding them. (49 Pa. Code 17.62).

Any program director who is dissatisfied with the decision of the ACGME or of the residency review committee with regard to accreditation of his program may ask for reconsideration of that decision by the residency review committee and, if still dissatisfied, may have an appeal hearing before a panel of program directors selected by the chairman of the ACGME. The final decision on the appeal is made by the full ACGME after receiving the recommendations of the hearing panel and of the ACGME Subcommittee on Appeals.

The special requirements for each specialty are developed by the residency review committee for that specialty and approved by the ACGME after review and recommendations by the sponsoring organizations of that residency review committee. The document sets forth the requirements for the essential educational content, instructional activities, patient-care responsibilities, supervision, and facilities that should be provided by any program in that particular specialty, and are revised frequently as the practice of that specialty develops.

The accreditation and review of residency training programs give rise to the same antitrust considerations as does certification. Although the requirements and essentials are designed to maintain certain levels of quality in the training of specialists, they also can have an effect on competition. First, because one essentially private organization controls program approval, and hence access to eventual financial benefits for the specialists, the process according to which programs are approved merits close scrutiny. Second, because residency program approval can so dramatically affect the supply and mix of specialist manpower, it is important to assess whether the supply is being manipulated and by whom and for what reason. Since the antitrust and due process aspects are being covered by other speakers in this conference, I will not explore them further here.

General requirements

The general requirements of the *Essentials of Accredited Residencies* delineate training program requirements and responsibilities which are common to all residency review committees, institutions, and programs regardless of specialty. They have been established by the ACGME in collaboration with the residency review committees and their sponsoring organizations, and are approved by each of the five sponsoring organizations of the ACGME.

A comprehensive revision of the general requirements became effective July 1, 1982. Among other changes, increased emphasis was placed on the educational aspects of the training programs. This change was thought necessary because, too often, the patient-care duties of residents have taken precedence over their education and instruction. Although the primary mission of a hospital must be excellence in patient care, it has a secondary mission with regard to its residents—that of education, and frequently those two missions come into conflict, particularly with regard to economics and with regard to physician coverage for the patients of the institution.

The new general requirements stress the notion of corporate commitment and the responsibility of all elements of the institution for the teaching of its resident physicians. The board of directors, the administration, the medical departments, and the teaching staff must all demonstrate their commitment to the graduate medical education programs provided by the institution:

1. By a written statement setting forth the reasons why the institution sponsors graduate medical education. (1.1.1)
2. By a description of the process by which institutional resources are distributed for educational purposes. (1.1.2)
3. By an operational system involving the program directors, based on institutional policies, establishing how the sponsored programs provide for:

a. The appointment of teaching staff;
b. The selection of residents;
c. The apportionment of resident positions among programs;
d. The supervision of residents;
e. The evaluation and advancement of residents;
f. The dismissal of residents whose performance is unsatisfactory; and
g. The assurance of due process for residents and teaching staff. (1.1.3)
4. By a periodic analysis of each program. (1.1.4).

More specific detail with regard to each of these provisions is given in the general requirements, and I am attaching to my paper for publication in the proceedings of this conference a sample form of a statement on institutional responsibility that can be adopted by the various bodies of the institution I have mentioned above to provide the documentation necessary under the general requirements.

Compliance with each of the general requirements, as well as with each of the applicable special requirements, is checked each time a training program is reviewed by the ACGME. A tabulation of the types of deficiencies noted by the residency review committee in the programs operated by one specialty during a recent five-year period shows deficiencies in the following general requirements areas, in addition to those found in the training for that particular specialty:

Faculty
Leadership and supervision
Recruitment—critical mass
Special programs for FMGs
Formal conferences and seminars
Poor academic environment
Lack of well-structured and supervised training assignments
Inadequate correlative training and experience

Provisions are set forth in great detail in the general requirements with regard to program organization and responsibilities, the eligibility and selection of residents, the responsibilities of institutions and training programs, the responsibilities of resident physicians, and the form of written agreement that the ACGME urges institutions to enter into with their residents. I will make reference to only a few of those provisions here.

First, is one of very limited applicability, but one that can cause great distress to program directors and physicians seeking board certification. That is the provision that graduates from institutions in the United States accredited by the American Osteopathic Association are eligible to enter residency programs accredited by the ACGME. (3.1.2). A footnote to that provision states that holders of the degree of Doctor of Osteopathy are not admissible for board certification in some specialties. Although those specialites are now very few in number, directors of programs in those specialties should make sure that any resident they accept with a D.O. degree knows that it may be impossible to be admitted to the board examination even after successful completion of an accredited training program. There are now over 1,000 osteopathic physicians serving in accredited programs.

The general requirements also cover in some detail the eligibility of members of certain other groups to enter into accredited residency programs. These include foreign nationals and graduates of foreign medical schools and other medical schools not accredited by the Liaison Committee on Medical Education. (3.1 and 3.2).

The new provisions with regard to the responsibilities of institutions and programs have spelled them out in more detail than previously and provide for supervision consistent with the special requirements for each program, counseling, and evaluation and assessment—at least annually, but preferably semiannually—of the knowledge, skills, professional growth, and performance of each resident. (5.1.5).

In the new general requirements, there are also expanded provisions for institutional procedures that provide for due process for all parties potentially involved when actions are contemplated which could result in dismissal or could significantly threaten a resident's intended career development, or when there are grievances against a program or institution. (5.1.6). As recently as 1976, an examination of 129 house-staff manuals disclosed that only 15 contained explicit grievance procedures to resolve resident-initiated concerns, and only 13 included "due process" procedures for disciplinary actions taken by the institution or program against a resident.

Faculties have the authority to make decisions about academic progress and the conduct of students, but those decisions will not be supported by the courts unless fair procedures and adequate standards are in place and are scrupulously followed in making the decisions.

Since graduate medical education is a vital step on the path to specialty certification with all its implications, there is a heavy burden on each program director and faculty to be concientious in the training and evaluation of each resident. The boards consider the recommendations they receive from the program directors in regard to the performance of candidates to be of major importance in the credentialing process, and a serious problem is created for a board when an institution has given a candidate a certificate indicating successful completion of residency training but the program director indicates that in his opinion the candidate has not achieved the level of training and expertise necessary to be recommended for admission to the board's examinations. Such a situation leads also to problems for the program director and the institution and can be avoided only by making sure that everyone issued a certificate of satisfactory completion of training is considered by the program director to be qualified to sit for the board's examinations.

Conclusion

Although the title of this book is *Legal Aspects of Certification and Accreditation*, I have limited this paper to reviewing the standards themselves that affect residency training programs and some of the background for them. The legal principles applicable to these standards and to the approval and operation of residency training programs are certain to be covered adequately in the other papers being presented here. The areas of antitrust, due process, reasonableness, discrimination, and confidential information all apply to graduate medical education as well as to certification.

Just remember, the *Green Book* is your bible. It contains the rules of this game. "Don't leave home without it."

THE _____ HOSPITAL
Graduate Medical Education
RESPONSIBILITY OF THE INSTITUTION

This institution has responsibility for ensuring that each specialty residency program fully meets the special requirements for approval by its Residency Review Committee. The specifications set forth in this section delineate an institutional system involving the teaching staff for the allocation of educational resources and maintenance of the quality of all sponsored programs.

1.1.1. The mission of any major health care institution must be seen as a practical balance of roles in preventive services, patient care, medical/professional education, and research. The effort expended in each of these areas serves to structure the kind of institution a hospital will be and to determine its role in the health care system. As a major health care center, The _____ Hospital must maintain a role in medical education in order to provide excellent community hospital experience to physicians and medical students who will be serving the Hospital's service area or that of similar communities, to support its role as a progressive community general hospital, and to maintain a highly qualified, well-informed medical staff.

> The _____ Hospital is dedicated to the healing of the sick, to the comfort of the suffering, and to the conservation of the life of the community excellence in preventive services, patient care, the training and education of health care professionals and through involvement in clinical research.

The Board of Directors of the _____ Hospital, mindful of the advantages of formal, approved graduate medical education programs in upgrading of the quality of care provided by its medical staff, has made a commitment to provide for the operation of physician residency training programs within this institution. Such residency training programs are the professional responsibility of the department sponsoring such programs. Training programs shall be established only upon approval of the Education Committee of the Medical Staff, the Executive Committee of the Medical Staff, and the Board of Directors. Once approved, the Departmental Chairman and his associates are mandated by the institution to develop an effective program for the training of quality specialists in that field. (A program director, other than the Departmental Chairman, may be delegated the responsibility for individual residency programs.)

1.1.2. The educational purposes are financially undergirded through involvement in our budgetary process on an annual basis. Each residency program director prepares his budget request, and they flow to Administration where each is balanced against the needs of the other, and a final budget is approved. Those budgetary items common to all the residency programs flow through the office of the Director of Medical Education after approval by the medical staff Education Committee and are then incorporated into the Hospital's overall budget which is ultimately approved by the Board of Directors.

Needed changes in space requirements are submitted to the Administration of the Hospital for consideration, and changes are effected as conditions allow.

1.1.3. *Operational system involving the program directors*

A. Teaching Staff Appointment: Teaching staff are appointed and supervised by the respective clinical department director and are selected from the medical staff based on their individual professional qualifications as teachers and their demonstrated commitment to the Graduate Medical Education program.

  The teaching staff is selected from staff physicians or administrators who have demonstrated a strong interest in teaching and a willingness to devote the necessary time and effort to the educational program. Key members of the teaching staff must have had adequate special training and experience in their specialty as determined by the Residency Program Directors and give evidence of active participation in appropriate national scientific societies and in their own continuing education.

B. Selection of residents: Residents are selected by the clinical department director and/or the Residency Program Director from applicants who are graduates of approved schools or candidates in their final year for doctorate degrees in medicine of osteopathy, and foreign medical graduates who submit appropriate documentation that they have successfully passed the ECFMG or equivalent examination and who have registered with the National Residency Matching Program.

  Their qualifications are ascertained by reviewing the transcript of grade scores, deans' letters, and letters of recommendation—all of which are required for an applicant to be considered for a personal interview with the Residency Program Director. The personal interview is a firm requirement which provides the applicant with an opportunity to question the Program Director about the institution's training resources and to compare his own special learning objectives with the educational opportunities available to him in this institution. The Program Director matches the student's professional goals and past performance records with the characteristics of the program to determine mutual acceptability.

  The ultimate selection of residents is subject to approval by the Education Committee, the Executive Committee of the Medical Staff, and the Board of Directors.

C. The apportionment of resident positions among programs: The number of residents accepted in each residency training program is established by consideration of the following limiting factors:

1. The clinical resources—sufficient number and variety of clinical problems (patient population) to provide a broad learning experience consistent with the professional goals of the trainee.
2. The availability of a suitable number of qualified faculty within the specialty, including appropriate subspecialists, who are committed to provide the instructional needs of the resident.
3. Physical resources—the availability of adequate space and equipment for present-day diagnostic and therapeutic modalities, including conference rooms and classrooms equipped with proper audiovisual educational aids.

  A well-maintained and supervised modern medical library and interlibrary service, easily accessible to the residents.
4. Available funds necessary to finance the Graduate Medical Education pro-

grams sponsored by the institution, including Rotating Residents from affiliated programs from outside the institution.

The funding of the entire program of Graduate Medical Education, including residents' salaries, is subjected to annual review and approval by the Administration and the Board of Directors through a budget prepared by the Department of Medical Education.

Individual departmental budgets are prepared by the respective Clinical Department Directors for allocation of funds for their specific departmental needs. This budget is approved through the same administrative mechanisms.

Increases in the number of residents already apportioned to any program, or in the total number of residents in training within the institution, must be approved by the concerned Residency Program Director, the Director of Medical Education, the Education Committee, the Executive Committee of the Medical Staff, and Administration.

D. Supervision of residents: The responsibility of supervising the performance and the training program of residents is shared by the senior residents, the Service Chiefs or preceptors, and the Director of the Department to which the resident is attached.

The ultimate overall responsibility for the training and supervision of the resident physician is the Director of the appropriate Department, or the Director of the Department and the Residency Program Director in the event they are not the same person. The Attending Staff members, or teaching staff, to whose service the resident is assigned are responsible for immediate supervision of the residents during the period of their assignment with them.

At the conclusion of each rotation or every two months, whichever is shorter, the appropriate Service Chief will complete a report to evaluate the resident's performance during that period of his training. (cf E, below)

Each evaluation will be submitted to the Office of Medical Education and forwarded to the appropriate Director of the Department or the Residency Program Director sponsoring the resident. All evaluations will become a part of the resident's permanent file maintained in the Office of Medical Education.

Day-by-day supervision of junior residents is the responsibility of the senior resident(s) on the service.

E. Evaluation of residents for professional competence: The principal purpose of the residency program is to provide an educational process to physicians in postgraduate medical training. The resident's service-related role must be considered secondary to his primary function as a learner, and academic achievement should be stressed in all programs. A reasonable "service component" however, is an inseparable feature of the program which should be regulated to be properly proportionate and consistent with the concept of supervised on-the-job training.

The success of the program is judged by the quality of the resident training in that program, which in turn is measured through the specialty certification procedure and whether the residents are capable of meeting the requirements of their respective specialty board. A high failure rate in certification jeopardizes the program. Therefore, a scholarly approach to the discipline must be stressed, especially in the application of basic sciences to clinical medicine.

The academic performance and the progress of the resident toward these goals shall be evaluated regularly by the attendings to which the residents are assigned.

Didactic lectures and teaching conferences shall be established for each resident training program as deemed appropriate to supplement bedside teaching and direct patient care responsibilities of the resident. The residents in all programs must attend all teaching conferences designated essential to that program and attendance at a minimum of 75 percent of these conferences is a requirement for completion of their training program. If a resident attends less than this, and should this deficiency not be corrected, the resident will not be approved by the Department of Medical Education as having completed his residency training program for that year. It is understood that at certain times it may be necessary to make judgments to excuse a resident from conference attendance or other duties. Only an excuse approved by the Program Director of the department to which the resident is assigned is acceptable as valid reason for failure to attend official conference programs of the department.

Resident evaluation reports—A resident's performance evaluation form will be sent out by the Office of Medical Education to each Service Chief and selected Attendings on his service to which the resident has been assigned at the conclusion of the service rotation or every two months, whichever is less, unless otherwise indicated by the Program Director or the Service Chief. These reports shall be completed by the concerned Attending(s) and returned to the Office of Medical Education for inclusion in the resident's permanent file, after which the Director of Medical Education will transmit a copy of the report to each Program Director. (Appendix)

A *semi-annual report* shall also be completed by the Program Director. In addition, and after the quarterly reports have been submitted to the Office of Medical Education, a departmental residency committee shall meet at least quarterly for review of each resident's academic performance and a complete report on each resident shall be prepared utilizing all previously submitted evaluations and the Program Director's report. This composite report and the report of the Departmental Resident Committee will be maintained as part of the permanent record of the resident in the Office of Medical Education. A comprehensive evaluation shall be undertaken by the Education Committee annually prior to the advancement of the resident to his next year of training. Documentation of the resident's qualifications for promotion will be a part of the minutes covering the deliberation of The Education Committee.

All members of each department participating in the academic programs should be acquainted with the organization of the program, including rotations and objectives of the program. This includes adjunct services when residents are assigned to services outside the parent department.

A checksheet will be maintained by the Office of Medical Education so that a record is kept of all service reports submitted to that office and keep a running inventory of the status of reports by department as a service to the Program Directors. A copy of the semiannual review by the resident committee of each department will be submitted to the Residency Program Director and the Director of Medical Education for review and filing.

The residents' performance evaluation form (Appendix) will be sent out to the respective Chief Resident for each of the residents assigned to the department, and he shall evaluate each resident and submit his report as part of the formal evaluation of all residents under his surveillance for use by the Departmental Resident Committee.

In-process training examinations—Formal examinations may be used as *one* parameter in evaluating residents by Departmental Residency Committees to measure the professional competence of residents and their readiness for advancement to the next year of training.

In an effort to upgrade the quality of graduate medical education, some specialty boards have developed examinations which are available for administration to residents in the particular speciality. Residents will be objectively tested at least once in each year of training by instruments selected or designed by the respective Program Directors and their Resident Committees.

Flex and National Board Examinations—All residents shall be required to take and pass Part III of the National Board Examination, or the FLEX Examination, or its equivalent and present documentary evidence to this before second-year residents may be advanced to their third year of training. When results of the examination are not available before entry into the second year of training, the resident must document to the Director of Medical Education that he registered for the National Boards Part III and FLEX or its equivalent. Any resident who fails the above examination must retake the examination at the earliest possible date during the second year. Should the resident fail the re-examination, his appointment will be terminated at the end of that academic year.

Resident evaluation on other than parent services—Residents who rotate on other than the services of their parent department will be evaluated by the service of rotation on which the resident is training, and this evaluation in each instance will become a part of the resident's record. When a resident is assigned to an adjunct service, he is expected to perform in accordance with the objectives and duties agreed upon by the chairman of that department and the director of the program to which the resident belongs. If problems arise regarding scheduling, educational and service experiences, or expectations, or administrative matters, the respective Program Directors shall resolve such problems as rapidly as possible. If a resident's performance fails to meet with pre-established guidelines, the chairman of the adjunct department or the Attending to which he is assigned shall report the problem immediately to the resident's Program Director. The latter will attempt to correct the situation but, if unable to do so, the resident, the Director, and the adjunct department chairman will meet to discuss the problem. If, in their determination, the resident is not performing effectively, he will be so advised and informed of what possible action will be taken if he does not improve. If it is determined that further action should be taken, either at that time or at a later date, the matter will then be referred through the Director of Medical Education to The Education Committee to determine what type of action, if any, should be taken.

To receive credit for the rotation, each resident must meet the standards of academic performance of the department to which he is assigned.

F. Dismissal of residents: Whenever the Department Director, the Residency Program Director, or the respective House Officer becomes aware of actions of a resident that could possibly result in the suspension or discharge of the House Officer for cause, they shall promptly notify the House Officer and attempt to resolve the matter by discussion on an informal basis.

The Department Director or Residency Program Director involved may so act either singularly or in concert with one another.

If further disciplinary action is necessary, the involved Department Director and the Residency Program Director acting jointly may, after consultation with the Director of Medical Education and the Education Committee, place the House Officer on a *probationary status* for such period of time as deemed appropriate. The resident is notified in writing of his probationary status.

If the matter is not so resolved, the Department Director and the Residency Program Director acting jointly and with the agreement of the Director of Medical Education and the Education Committee, may request the Education Committee to *suspend* the House Officer from all or a portion of the House Officer's hospital duties and privileges.

By a decision made jointly by the Residency Program Director, the Department Director, the Director of Medical Education, and the Education Committee, the House Officer may be discharged permanently for just cause, including but not limited to the following: a violation of the House Officer's employment agreement, the House Staff Manual, or other established policies and procedures; failure to perform duties properly; or such other actions which may make it necessary in the best interest of the Hospital or its patients.

The House Officer who is suspended for cause shall not be entitled to salary or other benefits under the Contract during the period of the suspension unless notified in writing to the contrary by the involved Department Director or the involved Residency Program Director.

A House Officer who is found to have committed a serious infraction may be immediately suspended by the Residency Program Director or the Department Director or the Director of Medical Education, pending a decision made jointly with the Education Committee after study of the details which led to the action.

G. Due process: The House Staff Hearing procedure for use by suspended or discharged House Officers, which describes the right to initiate a hearing procedure is included in the House Staff Manual as follows:

Any suspended or discharged House Officer shall have the right to initiate the following hearing procedures:

1. *Notice of Suspension or Discharge*
   Within a reasonable period of time, normally not to exceed ten days following a suspension or discharge of a House Officer, the Director of Medical Education (DME) shall notify the House Officer in writing of the charges which form the basis for the suspension or discharge and of the House Officer's right to a hearing on the charges before a Hearing Committee of the Education Committee. The House Officer may, within thirty days following his receipt of such notification, make a written request for a hearing addressed to the DME. The suspension or discharge shall become

final if the House Officer fails to request such a hearing within such thirty-day period.
2. *Hearing Committee*
The Hearing Committe of the Education Committee which conducts the hearing shall consist of the Director of the Department who supervises the House Officer's residency training, three other members of the Education Committee selected by the Chairman of the Education Committee, and the Chairman of the Education Committee (or other Education Committee member designated by the Chairman of the Education Committee if the Chairman of the Education Committee is also Director of the Department involved). The Chairman of the Education Committee or his designee shall preside at the hearing.
3. *Time and Place of Hearing*
Within a reasonable period of time normally not to exceed fifteen days following receipt of the House Officer's request for a hearing, the Director of Medical Education shall notify the House Officer of the time and place of the hearing. The hearing shall be scheduled by the DME so that the House Officer has sufficient time to prepare for the hearing, but in no event shall the hearing be scheduled earlier than fifteen days following the date on which the notice of the hearing is sent to the House Officer unless the House Officer specifically requests an earlier date in his request for the hearing.
4. *Procedure at Hearing*
At the hearing, evidence shall be presented supporting the suspension or discharge and the House Officer may present evidence on his own behalf and in rebuttal of other evidence. There shall be a right to call witnesses to testify, to present other evidence, including written statements or affidavits of other witnesses, and to confront and cross-examine any witnesses who are present and testify at the hearing.
5. *Determination of Hearing Committee*
After the hearing, the members of the Hearing Committee shall deliberate alone and by majority vote determine whether or not to uphold the suspension or discharge of the House Officer. The Committee's determination shall be based on evidence presented at the hearing. The President of the Hospital and House Officer shall be notified in writing by the Hearing Committee of its determination and its specific findings of fact in support thereof within a reasonable period of time following the hearing.
6. *Review*
If the determination of the Hearing Committee is adverse to the House Officer, the House Officer may, within fifteen days following his receipt of notification of such determination, request in writing that the Executive Committee of the Medical Staff review the determination and submit written argument with respect to it. The determination of the Hearing Committee shall become final and effective at the end of the fifteen-day period unless the request is made. The Executive Committee shall make its decision with respect to the Hearing Committee's determination within a reasonable period of time and its decision shall be forwarded to the Board of Directors and become immediately effective and final. The President of the Medical Staff shall notify the President of the Hospital, the Direc-

tor of Medical Education, the involved Department Director, the involved Residency Program Director, and the House Officer in writing of the Executive Committee's decision within a reasonable period of time after the decision is made.

1.1.4. Each residency program will be subjected to analysis annually by representatives of the concerned departments, the residents, and the administration.

The results of each annual evaluation of the residency training programs will be presented for review at a regular meeting of the Education Committee and will include the following documented issues:

1. Review of goals and objectives of the Residency Training Program.
2. Institutional plans formulated to achieve these goals.
3. A measurement process, designed by the Residency Program Director and approved by the Education Committee and the Executive Committee of the Medical Staff, that evaluates the effectiveness of the program in:
    a. Meeting its educational goals.
    b. The effectiveness of utilization of the available resources.
    c. Specific recommendations to correct identified deficiencies.

A report of this annual evaluation of each Graduate Medical Education program will be forwarded, with comments by the Education Committee, to the Executive Committee of the Medical Staff and then to the Board of Directors.

House Staff Manual

All established policy and procedure relating to the residents' relationship with the training program and the institution are stated in detail in the House Staff Manual. The manual is updated annually by each residency program director and the Director of Medical Education. Every member of the House Staff and the Residency Program Directors are provided with a current copy of the House Staff Manual at the beginning of each training year.

Approved: Education Committee
Residency Program Directors
Executive Committee of the Medical Staff
Director of Medical Education
Board of Directors

Revision: Revision of this policy requires review and approval by the Medical Staff Education Committee, the Director of Medical Education, and the Executive Committee of the Medical Staff.

Judicial Review: Liability in Tort For Certification or Accreditation Activities

David E. Willett, J.D.

The title "Judicial Review," takes in a good deal of territory. In today's world, our interest seems to focus on the judicial review of antitrust issues. These concerns are being addressed very capably by other chapters and this one will discuss another area of the law where there may be judicial review of accreditation activities.

The fear of antitrust liability, if not entirely new, is at least the particular concern of those involved in accreditation. However, we should not forget older—perhaps more prosaic—legal concerns. Tort liability—liability attributable to some error or negligence that contributes to personal injury—is a threat. Therefore, we should discuss harm or injury which might have been avoided but for some "glitch" in the accreditation or certification process.

Certification or accreditation activities may be applicable to individuals (particularly when we discuss the medical specialties), to programs, or to facilities. An example in the second category is the accreditation of continuing education, and an example relating to facilities is, of course, the JCAH program. Regardless of the nature of the program, and particularly in the health field, someone may claim that you didn't do a good enough job, when it was your obligation to do a good job, and that your negligence contributed to an injury. On a somewhat different theory, someone else may claim that you told the public that you are doing more than you really do and that the consequence of reliance on such unduly expansive representations was an injury that might have been avoided had the injured party not been misled.

California is sometimes renowned for its aberrations, and certainly there was an attitude for some years that only in California could lawyers invent and courts adopt what might appear to be far-fetched theories of liability. This is no longer the case. The "litigation explosion" exists throughout the country, particularly in the field of personal injury. We need only point to the asbestos cases—which are clogging courts throughout the land and threatening the solvency of some very large organizations—to show that the personal injury field continues to attract more than its share of plaintiffs' lawyers and hence potential plaintiffs.

There is no question but that organizations involved in certification or accreditation activities are different from commercial enterprises. These organizations frequently are characterized by their spirit of public service. Unhappily, the doctrine of charitable immunity has long ago fallen by the wayside in the United States, and noble motives or good intentions will not protect organizations from liability. Nonetheless, you may still wonder if many concerns are not far-fetched and remote from the real world. Sad to say, a headline on the front page of the April 4 issue of *Business Insurance* describes a new lawsuit which may dispel such notions. An organization that establishes standards, inspects for compliance, and issues certification—activities familiar to many of you—has been sued for over a billion dollars. The particular organization is the American Bureau of Shipping. The owners of that oil rig which capsized off Newfoundland last year—perhaps inadequately insured—are looking for someone else to share liability to survivors of decedents, injured workmen, and those sustaining property losses. It is suggested in the article that their insurance carriers may have been behind the suit against the certifying agency, as well as builders, suppliers, and others more directly involved. Although the activities of this organization may have a more commercial coloration than the activities of organizations more familiar to you, you must expect lawyers to recognize the analogy when they are casting about for additional defendants.

We have noted that there are two different theories on which liability may be claimed. The first theory is the ascertion that "you goofed": negligence. The second theory is that you didn't tell the truth: you misrepresented, exaggerated, or carelessly created a wrong impression which the injured party believed and relied on—an injured party who might have avoided the injury if he had not believed you.

Where may negligence occur? If you are also the standard-setting agency, there may be negligence in the development or promulgation of standards. Perhaps more frequently, negligence may occur in the certification process itself.

In either case the burden of proof is on the plaintiff, usually, but not always—the injured party. How will negligence be proved? In the overwhelming majority of cases, *from your own records*. We emphasize the importance of your records, because your adversary will probably depend on those records. The plaintiff will want to review everything you have that describes the *purpose* of your organization. Next, the plaintiff will want to review all the documents that describe the *process* you follow. This includes procedures, protocols, and the agreement of application that set events in motion. Finally, the plaintiff will review the record made in the process of certification.

First, the plaintiff will seek to determine whether yours is a *reasonable* process, measured against your stated purpose: Does it ignore the necessary or perhaps even the obvious? Most of all, the plaintiff will want to determine whether you followed your own rules! Although depositions may be taken from those involved, it is the written record that generally furnishes the most useful information as to what occurred.

There is a circumstance that deserves special mention. Adversaries will be reviewing your certification process to see if a red flag was run up at some point, and then ignored. I am referring particularly to the so-called Tarasoff rule. In the Tarasoff case (*Tarasoff v. Regents of University of California*, 17 Cal. 3d. 425, 131 Cal. Rptr. 14, 551 P. 2d. 334), an outpatient at a university clinic confided to his therapist that he intended to kill his girlfriend. Although the therapist enlisted the aid of campus police to deter the patient, superiors countermanded his instructions, directed that copies of communications to campus police be destroyed, and caused no action to be taken. Subsequently, the patient killed his girlfriend. In *Tarasoff*, the court concluded that a special relationship to either the person whose conduct needs to be controlled or to the forseeable victim of that conduct gives rise to a duty to exercise reasonable care to protect others from foreseeable injury. Although the decision has been severely criticized by professionals, particularly because of the impact it may have on the success of patient care and because of the difficulty in determining when actual risks of harm are present, the case has been cited with approval in other jurisdictions. An organization whose public pronouncements stress the public benefits of certification and the protection afforded the public is likely to be at peril if it ignores a situation that demands some action. The precise action that must be taken will depend entirely on the circumstances; however, closing one's eyes to a dangerous situation because that situation cannot be addressed within the matrix of the existing process may produce a claim against the organization or individuals involved.

Let us now discuss the consequences of extravagent statements. As a general proposition, the law provides that one who undertakes—even voluntarily—to provide services for the protection of a third party may be liable if that third party suffers harm because the person undertaking to provide services fails to exercise reasonable care, if any of three circumstances exist. As a certifying agency, you may be liable if the third party has relied upon your performance, or if your negligence actually increased the risk to the third party, or if you undertook to discharge a duty which someone else owed the third party. For example, a third party deliberately seeking out a board-certified specialist may contend that he has relied specifically upon your negligently bestowed certification. In a different example, take the case of a physician who has been certified as competent in CPR without any reasonable demonstration of proficiency. Even though his patient did not rely upon this certification, the patient has been exposed to a greater risk if the physician was able to obtain surgical privileges on the basis of the negligently granted certification. Finally, if a certifying agency contractually assumes a credentialling function on behalf of some institution, it may assume that institution's legal responsibility to ascertain the fitness of persons awarded privileges. In any of these examples, negligence in the granting of certification may be grounds for liability.

Let us now discuss the potential consequences of extravagent representations as to the nature or effects of your certification program. Two appellate cases are pertinent. The first case, *Collins v. American Optometric Association*, 693 F.2d. 636 was decided last year. The plaintiff had successively seen three different optometrists. None detected his glaucoma. He sued all three optometrists plus the American Optometric Association. With respect to AOA, Collins alleged that the association "negligently advertised, informed and represented to the public, including the plaintiff, that optometrists were educated and qualified to detect and diagnose glaucoma and to give the best vision care possible."While there was evidence that the American Optometric Association in fact had engaged in advertising, Collins lost his case because he could not prove that he had seen any of the ads or that he had relied on this advertising in deciding to be treated by an optometrist. Significantly, the U.S. Court of Appeal's decision concludes with the observation that its "resolution of the instant case might well be different if the plaintiff had been able to show that he relied specifically on any AOA representations in selecting or seeking the assistance of any of the optometrists he visited."

Let us look at another case. Colloquially, it's not uncommon to hear some certification referred to as the "Good Housekeeping Seal of Approval." *Hanberry v. Hearst Corporation* (1969) 276 Cal.App.2d 680, 81 Cal.Rptr. 519, involved the "Good Housekeeping Seal of Approval." Hanberry claimed that the pair of shoes she bought had soles so slippery that they were unsuitable for wearing on common floor coverings, including vinyl floors. The shoes carried the "Good Housekeeping Seal." Hanberry claimed that Hearst, the publisher of *Good Housekeeping Magazine*, made no examination, test, or investigation before its seal and certification were awarded. Hearst claimed that it had no responsibility to Hanberry. The court held, however, that "Implicit in the seal and certification is the representation respondent has taken reasonable steps to make an independent examination of the product endorsed, with some degree of expertise, and found it satisfactory." The court held that Hearst had the duty to use ordinary care, and this was a duty owed the public, including Hanberry. The magazine held itself out as a disinterested third party, and the public could assume that the magazine possessed superior knowledge and special information. It was held that Hearst may be liable for negligent representations of either fact or opinion under these circumstances.

These two cases tell us that an organization which certifies, or which tells the public it may rely upon some organizational affiliation or seal of approval, may be liable if that certification or seal of approval is granted without adequate investigation or effort.

At this point in the discussion we should summarize points to be noted. First and foremost, certifying activities carry with them the risk of liability to third parties. As a result, organizations that are engaged in certification or accreditation must take a critical look at all aspects of that activity, asking the following questions:

1. Is the organization accurately describing the purpose of its activities?
2. Have unobtainable goals been described as realities? For instance, accreditation should not be described as a "guarantee of quality." More often, accreditation is the representation that an institution has been inspected and, on the basis of such inspection, found to conform to the standards of the accrediting organization.
3. Are those who are accredited or certified being allowed to misrepre-

sent the meaning of accreditation or certification? An organization should not knowingly permit those granted certification or accreditation to lead the public astray as to the value or meaning of that award.
4. Are the standards which are the basis of certification reasonably suited to achieve the stated purposes?
5. Are the steps taken in determining compliance with those standards sufficient to make a reasonable determination?
6. Are the processes described in organizational protocols the processes actually followed? A variance between what is actually done and what the organization says it does will have to be explained, perhaps in court. If protocols are outmoded, and aren't being followed, amend the protocols before being placed on the defensive.
7. Are the individuals involved in the process, particularly those who must make "judgment calls," aware of organizational responsibilities? The individuals responsible for carrying out these tasks should be aware of the legal significance of their activities. They should also be aware that legal responsibilities may extend beyond the specific bounds of the certification process. "Red flags" should be observed. When inquiries are indicated, inquiries ought to be made.
8. Is documentation adequate? Do organizational records demonstrate that essential steps have been taken? If documentation is complete and credible, litigation may be avoided.
9. Finally, there are some miscellaneous inquiries. Does the organization maintain adequate insurance, sufficiently comprehensive to provide coverage against the liabilities we have discussed? Is certification or accreditation being extended to facilities of organizations that benefit as a result? If so, exculpatory or indemnification provisions (even though often avoided or narrowly construed by the courts) may have a place.
10. Are statutory protections available? Some organizations involved in certification or accreditation activities may be able to claim the benefit of statutory provisions which provide for the confidentiality of records or the immunity of individuals involved in the peer review process. A California statute (Civil Code Section 43.7), for instance, provides immunity for committee members of professional societies when the purpose of a committee "is to review the quality of medical services rendered by physicians." The manner in which a certification activity is described may affect the availability of this defense to individual participants. Similarly, another Califorina

statute (Evidence Code Section 1157)—which has been adopted in numerous other jurisdictions—protects medical society records from subpoena. Another statute (Evidence Code Section 1157.5) extends this protection to some other organizations. Here again, the manner in which the organization describes its purposes and the purposes of certification may affect the availability of this statutory protection. Many states have enacted statutes that are designed to protect "peer review" functions particularly by medical staffs or medical societies. The wording of such statutes varies from state to state. Even though certification activities may not immediately appear to be within the scope of these statutory provisions, reflection may lead to the conclusion that an organization's activities are fundamentally for purposes granted this protection, warranting efforts to describe certification functions and purposes to clearly bring the organization within the scope of statutory protections.

Summary

Organizations involved in certification or accreditation activities should anticipate that their role may be scrutinized by persons interested in expanding the scope of responsibility for personal injuries. This discussion briefly describes grounds for potential liability and countermeasures that might be taken.

The Role of Trade Names and Trademarks in Medical Specialty Certification

Daniel W. Vittum, Jr., J.D.

Introduction

It may seem that a discussion of trademarks and trade names in a book devoted to the discussion of medical certification and accreditation, even the legal aspects thereof, is inappropriate. Although many of us may be familiar with the legal battles over familiar trademarks like Monopoly, Xerox, and Thermos, we are more likely to associate those trademark issues with Madison Avenue and advertising and are much less likely to associate such issues with the Hippocratic Oath.

Nevertheless, the medical profession, like the legal profession, has begun to recognize that trademark issues are as intimately related to the delivery of health care as they are to the rendering of any other service to a public which is surrounded by instant communications and sophisticated advertising.

It is in just this environment that the law of trademarks is designed to function. As was stated by Justice Felix Frankfurter: "(T)he protection of trade-marks is the law's recognition of the psychological function of symbols." *Mishawaka Rubber and Woolen Mfg. Company v. S.S. Kresge Co.*, 316 U.S. 203, 205 (1942).

The focus of this presentation will be the statutory protection accorded to trademarks. The primary statute is the federal Trademark Act, 15 U.S.C. § 1051-§ 1127, known as the Lanham Act after its sponsor in the

the Congress. In particular, we will be looking at the ways in which certifying and accrediting organizations may use the Lanham Act to assist the public in selecting the medical specialties they want and to protect the public from bogus organizations who rely on deception and confusion to attract customers.

At the outset, it is important to distinguish trademarks from patents and copyrights. Unlike a patent or a copyright, a trademark is not the grant of a monopoly to a trademark owner to absolutely prohibit the use of a word or words by others. A trademark is quite different from a monopoly. According to the legislative history of the Lanham Act, trademarks are "the essence of competition, because they make possible a choice between competing articles by enabling the buyer to distinguish one from another." *1946 U.S. Code Cong. & Ad. News* 1274, 1275. Trademark protection only goes so far as to allow the owner to prohibit the use of his mark in order to protect his goodwill against the sale of another's product or service as his. *See Prestonettes v. Coty*, 264 U.S. 359, 368 (1924).

It is also important to distinguish between pure trade names, which are not registered, and trade names which are used as trademarks, e.g., Gulf, Pillsbury, or DuPont, which are registerable. The use by certifying and accrediting organizations of their trade names to certify their services qualifies those names for protection under the trademark law. *See Communications Satellite Corp. v. Comcet, Inc.*, 429 F.2d 1245 (4th Cir.), *cert. denied*, 400 U.S. 942 (1970) (COMSAT protected as corporate trade name and federally registered service mark); *Ex parte The Supreme Shrine of the Order of the White Shrine of Jerusalem*, 109 U.S.P.Q. 248, 249-50 (Comm'r Pat. 1956) (identifying and distinguishing mark registerable even though a trade name).

The importance of protecting the trade name and trademark of the certifying body

The benefits of and the challenges to the certification and accreditation process are well suited to trademark protection. According to the legislative history of the 1946 Lanham Act, a purpose of the statute is to protect the purchasing public. Thus, a consumer of medical services is entitled to be confident that, in purchasing a service, he will get the service he asks for and that the service will be performed by someone qualified to deliver it.

The adoption and use of trademarks and trade names by certifying and accrediting bodies perform the first function of protection by identifying to the public a source of quality professional care. The public trust and confidence accrues to the individual practitioner and his or her profession as well as to the certifying and accrediting organization which has lent its trade name or trademark to the practitioner and the profession.

The use of trademark symbols, like the name or seal of a certifying or accediting organization, has several important benefits. First, the consumer of health care services is likely to associate the high-quality health care he or she receives with the certifying or accrediting organization. Second, the consumer is likely to look for that symbol when seeking additional health care services.

However, there are of course obvious disadvantages to the use of symbols to guide consumer choice in the health care field. For example, a consumer is not likely to inquire into the particular standards a health care practitioner must meet before being allowed to use the name or seal of a certifying or accrediting organization. In the health care field, those standards can vary widely. Thus, bogus certifying organizations or unscrupulous practitioners, unwilling or unable to satisfy rigorous standards of certification and accreditation, are quick to recognize and to appropriate the valuable certification and accreditation symbols of others in order to sell their own services.

The Lanham Act protects the accrediting and certifying bodies from other organizations which adopt and use a similar name, logo, or seal because the law recognizes that, if allowed to continue, such use (1) would dilute the investment of energy, time, and money in the trademark or trade name of the certifying body; (2) would affect the public trust and confidence that the public has in a particular profession; (3) may impact adversely upon the quality of professional service the public has come to expect; and (4) may ultimately expose the legitimate certifier to liability if the certifier has not acted to protect the public from the unauthorized use of the legitimate certifier's mark or name.

The names and symbols of certifying groups are readily protectible

Certification and Collective Marks. Registration of trademarks for accrediting and certifying organizations was streamlined by the enactment of the Lanham Act in 1946. Before 1946, federal trademark registration was limited to *trademarks* that had been used by the trademark *owner* on *goods* in interstate commerce. The 1946 Lanham Act opened up registration to certain types of marks that were not used by the *owner* on *goods* but were still deserving of protection. For example, the 1946 Act allows the registration of marks that are used in connection with the sale or advertising of services as opposed to goods. More significant for present purposes, the Lanham Act (1) allows someone other than the owner to actually use those marks on goods and services in commerce and (2) allows groups, associations, and other collective organizations to serve as owners. The specialized types of marks that resulted form these important changes are termed Certification Marks and Collective Marks.

The term "Certification Mark" means "a mark used upon or in connection with the products or services of one or more persons other than the owner of the mark to certify regional or other origin, mode or manufacture, quality, accuracy or other characteristics of such goods or services or that the work or labor on the goods or services was performed by members of a union or other organization." 15 U.S.C. § 1027.

A certification mark, unlike a trademark, does not distinguish among producers but only certifies some characteristic common to the goods or services of many persons. Familiar examples of certification marks are the Underwriters Laboratories' symbol and the Good Housekeeping Seal of Approval. More recent examples of certification marks for goods (Class A) and services (Class B) are shown in Exhibit 1.

Before a mark will be registered as a certification mark, the applicant must show that the purchaser is aware that the mark is being used as a certification mark. If not, the application for registration will be refused. *Ex parte Van Winkle*, 117 U.S.P.Q. 450 (Comm'r Pat. 1958).

The term "Collective Mark" means "a trademark or service mark used by members of a cooperative, an association or other collective group or organization and includes marks used to indicate membership in a union, an association or other organization." 15 U.S.C. § 1027.

The collective mark was created for those situations where members of an association or other group desired to indicate their membership in the group. Examples of such collective marks include National Trailways, The Douglas Fir Plywood Association, the PGA, and The Quality Court Motels. Other examples are shown in Exhibit 2.

A collective mark *must* be used in a way such that membership is indicated. *See In Re Safe Electrical Cord Committee*, or 125 U.S.P.Q. 310 (T.T.A.B. 1960) ("U.L. Inc. Inspected" refused registration because membership not indicated). It has been held that the essential characteristic of a collective mark is the existence of contract or license between applicant for a collective mark and the applicant's members. *Huber Baking Co. v. Stroehmann Brothers Co.*, 252 F. 2d. 945, 116 U.S.P.Q. 348, 353 (2nd Cir. 1958), *cert. denied*, 358 U.S. 829 (1958).

Collective and certification marks are not necessarily mutually exclusive. A comparison of the statutory definition shows that members of "a union or other" organization are entitled to use certification marks and collective marks. In fact, a collective mark can also serve as a certification mark. See *Ex parte Douglas Fir Plywood Ass'n*, 118 U.S.P.Q. 162 (Comm'r Pat. 1958) ("DFPA" mark for plywood was registerable as collective trademark even though mark performed a certification function as well). This result follows from the different but compatible purposes these two marks are designed to achieve. A certification mark symbolizes that goods or services meet a certain standard, while a collective mark symbolizes membership in a group or organization. It is only logical that a group formed around a particular good or service will in turn establish standards for the particular product.

An example of a situation in which a collective mark can also act as a certification mark is characterized by the statement "Look for the Union Label." For example, a union seal or logo would certainly qualify under the statute as a collective mark. In addition, when union labels are placed on goods like clothing, machinery, or food, they certify that the goods were produced by members of the union. For the purposes of a trademark application, the Trademark Office would classify the union label within Class A, a certification mark for goods.

Where a union label is displayed in a service establishment like a barber shop or beauty parlor, the label certifies that the service was performed by a member of the union. The application in this case would designate the union label as a certification mark in Class B, Services.

In those situations where there is some confusion about whether a certification mark involves goods or services, the trademark examiner who reviews the owner's application is likely to consider a number of factors. The primary factor is the manner in which the business is conducted.

One characteristic that is common to both certification and collective marks is that the owner must exercise some degree of control over the mark. For example, if the owner contracts away that right, the mark cannot be registered as either a collective mark or a certification mark. See *R. M. Hollingshead Corp. v. Davies-Young Soap Co.*, 121 F.2d 500, 504, 50 U.S.P.Q. 71 (C.C.P.A. 1941).

A second common characteristic of certification and collective marks is that the owner of the mark cannot use the mark on its own goods or services. See *National Trailways Bus System v. Trailway Van Lines*, 222 F.Supp. 143, 139 U.S.P.Q. 54, 56 (E.D.N.Y. 1963) (collective mark, not service mark, should be sought where applicant's members and not applicant provides the services). On at least one occasion, this distinction has been strictly interpreted. In the case of *In Re Florida Citrus Commission*, 160 U.S.P.Q. 495 (T.T.A.B. 1968), the Board of Trademark Trials and Appeals held that the fact that the Florida Citrus Commission had registered the mark "OJ" as a service mark for its own goods barred the commission from registering the same mark as a certification mark for Florida orange juice products.

Although this holding is a strict interpretation of the distinction between these special purpose marks and common trademarks, it does follow from the fact that the initial service mark registration asserted that the Florida Citrus Commission was the provider of the services bearing their mark "OJ." As noted above, the statutory exception for certification marks and collective marks was created specifically for that situation where the mark is used in connection with products or services of one or more persons "other than the owner of the mark." However, there is nothing to preclude the owner of a certification or collective mark from selling goods or services under a different mark. The only condition is that the two marks be "separate and distinct." *In Re Monsanto Co.,* 201 U.S.P.Q. 864, 869 (T.T.A.B. 1978).

To illustrate the difference between collective and certification marks, consider the American Board of Medical Specialties and its members. The American Board of Medical Specialties and its seal are registered *collective* marks because they are used primarily to indicate membership. In contrast, the names of the member boards are used primarily to certify and accredit practitioners in the health care field. Thus, these marks would logically be classified as *certification* marks.

Registration

Applications for registration of collective or certification marks are made in the same way as are applications for trademarks.

An application is filed in the Patent and Trademark Office, where the application is reviewed by a trademark examiner. The applicant may file and prosecute his own application or the applicant may be represented by an attorney.

An application must include the name of the applicant, citizenship, and address. The applicant must provide a drawing showing the mark and must certify that he has adopted the mark and that he is using it in commerce. The applicant must specify the date of first use of the mark, the date of first use of the mark in commerce, and the manner in which the mark is being used.

An applicant can expect the first comment on the application by an examiner to occur about nine to twelve months after filing. A typical period from time of application to registration is about two years. Applications for certification and collective marks include some special features. An application for a certification mark must state that the applicant is exercising legitimate control over the use of the certification mark. It must also state that the mark was first used under the authority of the applicant because the certification mark cannot be used by the applicant himself. Moreover, the application must contain a statement of the characteristic or other feature that is certified by the mark. For example, an application would read as follows: "The certification mark, as used by persons authorized by applicant, certifies that . . . ."

All the characteristics the mark certifies should be included, and a mark need not be limited to certifying a single characteristic. According to the *Manual for Trademark of Examining Procedure* (MTEP), the characteristic should be stated with some specificity. For example, material strength or purity is preferred to a statement that the certification relates to quality. The application must contain a statement to the effect that the applicant does not engage in the production or marketing of any goods or services to which the mark sought to be registered is applied.

A collective mark application also has some particular features. The application must state that the applicant is exercising legitimate control over the use of the mark instead of the normal statement to the effect that the applicant is using the mark. Moreover, in setting up the dates of use of goods or services, the application must state that the mark was first used by a member or members of the applicant.

Tests for registration

Before a certification mark or a collective mark will be accepted for registration, the trademark examiner must be satisfied that the mark is not confusingly similar to other marks and is not descriptive. Marks that are descriptive or deceptively misdescriptive are statutorily barred from registration as trademarks. This often may be the most difficult part of the application process.

With respect to confusion with other marks, an applicant can anticipate and perhaps avoid some problems if he initiates a search of similar terms that might already have been registered with the Trademark Office. The cost of this search is dependent on a number of factors to include: the number of marks in that particular area, the particular words or symbols used in the mark, and the detail of the search.

Certifying and accrediting organizations might be vulnerable to a claim of confusion if other societies have similar marks. For example, the names of organizations that certify or accredit the practitioners in the fields of psychiatry and psychology may be confusingly similar. Although one who practices in these fields may readily be able to distinguish between the two, the applicant must convince the trademark examiner that a reasonable *purchaser* of those services is not likely to be confused by the similarity in the names of the organizations.

The legal standard of confusion is difficult to define precisely. It will depend on the facts in the individual case. For example, in *Aloe Creme Laboratories, Inc. v. American Society for Aesthetic Plastic Surgery, Inc.*, 192 U.S.P.Q. 170 (T.T.A.B. 1976), the board faced the question of whether a figure used in the plaintiff's trademark could be incorporated into the defendant's collective mark. The board allowed the registration of the mark because the sole function of the mark was to identify membership in the group and not to sell goods or services. Although the statement of law appears to be correct, there is some question whether that result was proper given the facts of the case. In the *Aloe* case, the defendant society incorporated into its collective mark the familiar trademark of the plaintiff, which was used on a line of cosmetics that was particularly beneficial to persons who had recently undergone plastic surgery. Under these facts, there appears to be sufficient evidence to support a finding of likelihood of confusion. Even though there was no such finding based on the fact that the collective mark at issue would not be used on competing goods or services, it seems likely that similar conduct would not be condoned in a future case.

Although the standard of confusion is difficult to define precisely, it is helpful for an applicant to recall the basic limitations of trademarks. The owner of a trademark is not granted a monopoly. The scope of a registrant's legal rights is limited to those situations where there is confusion as to source or quality or if there is a danger that a registrant's investment will be threatened by unscrupulous competitors. *See National Science Foundation v. National Sanitation Foundation Testing Laboratory, Inc.*, 207 U.S.P.Q. 323 (T.T.A.B. 1980) (oppositions by National Science Foundation to registration of National Sanitation Foundation dismissed where evidence showed that both parties had operated in particular areas for over twenty-five years).

In addition to the likelihood of confusion, the trademark examiner may claim that a mark is descriptive. Once again, the names of certifying and accrediting groups are likely to be challenged on this ground. It has been held that a certification mark is descriptive where an educational degree or title is used solely as a personal title or degree. When used descriptively, titles and degrees indicate qualifications or attainments of a person and do not pertain to or certify services that have been performed by the person. *In Re Professional Photographers of Ohio, Inc.*, 149 U.S.P.Q. 857 (T.T.A.B. 1966).

Once again, descriptiveness is not an absolute standard, but a matter of degree. In most cases, the application of reasonable rules of policy leads to the correct result as to whether a particular word or words should qualify as a trademark. The Trademark Office cannot allow one party to remove from the commercial vocabulary certain descriptive terms that anyone in a particular profession might require in his business. In the *Professional Photographers* case, to allow one organization of professional photographers in Ohio to register such a certification mark would have seriously disadvantaged the remaining professional photographers in Ohio who were not certified by this organization.

Moreover, the certification mark in question did not perform the function of identifying to the public that a particular service was being certified. The title merely indicated that the photographer took photographs for a living. *See In Re Institute of Certified Professional Business Consultants*, 216 U.S.P.Q. 338, 339 (T.T.A.B. 1982) (certification mark for initials "CPBC" registerable only if circumstances surrounding the use of the mark gave certification significance to the mark in the marketplace).

Descriptiveness is also a factor in the decision to award a collective mark. For example, in the case *In Re National Society of Cardiopulmonary Technologists, Inc.*, 173 U.S.P.Q. 511 (T.T.A.B. 1972), the board upheld the decision to refuse a registration where the society sought to register certain titles: "CPT" (Cardiopulmonary Technologists), "PUT" (Pulmonary Technologists), or "CVT" (Cardiovascular Technologists). The board held that the titles were merely descriptive and did not designate membership in the society as was required of collective marks.

Benefits of federal registration

Federal registration has many advantages. First, federal registration is considered to be constructive notice within the United States. 15 U.S.C. § 1072. This means that the trademark owner need not show that the infringer had an intent to infringe on the plaintiff's mark. A good-faith user of the mark can still be held liable for infringement. The general rule is that the senior user who has a federal registration has superior rights throughout the United States. The owner of a federal registration has the security of knowing that no one else may henceforth legitimately adopt his trademark and create rights in another area of the country superior to his own. *Application of Beatrice Foods Company*, 429 F.2d 466, 472-73, 166 U.S.P.Q. 431 (C.C.P.A. 1970).

Second, federal registration is prima facie evidence of the validity of the registrant's ownership of the mark and the registrant's exclusive right to use the mark in commerce. 15 U.S.C. § 1057(b). This simplifies questions of proof.

Third, after five years, the trademarks becomes incontestable and constitutes *conclusive* evidence of the registrant's exclusive right to use the mark. 15 U.S.C. §§ 1065, 1115(b).

Fourth, federal registration gives a registrant the right to institute trademark actions in federal courts, without regard to diversity of citizenship or the amount in controversy. 15 U.S.C. § 1121.

Fifth, a registrant may obtain treble damages and other remedies in civil actions for infringement. 15 U.S.C. § 1116-1120.

The cost of registration is likely not to be significant. A simple application costs no more than about $250 to file. If an application is submitted for a design or logo, the cost might be about $350. The total cost of pursuing the registration would, except in unusual cases, be significantly less than $1000.

State registration of trademarks is also available. *See* Ill. Rev. Stat. ch. 140, § 9. Although an Illinois registration of a trademark or trade name does not enlarge the substantive rights accorded to that mark insofar as trademark infringement remedies are concerned, *see Underwriters Laboratories, Inc. v. United Laboratories, Inc.*, 203 U.S.P.Q. 180, 184 (N.D.Ill. 1978) (federal relief made state relief unnecessary), registration does create certain presumptions that may assist the registrant in protecting the symbol in any later litigation. Registration is prima facie evidence that the mark was being used on the date of that registration, and registration creates a presumption that the mark is not descriptive. Although the owner of an unregistered mark may sue for an injunction under Section 22 of the Act, a registrant may also seek recovery of the defendant's profits as well as money damages. Ill. Rev. Stat. ch. 140, §§ 19, 20 and 22.

Remedies for Infringement

The traditional remedies involve injunctions, damages, profits, and attorneys' fees. Injunctive relief is ordinarily the principal remedy, and its terms may be tailored to the facts of each individual case. If the circumstances warrant, additional remedies may be granted. For example, a registrant may recover the defendant's profits, any damages sustained (which may be tripled), and the costs of the action. 15 U.S.C. § 1117. In addition, the court may order registration of a mark or cancellation of a registration in whole or in part and may order the defendant to deliver up for destruction all labels, packages, wrappers, and advertisements bearing the infringing mark as well as the plates, molds, matrices, and other means of making or reproducing the infringing mark. 15 U.S.C. § 1118.

It is also possible for the court to order an accounting for profits. Before a registrant may request profits, however, the registrant must show that he has not himself engaged in inequitable conduct, that he has taken prompt action against the infringer, and that he has given notice of the registration of his mark. 15 U.S.C. § 1117. It seems well established that, for an accounting to be ordered, the infringing party must be a competitor selling the same product. Otherwise, the plaintiff could not have lost any sales. In *Underwriters Laboratories, Inc. v. United Laboratories, Inc.*, 203 U.S.P.Q. 180, 183-84 (N.D.Ill. 1978), the court ordered an accounting of defendant's wrongful profits and payment of plaintiff's attorney's fees because the court found that an injunction alone would have permitted the infringing defendant to retain the benefits of its *intentional* infringement of the plaintiff's famous mark.

It should be noted that the burden is on the infringer to prove that his infringement had no cash value in sales made by him. If the infringer does not do so, the profits made on sales of goods bearing the infringing mark properly belong to the owner of the mark.

Actual damages may also be awarded in addition to the defendant's profits. Damages may only be likely, however, where the defendant's acts have been intentional and the entry of an injunction and the award of profits will not adequately compensate the registrant.

Finally, since 1975, a reasonable attorney's fee may be awarded in "exceptional" cases. 15 U.S.C. § 1117.

Once registered, vigorous protection of trademarks is important

Once a trademark is obtained, a registrant must be careful how the trademark is used and how that trademark is policed.

Other speakers have discussed in detail the legal constraints on the use of certification and accreditation, and those issues will not be repeated. It is enough to say that a certification mark is subject to cancellation if an organization refuses to certify those who satisfy the certification standards *See American Automobile Ass'n v. National Automobile Ass'n*, 127 U.S.P.Q. 423, 427 (T.T.A.B. 1960).

One antitrust issue worth noting is a defendant's tactic of raising antitrust violations as a defense to charges of trademark infringement. However, such a defense is not likely to succeed unless the defendant can meet the "heavy burden" of showing that "the mark itself has been the basic and fundamental vehicle required and used to accomplish the (antitrust) violation." *Carl Zeiss Stiftung v. V.E.B. Carl Zeiss, Jena*, 298 F. Supp. 1309, 1315, 161 U.S.P.Q. 414, 419 (S.D.N.Y. 1969), *modif'd on other grounds*, 433 F.2d 686 (2nd Cir. 1970). *cert. denied*, 403 U.S. 905 (1971). This indeed has been a heavy burden, because at least one court has been unwilling to convert a straightforward trademark infringement case into a complex antitrust case without a showing by the defendant that the trademark had an "immediate and necessary relationship" to the defendant's antitrust claim. *Coca-Cola Co. v. Howard Johnson Co.*, 386 F. Supp. 330, 337, 184 U.S.P.Q. 549, 554 (N.D. Ga. 1974). It seems that the marks of certifying and accrediting health care organizations would not constitute a "necessary" part of an antitrust violation and thus would not defeat a suit for trademark infringement.

The only other issue of use (which might not be mentioned in other presentations and merits at least passing reference) is that an owner should attempt to indicate that his mark is registered whenever possible. Use of a circled "R" or different typeface is usually satisfactory. The danger to be avoided is the situation into which "aspirin" or "escalator" have fallen: i.e., they have become generic. *See Community of Roquefort v. William Faehndrich, Inc.*, 303 F.2d 494, 133 U.S.P.Q. 633 (2nd Cir. 1962) (Roquefort for cheese had not become generic due to proper use and enforcement by the owners).

Failure to properly police infringements can also limit the effectiveness of registration. For example, there are three standard defenses a defendant can be expected to make to any charge of infringement. Those three defenses are laches, abandonment, and estoppel. Laches is negligence or delay by a registrant in asserting his rights or the registrant's failure to take prompt affirmative action to protect his rights. If the delay was brought about because the registrant was unaware of another's infringement, the registrant's right to relief is unaffected. However, a registrant need not have actual knowledge of another's infringement. He may be charged with knowledge, i.e., constructive knowledge, if the registrant knows facts from which a reasonable man would infer the infringement.

The registrant is not required to bring an action on first suspicion of wrongdoing. He is entitled to take time to make an investigation to ensure the success of his action once brought. A registrant who has been guilty of laches with respect to his trademark rights does not forfeit his rights. He may obtain injunctive relief against further infringements. He may, however, be barred from obtaining a preliminary injunction and from all damages and profits that might have accrued prior to bringing the action. A preliminary injunction is usually obtainable only where a plaintiff can show that irreparable harm will result if the action is not ceased. A registrant who sits on his rights will have a hard time showing that any further delay will create the necessary irreparable harm. However, laches has been held not to bar the remedies of damages and attorney's fees where a defendant has intentionally infringed a certification mark. *Underwriters Laboratories, Inc. v. United Laboratories Inc.*, 203 U.S.P.Q. 180, 182 (N.D. Ill. 1978).

Abandonment or acquiescence is a similar concept. Abandonment usually refers to those situations where a registrant has been so lacking in diligence and so inactive in protecting his rights that it is fair for a court to deny him any kind of relief at all. Where a registrant had been inactive for twenty years during which time numerous infringers had used a mark, the Supreme Court held that it was too late for the registrant to "resuscitate her original title." *Saxlehner v. Eisner & Mendelson Co.*, 179 U.S. 19, 37 (1900). Another famous case involved the trademark, Milk of Magnesia. In that case the registrant had stood silently by for nineteen years while others had used the mark as a name for their products. In that case, the registration was canceled. *McKesson & Robbin v. Phillips Chemical Co.*, 53 F.2d 342 (2d Cir. 1931), *cert. denied*, 285 U.S. 552 (1932).

The third situation involves estoppel. The term refers to those cases where a court finds that it would be inequitable for a registrant to be permitted to enforce its trademark rights over a mark that still possesses some distinctiveness. Unlike abandonment, estoppel does not divest an owner of all his rights. This means that, in an estoppel situation, a registrant might be estopped to assert his right against one particular defendent but permitted to enforce his rights against other defendants.

The concepts of laches, abandonment, and estoppel lead to several clear rules for trademark registrants to follow. First, the advantages of registration can be lost if violators are not promptly pursued. Second, the organization should make known to its members that it is interested in learning of and pursuing trademark violations. Third, notice of a trademark violation should be given in a timely manner because notice permits the registrant to obtain damages and profits. Fourth and perhaps most important, once the registrant learns of a violation and has given notice and the infringer continues to infringe, the registrant should pursue the violator and litigate the matter if necessary.

Although the program of enforcement discussed above is not self-executing, neither is it difficult, complex, or in need of an enforcement bureaucracy. The best enforcement programs rely on existing resources, such as the staff and membership of a certifying or accrediting organization. Enforcement may be merely a matter of raising the consciousness of those who are involved in the business of certification or accreditation. An effective in-house program avoids litigation and the burden of attorney's fees because most infringements can be handled with a warning letter which gives the infringer notice of federal trademark registration.

Conclusion

Trademark law provides inexpensive and effective protection for the most valuable symbol of an accrediting or certifying organization: the organization's name and design.

Collective and certification marks of certifying and accrediting organizations are appropriate marks for trademark protection because a consumer of health care services is likely to associate high-quality health care with a particular mark and to look for that mark in the future. Consumers as well as registrants are entitled to protection from bogus certifying and accrediting organizations and practitioners who would trade on a consumer's association with a valid mark to pass off health care services that do not meet certification or accreditation standards.

There are two main showings that an applicant must make to the trademark examiner before the applicant may obtain a trademark registration. First the applicant must satisfy the examiner that the proposed mark is sufficiently distinctive of the applicant's services so as not to be merely descriptive of the products and thus capable of performing the traditional identification function of a trademark. Second, an applicant must satisfy the examiner that the proposed mark is not confusingly similar to other marks already in use.

Once registered, a trademark is only as good as the quality of the registrant's use and enforcement. Reasonable use of the mark and prompt enforcement right from the outset will ensure that a registrant can take full advantage of the wide range of federal and state remedies available to a trademark owner in the event that the mere presence of those remedies is not sufficient to deter infringers.

Exhibit 1. Examples of Certification Marks

Class A Certification–Goods

American Society Of Sanitary Engineering and Design
Farmworkers AFL-CIO and Eagle and Flag Design
Florida Sunshine Tree
International Ladies Garment Workers Union
Irish Poplin and Design
Kevlar Design
Liebfraumilch
Teflon
Underwriters Laboratories
USDA Shield

Class B Certification–Services

Full Service Wholesaler and Design
Certified Trichologist, Design
Gellert Certified Systems and Design
Teamsters and Design

Exhibit 2. Collective Membership Marks

Class 200

American Board of Medical Specialties and Design
American Board of Ambulatory Anesthesia
American Board of Quality Assurance and Utilization Review of Physicians
National Association of Boards of Pharmacy
National Society of Daughters of The American Colonists and Design
Pan-American Psychological Association
Quality Courts and Design

Standardized Testing Legislation: Consumer Protection or Consumer Fraud?

James B. Erdmann, Ph.D.

Would you like to be known as an opponent of "truth in testing?" Are you not concerned about *fairness* in testing? Do you oppose *openness* in testing? Do you not think people have a right to see what they pay for? Do you not believe that students should know where they have made their mistakes so they can do better the next time? Don't you think that secrecy and mystery must be taken out of testing? Should testing companies not be made *accountable* to somebody? Is it not important that researchers, not connected with the test sponsor, conduct studies of its usefulness? Are you concerned about these coaching courses that give the wealthy an unfair advantage? Don't you agree that test bias must be eliminated? Should tests be allowed to determine a person's future? Do you trust the accuracy of the scores reported? Should you not be allowed to verify personally the answers considered correct? Do you know that test takers from privileged backgrounds get higher test scores? Did you hear about the right answers that were marked wrong in a recent SAT and PSAT? Do you know that a certain nonprofit testing company has a budget of over 100 million dollars and is located on a beautiful campus with its own lake and conference center?

Should these reflections not be persuasive at the moment, project your feelings if either you or a family member were to receive unfavorable consideration, ostensibly, at least, because of poor test scores.

Are you now prepared to support "truth-in-testing" legislation?

Sponsors of such legislative action claim that these are the issues with which they are dealing. Before lending your support prematurely, it may be wise to examine so-called truth-in-testing legislation a little more closely.

Where are the remedies this kind of legislation offers

First and foremost are the "disclosure" provisions. Almost all proponents use the term "disclosure" in this connection because of the obvious suggestion that something is being wrongfully concealed. Similarly, most of the bills are referred to, if not actually entitled, "truth-in-testing" laws to gain the credibility and sympathy associated with truth-in-packaging, truth-in-lending, and truth-in-advertising laws.

"Disclosure" is usually defined to have two applications: one to the test contents and the other to the studies, analyses, and evaluations conducted in connection with the use of the test. In its "purest" form, disclosure of content requires the *exposure* of all scored test questions and answers after every administration of every test. Various versions of these bills are now appearing in which the operational definition of "disclosure" is being modified to exclude some test programs altogether, the stated reason usually being program size. In the case of the Medical College Admission Test (MCAT), one recent proponent admitted he wanted to avoid a legal hassle. He was referring to the suit brought by the AAMC against the State of New York to protect the Medical College Admission Test.

Disclosure may also be limited to certain administrations of a test. These modifications usually have little rational support. Rather they are mostly the result of political compromise. I have yet to hear anyone, including Mr. La Valle (the sponsor of the New York law) attempt to defend how he determines that a program is sufficiently small to merit exclusion from the provisions of his bill. It is also interesting to note that civil service exams, other government tests, and examinations developed by a particular school or teacher for their exclusive use are usually specifically exempted. You may be aware that—save some notable exceptions—most early proposals, especially, limited coverage to tests designed for and/or used in admissions decisions for post-secondary education. Some quarters may only be awakening to the consolation offered by this kind of legislation, however. In several states bills have appeared that include tests used in elementary and secondary schools, and, in two states, tests used in occupational, licensing, and certification settings as well. The latter two states are Pennsylvania and Illinois. The Illinois bill has yet to be reintroduced, though the sponsor has resubmitted his measure for post-secondary education during the current session.

Beyond the impact of disclosure on the continuing quality of test questions and content coverage is its impact on equating and test development. The restriction of disclosure to those questions used in developing an examinee's score is considered by the authors of these bills to eliminate all the equating and new-question-development problems of earlier versions of the bills. Such is clearly not the case.

The other area to which disclosure is applied encompasses all studies, analyses, and evaluations that test sponsors prepare or cause to have prepared. Proponents admit that this reflects their belief that test sponsors conceal unfavorable results and report only the favorable. The implication is that researchers independent of the test program are unable to conduct studies without having access to data under the exclusive control of the test sponsor. Studies reported in the literature by independent researchers on the usefulness of test scores sent to their institutions are conveniently ignored. Also overlooked by this provision is the need to evaluate the quality of questions in development and the corresponding necessity to prevent their being compromised prior to actual use as scored material. The filing of all analyses as public documents hardly seems consistent with that need for confidentiality.

Perhaps most important, this provision interferes with the obligation of the investigator to assume responsibility for the reporting of research results. The stability and validity of results and their educational and social impact can no longer be factors weighed by the researcher in disseminating findings.

Quite recently a new set of issues has been injected into this arena. In California, prompted by the action of the Education Testing Service (ETS) in canceling the scores of a large number of examinees at a single test center, State Senator Torres from Los Angeles has offered legislation that specifies procedures to be followed in reviewing and deciding cases of suspected irregularities. Obviously, little regard can be given to candidate and program differences. This matter is yet to be resolved.

The remaining provisions of these bills do little more than codify the current practice of most test sponsors. They require a spelling out of the purposes for which a test was designed, the areas to be examined on the test, rules for converting raw scores to reported scores, the interval that will elapse between the taking of the examination and the distribution and of the scores, the right of the examinee to be the sole determiner of the destinations to which individually identified scores will be sent, and so on. Although no agency has objected to the substance of these requirements, there is general agreement that, since a law was not necessary to institute such policies, collegial pressure and the standards of the profession will be sufficient to sustain and refine them.

How have these legislative proposals fared?

The legislation described was advanced first in New York in 1977. No hearings were conducted on the '77 New York Bill, and the fact that it seemed to attract so little support possibly provided a false sense of security when the 1979 version was introduced. In 1978, the Harrington Bill had been introduced in the U.S. House, but no hearings took place there either. In the same year, however, the idea gained serious consideration on the West Coast, and California began consideration of a testing bill in the spring. The initial version of the California bill with the more "pure" form of disclosure, was modified significantly. In place of the exposure of test contents after every administration, a requirement to place on file a nonsecure form of the kind used during the last three years was substituted. If that was not available, a representative sample of material reflecting the content and format of the test in current use would suffice. The requirement regarding the publishing of studies and analyses was framed to conform with the corresponding guidelines contained in the Standards for Educational and Psychological Tests prepared jointly by the American Psychological Association, American Educational Research Association, and National Council on Measurement in Education. This version was enacted into law in the summer of 1978. The camel's nose was in the tent. Three years later, the law was amended to stiffen the disclosure requirements for admission tests to college and university programs. Attempts to extend stiffer disclosure measures to post-secondary education were successfully resisted at that time.

In the summer of 1979, the New York Law became a reality, causing 20 of 26 test programs to announce they were withdrawing from the state. Within months, two lawsuits were filed; one by the college boards on a jurisdictional matter, the other by the Association of American Medical Colleges (AAMC) on the basis of rights guaranteed under the Federal Copyright Statute, the U.S. Constitution, and the Constitution of the State of New York. The AAMC sought injunctive and declaratory relief in the U.S. District Court, Northern District of New York. Its complaint argued copyright, due process, and equal protection issues. The College Board case was resolved by amendments to the New York law in 1980; in the same year, the AAMC was granted a preliminary injunction prohibiting enforcement of the New York disclosure provisions against the MCAT, during the pendency of its litigation. The latter case is still before the court.

Shortly after passage of the New York law, hearings were begun in the elementary, secondary, and vocational education subcommittee of the

Education and Labor Committee in the U.S. House of Representatives. Two bills had been introduced, one by Mr. Weiss from New York that was modeled very closely on the Harringtion and New York bills, and one by Mr. Gibbons from Florida. The Gibbons bill extended its coverage to all tests, including those used in occupational settings, but it did not require disclosure. It did seem to rule out the use of norm-referenced scores, even though other provisions of the bill could not be accomplished without norming. After an additional set of hearings in the fall of 1979, Mr. Weiss withdrew his bill before action by the subcommittee. He reintroduced his measure in the spring of 1980, and a further set of hearings was held in June. The hearings concluded with concurrent jurisdiction being assigned to the Post-Secondary Education Subcommittee. No action occurred in that forum before the end of the congressional session. Both bills were reintroduced in the new congress (1981), hearings were held, but no action was taken. There is currently no pending legislation in this arena in the U.S. Congress.

Returning to state activity: After the 1979 enactment of the New York law, almost 25 states exhibited some form of interest in this type of legislation by the summer of 1980. Hearings were held in only about a third of those states, and in no instance did a bill get to the floor of either house. Four states either by administrative or committee action did decide to initiate further study of the matter.

During 1981, legislation appeared in about 15 states. Somewhat fewer considered bills in 1982 and fewer still in 1983. Some of the regulars who seem unable to "let go" of the notion include Massachusetts, Connecticut, New Jersey, Pennsylvania, Kentucky, Illinois, Missouri, Louisiana, Oregon, and, of course, California.

Just about the time that a certain amount of complacency seems justified, various events conspire to keep the issue alive. Currently there is the ruling of the NCAA setting a minimum score on the SAT in order to qualify for participation in NCAA-sponsored athletic events. In addition, several states have set minimum test scores for entrance into state-supported systems of higher education as a way of raising standards and saving money. Both steps have stimulated heated debates that are almost sure to reawaken interest in regulating tests.

Some personal observations

Advocates of the so-called truth-in-testing legislation are obviously not interested in "truth-in-education." They prefer to hide the truth about the educational system by killing the messenger that brings them news they prefer not to hear. In some instances they have persuaded representatives of minority groups to support their cause by raising once again the tired spectre of bias in standardized testing. These advocates would have society believe that "good" tests would reflect no differences between minority and majority groups and that there are no inequities in educational opportunity that might explain exisiting differences. And, of course, by sounding the death knell for standardized testing through their current legislative efforts, proponents of these bills consciously or unconsciously are going to make sure there are no more messengers to tell us how great the needs of educationally deprived groups are. Nor do supporters of such legislation appear to see a role for tests in the identification of deficiencies and in monitoring efforts to remedy problems. If there are those who prefer that such questions not be addressed, standardized testing is a convenient scapegoat and the logical party to silence.

Minorities are not the only group likely to suffer with the disappearance or weakening of standardized tests. The older applicants, whose formal training occurred some years back, will surely have a more difficult time supporting their qualifications. Competitive applicants from less-well-known undergraduate programs will find it difficult to persuade the admissions committee that their credentials are so good if not better than those of candidates from prestigious schools. After all, how does one interpret an "A" from a known school compared to an "A" from an unknown school? Is a "B" from a prestigious institution equivalent to an "A" somewhere else? For that matter, what does a "pass" mean, regardless of the source? Even from the same school, how can applicants with different majors or even the same majors with different programs be compared with some objectivity? It is difficult to see how the charges of arbitrariness and favoritism in admissions decisions that existed prior to the advent of standardized testing could be resisted successfully should this form of measurement be eliminated.

The irony of this entire experience is that these bills, supposedly representing the interests of the consumer and the disadvantaged, will in all likelihood accomplish just the opposite of what is intended. The consumer in New York has already been beset by confusion and by loss of service and by higher costs.

- If an objective of the legislation is to equalize access to information about tests and thereby reduce the alleged advantage of coaching

courses, it seems safe to expect just the opposite outcome. The disclosure of test contents on a continuing basis is going to make it all the easier for coaching courses to prepare more specific and detailed materials to the greater advantage of those who have the resources to use that approach to preparation.
- If the objective is to minimize the alleged monopolistic nature of the testing industry today, once again the opposite will be achieved. As was noted in New York, it is particularly the smaller test sponsors that will have the greatest difficulty in continuing to offer their programs under conditions of such legislation.
- If the objective is to enhance the quality of testing materials, it seems foolish to believe that the production of more materials in a shorter period would enhance the quality of the emerging product. Quality seems clearly at risk if items of demonstrated value cannot be reused.
- If there are legitimate questions to be answered regarding the accuracy of questions and answers and of the scores that are reported, disclosure of test contents to every examinee is hardly the most effective or efficient way to satisfy those concerns.
- If it is a question of improving feedback to the examinees on their performances so that they may better guide their preparations for subsequent attempts, uninterpreted feedback in the form of the answer to every question on the test is not likely to be as valuable to the candidates as a set of subscores that would identify specific strengths and weaknesses in the various topical areas covered by the examination. This latter suggestion was made by the AAMC and was rejected by the sponsor of the law in New York as not satisfying his interests for feedback to the examinee.

Though the present focus has been on the tests. It is important to recognize these legislative initiatives as a first step in the government determination of admissions and certification policies and practices in our colleges, universities, professional schools and in the professions. Self-regulating behavior in this area by faculties and professional organizations is clearly being characterized as irresponsible, uninformed, and inadequate.

In the final analysis, the most frustrating, insidious, and destructive aspect of this entire movement is the effect it has had in distracting the energies and resources of test sponsors from conducting the kinds of studies, from introducing the kinds of refinement and innovation into test programs that will achieve a better instrument and ultimately lead to better evaluation procedures. These energies and resources must now be mobilized to protect the basic integrity and viability of the testing program. It appears that once again we are prepared to ignore history's lesson and insist on killing the messenger in a futile effort to avoid the "truth about education."

Where to next?

I began by posing a series of questions that represent the stated concerns of proponents of standardized testing legislation. I suspect that each of us would have found it difficult to argue that none of the concerns had merit. Therein, I suspect, lies an important reason for the continuing interest displayed in these bills.

- We *can* provide more information about our tests, i.e., the knowlege and skills they are designed to measure and the manner in which the tests expect to make those measurements.
- We *can* provide more information about how the scores are derived and what standards for interpretation are used or suggested.
- We *can* incorporate various safeguards for assuring fairness and inform the consumer of these practices.
- We *can* report the results of research and studies that provide the bases for the use to which test results are put.
- We *can* make more explicit our review and appeal mechanisms for instances of questionable authenticity and validity.
- We *can* publicize our steps for ensuring accuracy of test answers and test scores.
- We *may* be able to provide more feedback about test performance than a single score or the ultimate outcome to which the score contributed.

The list could be expanded considerably. The message, however, seems clear. Some perceived needs and some abuses do exist. Wisdom suggests responding to the needs that have been identified, as well as assuming more responsibility for halting any abuses of which we are aware. At this point, however, it is not a case of preventive medicine. It is a matter of stopping the spread of an epidemic.

From another perspective, we have ample evidence that legislators, congressmen, and their staffs do listen. They may listen more attentively if the arguments are couched in terms they are most likely to understand. But they do listen. In many instances, there is clearly a significant degree of confusion and misunderstanding that must and can be dispelled, particularly if the information is provided before a hard position has been assumed publicly. Therefore, we must make our case. Do not be misled that advocates of testing legislation are interested only in secondary and post-secondary education. The bill proposing to regulate examinations used for certification has just recently been reintroduced into the Pennsylvania Legislature (House Bill 440).

As suggested by the title of my comments, I hope to raise certain issues that might assist you in deciding whether testing legislation was consumer protection or consumer fraud. I would like to conclude my remarks by drawing your attention to an article, "Representative Democracy, 'Men of Zeal,' and Testing Legislation," by Barbara Lerner, published in the March 1981 issue of *The American Psychologist*. I think you will find this a most provocative treatise of the consumer protection/fraud issue as it relates to testing legislation. Dr. Lerner reviews the data from ten different public opinion surveys and compares those expressions of public sentiment about tests and test use with positions taken by various groups, including so-called consumer and student groups.

She notes that in a 1979 Gallup poll, 81 percent of a sample of American parents found standardized tests "very useful" or "somewhat useful." In a 1977 Gallup poll, 81 percent of a sample of American adults favored use of ability test scores as the main consideration in allocating jobs and places in colleges *over* preferential treatment for women and minorities. In 1979, when the same question was put to students, essentially the same results were obtained.

Lerner also reported that data indicate that teachers are much more supportive of testing than the National Education Association (NEA) would have us believe. In the highly publicized area of minimum competency testing, only 16 percent favored the moratorium on testing called for by the NEA, while 62 percent endorsed the use of competence tests to determine high school graduation. Interestingly, at a meeting of leaders of the National School Boards Association where 1,000 attendees were surveyed, 69 percent agreed that teacher groups who call for the elimination of standardized testing are only trying to avoid being held accountable.

Dr. Lerner does suggest a note of caution for those of us who represent the interests of various constituencies. When members of the National Council on Measurement in Education were asked to estimate teacher and student attitudes toward standardized tests, they consistently overestimated the incidence of negative attitudes and underestimated positive ones.

Dr. Lerner teases us a bit with the suggestion that maybe there should be a truth-in-lobbying law. In closing, I would like to read a quotation that she cited early in her article. It was written by Justice Brandeis in his 1928 dissent in *Olmstead v. United States,* but seems to have renewed meaning today. He wrote,

Experience should teach us to be most on our guard to protect liberty when the government's purposes are beneficent. Men born to freedom are naturally alert to repel invasion of their liberty by evil-minded rulers. The greater dangers to liberty lurk in insidious encroachments by men of zeal, well-meaning but without understanding.

Disclosure of Confidential Information

Jerome S. Beigler, M.D.

By the nature of the doctor-patient relationship, the physician learns information, which, to protect the interests of both patient and profession, must not unilaterally be disclosed. Protecting the vulnerability of a person who becomes a patient has been codified as an ethical principle since the time of the Hippocratic Oath, which holds such information as "holy secrets."[1,2] On the other hand a complex society for its optimal functioning requires maximum access to information. A set of compromises has been evolved to determine the balance between these countervailing forces in areas such as litigation (malpractice; divorce proceedings; breach of contract to maintain privacy; personal injury); health care and health insurance; law enforcement (reporting communicable diseases, gunshot wounds, child abuse; warning third parties; investigation and trial of crimes); computer technology (access to private information without consent; "matching" programs; redisclosures). In addition, as will be discussed below, it seems the respect paid to the right of individual privacy is an inverse function of the emphasis on secrecy of government activities.

To provide further background, let us define three interrelated terms:

"Privilege" is a narrow, legalistic term pertaining to litigious situations of discovery of trial in which communications such as between patient and physician, lawyer and client, and priest and penitant or between spouses are protected by statute or public policy.

"Confidentiality" is a broader term with both legal and ethical meanings. It applies to the nondisclosure of communications in such spheres as health, insurance, employment, education, credit, and business.

"Privacy" is the broadest term, defined by Justice Brandeis as the "right to be left alone," and more recently found to have a constitutional basis.[3,4,5]

Antitrust aspects of confidentiality

The relevance of the above considerations to certification and accreditation can be illustrated by considering the antitrust suit brought by Doctor Pireno, a New York chiropractor, against the Union Labor Life Insurance Company and the New York Chiropractic Peer Review Committee, alleging their finding his professional practices unacceptable and his fees excessive as part of a "conspiracy to fix the prices that chiropractors would be permitted to charge for their services." The Peer Review Committee claimed immunity from antitrust scrutiny on the basis their deliberations were part of administering the "business of insurance." The U.S. Supreme Court affirmed an appeals court ruling that the committee, rather than being part of the "business of insurance," which pertains to state-regulated and antitrust-immune cooperation between insurance companies for actuarial purposes, was really part of the "insurance business" (which involves competitive selling of insurance and setting premium rates), which *is* liable to antitrust litigation, and remanded the case for trial.[6]

From a confidentiality perspective it was determined that, although state statutes protected the deliberations of peer review and other professional-regulatory committees from discovery, thus enabling their function in the interest of society and profession, the statutes could be preempted in federal jurisdictions. Except for specific regulations regarding professional standards review organizations (PSROs) and alcohol and drug abuse programs, there is no federal confidentiality law, and, as has been cited in other antitrust suits brought by physicians against their hospitals and hospital staffs, the Supremacy Clause of the U.S. Constitution prevails.[7]

Of further practical significance is that malpractice and general liability insurance provide only limited coverage for antitrust legal representation and, because antitrust action may be a crime and crimes cannot be protected by insurance, there is no coverage for antitrust (treble) damages. In view of the increasing likelihood of antitrust litigation against the professions, it is wise to review carefully individual and board malpractice and liability insurance and to have in mind the vulnerability of the deliberations of professional bodies to discovery in federal jurisdictions.

Erosion of privacy and increase of government secrecy

Let us now turn to an overview of national trends regarding the erosion of personal privacy while there is a concurrent increase in the secrecy of government-agency operations. Personal privacy is being encroached upon in two areas: the increased efficiency of computers due to technological advances; and the increased use of medical information for law-enforcement purposes (Ref. 2, pp.228–32; Ref. 8, pp. 81–86).

Because of the advances made in computer technology and the numbers of computers available, new federal programs allow for the matching of Internal Revenue Service (IRS) records and welfare payments, selective service registration, delinquent debtors, and the tracing of parents who abandon responsibilities for their children. On the one hand such programs may help detect and trace fraud and delinquency, but, on the other hand, the use of such previously confidential records will lessen trust in government and contribute to the general loss of discipline regarding confidentiality and respect for privacy.

Similarly the Secret Service tentatively has been authorized to use the FBI's computer system to keep track of persons who may pose a threat to officials. Until now, the FBI computers hold information only about those officially accused of crime, but the proposed program allows inclusion of those viewed as suspects.[9]

Another computer-related problem is that the new technology enables small employers to provide and administer their own health-insurance programs. Self-insured programs are not state-regulated, and employers have complete access to utilization histories of individual employees, thus enabling discriminatory decisions regarding employment. The only defense in such a program is not to use one's insurance benefits.[10] Health insurance programs of larger corporations use only periodic reports of utilization profiles on aggregates of anonymous patients, thereby lessening this risk.

Further evidence of the trend to efface privacy is the new federal rule requiring notification of parents of adolescents who obtain sex counseling and contraception and the move to end the confidentiality of juvenile criminal records.[11]

The increased use of medical information for law-enforcement purposes is additional evidence of this trend.[2,8] It is understandable that physicians be required to report communicable diseases, gunshot wounds, and child abuse, but there have been judicial developments that impose on a physician a limited duty to warn the presumed victim of his patient's aggression.[2,8,12] The status of this problem is still in process of evolving but has been the source of much uncertainty and has added further limitations to a physician's ability to ensure confidentiality.

The Privacy Protection Act of 1980, Public Law 96-440, was passed to protect the media from the consequences of the *Zurcher v. Standford Daily* decision, which upheld the validity of a warrant to search the premises of the Standford Daily newspaper for pictures of a student altercation. Search warrrants are issued only against those suspected of a crime; warrants against innocent third parties is new. If it had been available, *Zurcher* would have enabled Nixon's "plumbers" a warrant to search Doctor Fielding's office for information on Ellsberg (of the Pentagon Papers) rather than necessitating burglary.

The Privacy Protection Act of 1980 protects the media from surprise searches, but it leaves the rest of us vulnerable. Should a federal law-enforcement agency believe that we may have information relevant to the investigation of a suspected criminal, a warrant can be issued to search our offices, homes, or cars even without our presence. There is little legal recourse except after the fact. In the three years after the *Zurcher* decision there were at least 23 searches or attempted searches against third-party professionals.[13] Most of these were against lawyers (often public defenders) and journalists, but four were against health professionals (including a psychiatric-resident-in-training, a drug-abuse clinic and a psychologist in private practice).

Lawyers are familiar with subpoenas, but specific expertise is required to cope with a warrant. Because there are limited, legal self-protective actions that can be taken, a set a guidelines has been devised for those confronted with the service of a warrant. The guidelines have been published in several professional publications including the "Record" of the American Board of Medical Specialties.[14]

Another similar potential legislative problem involves the enactment thus far in seven states of the National Association of Insurance Commissioners' "Insurance Information and Privacy Protection Model Act." It is an industry-designed bill regarding the gathering and management of insurance-related information. "Section 13. Disclosure Limitations and Conditions" permits redisclosure of information without consent or notification of patient or doctor to law-enforcement authorities on the initiative and discretion of the insurance carrier. The intent was to facilitate the reporting of arson suspects, but the language allows the redisclosure of any information, thus eroding further the ability of physicians to protect the confidence of patients.[15]

The pressures of the medical profession to become agents of social control are also felt by the accountants and lawyers, as evidenced by the current controversy within the American Bar Association to change its ethical code to require reporting the crimes of clients.[15a]

Accompanying the above-outlined trend of eroding medical and professional privacy is a broader trend reflecting the increasing intrusiveness of government agencies, a growing disrespect for individual rights and an increasing secrecy that prevents oversight of government agencies by the public and its representatives. An early manifestation of the problem was a complex national security problem regarding the funding of academic research in cryptology resulting in a compromise in which the National Security Agency has requested it review cryptology-research papers before publication.[16,17]

Another manifestation of the trend toward government secrecy was a controversial Executive Order on April 2, 1982, regarding the reclassification of information, reversing a 30-year trend toward reducing classified information. Under the Carter Administration, a government official was not to classify information in case of doubt; under the Reagan order, when there is doubt regarding classification, the material is to be "safeguarded" by classifying it for 30 days, during which time government authorities would determine its classification.[18] The increase in classification hinders access to documents by the public under the Freedom of Information Act (FOIA).

The Reagan Administration has thus far unsuccessfully urged Congress to narrow the FOIA; instead the Justice Department has issued new guidelines reducing the number of requests that are granted free of charge.[19]

The relaxation of restrictions on CIA counter-intelligence activities has also been fostered, enabling domestic spying and early infiltration of domestic organizations.[20]

The Right to Financial Privacy Act (RFPA) was amended in 1980 to allow the Securities and Exchange Commission to obtain personal financial records from financial institutions without notifying the individual; secret charges can be filed and kept sealed without the person's knowledge.[21]

"Efforts by Members of the Reagan Administration to impose a variety of new restrictions on the open communication of unclassified scientific information in the name of national security are for the most part unwarranted and likely to be counterproductive," is the main conclusion of a joint committee of the National Academy of Sciences, the National Academy of Engineering, and the Institute of Medicine in a two-volume report. The study was provoked by a series of government censorship conflicts with the university-based research community. Micro-electronic data could not be routinely disseminated without prior government approval. "On several occasions unclassified papers were withdrawn on short notice from international scientific conferences at the insistence of government officials, and permission for visits by foreign scientists has been abruptly denied. In addition, universities have been asked to help in monitoring and enforcing restrictions on the movements of foreign scientists and foreign students on campus."[22]

These measures were justified by officials on the basis of preventing a growing "leakage" of militarily significant scientific information to "adversary nations." The independent panel verified a "substantial transfer of U.S. technology to the Soviet Union from diverse sources" but very little of this was attributable to universities and the open scientific communications. "U.S. openness gives [us] access to Soviet science . . . and useful insights into Soviet institutions and society."[22]

The panel felt tighter controls would counter-productively inhibit research, interaction, and training. "[T]he costs of even a small advance toward government censorship in American society are high. The First Amendment guarantees of free speech and free press help account for the resiliency of the nation." A "trust in Government . . . is promoted by openness and eroded by secrecy. Openness also makes possible the flow of information that is indispensable to the well-informed electorate essential for a healthy democracy."[22]

Rather than censorship, the panel advises reliance on security by accomplishment based on open and free scientific communication. The risks of such a strategy are balanced by our capacity to develop new technology faster than our adversaries. Interference with basic research by a military censorship would be damaging to scientific and economic as well as military progress; open communication accelerates scientific progress and the welfare of the nation. The panel recommends the vast majority of university research should be subject to no limitations on access or communications. In the rare case of government-supported research leading to short-term military applications, classification should be considered; other situations could be managed by limited control measures specified by contract, but not by extending existing export regulations.[22]

These recommendations are in considerable contrast to the last-minute withdrawal, demanded by the DOD, of 100 unclassified papers that were to be presented at the 26th International Technical Symposium of the Society of the of the Photo-Optical Instrumentation Engineers in San Diego, California, in September 1982 on the basis that the Russians derive intolerable benefits from such presentations.[23]

More subtle, but also significant, is President Reagan's 1984 budget proposals for research and development. There is a major increase in research allocations, but with a distinct emphasis on defense-oriented projects and job creation, yet accompanied by the blocking of "channels of scientific communication and technology transfer . . . enmeshing the scientific and engineering communities in the toils of political accountability. . . . What bears thinking about is the escalating instrumental function of the sciences in the business of the state and what, in the long run, may come of it."[23a]

Recently reporters, prior to being briefed on Russian military strength, were asked to sign a secrecy pledge promising disclosures to no one, including their own editors. The reporters refused so unprecedented a request, but were briefed after giving verbal reassurances of nonreporting. The fact that the DOD felt free to make such a request reflects on the recent changes in political ambience.

Futher evidence of this trend toward censorship and restriction of individual rights is the first loosening in seven years of guidelines for FBI investigations. The new guidelines allow investigations when there are indications "that two or more persons are engaged in an enterprise for the purpose of furthering political or social goals . . . through activities that involve force or violence."[24] Congressman Don Edwards (D., California), Chairman of the House Subcommittee on Civil and Constitutional Rights, expressed concern that "The Guidelines permit the launching of a full investigation based on 'advocacy' alone. . . . Mere advocacy is not enough to warrant prosecution, yet the FBI wants to investigate speech, [thereby chilling] legitimate First Amendment activity."[24] The guidelines have been ruled by Federal Judge Getzendanner as being in violation of a 1981 consent decree approved by the bureau in the settlement of "police spying" litigation.[24a]

Another restriction of free speech was effected by an executive order requiring several governmental agencies to review speeches and publications of their present and former employees as does the CIA, which has a Publications Review Board. The new order enables strict censorship over the writings of former officials, especially diplomats and military officers, making it difficult for them to participate in public debate and the political process. Officials will be governed by this order for the rest of their lives, even should they write novels or short stories.[25]

In the same vein, "President Reagan is moving quickly before the United States Supreme Court and the Congress to overturn the exclusionary rule, which prohibits prosecutors from using illegally seized evidence . . . to convict a defendant."[26] Since 1914, Supreme Court decisions interpreting the Constitution have deemed illegally obtained evidence inadmissable against a defendant. The Reagan Administration is seeking in a case before the Court[26] and in a bill introduced in Congress, a "good-faith" exception to this constitutional rule, which would authorize use of the evidence if the judge and jury conclude a law-enforcement officer had acted in good faith even though he had acted illegally and unconstitutionally. If adopted, this exception will foster further erosion of constitutional rights and encourage law-enforcement dishonesty. It would give license to courts, prosecutors, and police to ignore constitutional protection, thereby setting an example for the citizens of this country also to ignore the law[26] and adding to the considerable momentum to override the rights of members of a democracy.

Further evidence of the trend to restrict constitutional rights, especially freedom of speech, was embodied in Circular A-122 from the Office of Management and Budget, which would prohibit lobbying and advocacy by all nonprofit organizations that receive federal funds. Present regulations properly forbid the use of government dollars to influence legislation; the proposed new regulations would preclude the use of private funds for lobbying and also any form of intervention in the governmental decision-making process, including the submission of *amicus curiae* briefs, and would prohibit contact with public officials for purposes of debate or even cooperation such as education regarding objective research findings. The outpouring of public objections to the proposal was intense enough to effect its withdrawal for purposes of modification and resubmittal.[27] But again the evidence of overkill in the direction of censorship is disquieting. The promulgators of these liberty-restricting edicts no doubt are sincere and convinced of their rectitude. One is reminded of Justice Louis Brandeis, who wrote in 1928: "Experience should teach us to be most on our guard to protect liberty when the government's purposes are beneficent. . . . The greatest dangers to liberty lurk in insidious encroachment by men of zeal, well-meaing, but without understanding.[28]

Countervailing legislation and judicial decisions

In view of such manifestations of a regressive movement regarding privacy, government intrusion, and government secrecy, what can be done, and is there evidence of balancing forces? Our government has been through such crises in the past as for example during the Joe McCarthy era and the Nixon Administration. It is to be hoped that, if the democratic process prevails, we will manage through this one as well. There are bits of evidence in the form of judicial decisions and new legislation that may be reassuring. The Supreme Court unanimously judged that the Bureau of the Census need not disclose its master address lists to state and local officials challenging the accuracy of the 1980 census. The court agreed with the bureau's argument that census data must be kept confidential so that people would respond to the census without fear of invasion of their privacy.[29]

There have been three developments in response to the vulnerability of professional offices to innocent third-party search warrants. The Minnesota Supreme Court found searches of lawyers' offices "unreasonable" on the basis of violating attorney-client confidentiality and the work-product doctrine. The lawyer can be effective only if the client is assured of confidentiality and can disclose all the facts. The lawyer's ethical obligation to protect confidences is broader than the attorney-client privilege as is the work-product doctrine; allowing such searches unacceptably limits a defendant's right to effective counsel. The court based its decision on the Minnesota constitution and advised the use of subpoenas rather than warrants.[30]

California passed legislation mandating the presence of a special master at such searches to deter disruptive searches and to seal documents for which privilege is claimed pending adjudication.[30]

In 1978, Hawaii passed its Law 105, the Hawaii Medicaid Fraud Law. Section 8 authorizes warrants to search psychotherapists' offices for evidence of Medicaid fraud when "in the public interest." This meant that a warrant may be issued on the mere statement of a state official that fraud might exist. A psychologist was served such a warrant and many of his records were seized. The Hawaii Psychiatric Society sued to enjoin implementation of Section 8. On October 22, 1979, Federal District Judge Matthew Byrne issued a preliminary injunction pending trial, declaring Section 8 unconstitutional. (Judge Byrne of Los Angeles was also the judge in the Ellsberg [Pentagon Papers] break-in case involving similar issues.) On December 27, 1982 he issued a permanent injunction in a learned decision which recognizes a constitutional right to privacy, including the right of a patient to make an informed decision whether or not to undergo psychotherapy. Surprise searches expose a patient to loss of privacy; therefore, he cannot make an unencumbered decision regarding his own welfare. The statute was also held unconstitutional on the basis of violating the right to privacy by hazarding the forced disclosure of confidences made voluntarily in the course of psychotherapy. These are landmark adjudications defining a constitutional right to privacy, which includes a right to make unencumbered decisions about one's health and a right to maintain psychotherapeutic confidentiality.[2,5,31] The decision has been appealed by Governor Ariyoshi. It is hoped the case will reach the U.S. Supreme Court for important definition. Should it do so, there will be significant *amicus* work to do.

Also of favorable significance is a Seventh Circuit U.S. Court of Appeals decision that supports academic freedom by denying to Dow Chemical access to the unpublished data of a University of Wisconsin researcher. The University's attorney argued that "a scientist has to be free to take his inquiries where they lead him, and that a scientist should not be forced to disclose his research data until he has results he is willing to stand behind."[32] This important decision supports the privacy of a scientist's work product.

There have been three interesting decisions regarding peer review, PSROs, and adults. A federal trial court in Connecticut ruled that the proceedings of a hospital medical review committee conducting peer review were not discoverable in a malpractice suit. The court ruled that state law barring discovery of peer review proceedings unrelated to the subject matter of the suit prevailed, thus encouraging physicians to evaluate their peers without fear of disclosure, which purpose would be hampered by the release of any proceedings, not just those of the plaintiff patient. The function of the review committees to the profession and the public required an atmosphere of complete confidentiality. The principle of specific confidentiality in the interest of society's greater good prevailed.[33]

The confidentiality status of PSROs, which review Medicare and Medicaid cases according to federal statutory criteria, is in process of change. The District of Columbia Appeals Court struck down Judge Gesell's lower-court decision that PSROs are federal agencies subject to the release of information under the Freedom of Information Act (FOIA), but the Health Care Financing Administration (HCFA) sponsored a prestigious Institute of Medicine (IOM) Study which recommended implementation of HCFA's 1979 proposed loosening of PSRO confidentiality regulations. In the meantime, Rep. Henry Waxman (D., California), Chairman of the House Commerce Health Subcommittee, intends to use the IOM study as a guide for legislation pending further judicial decisions.[34]

Also relevant to Medicare and Medicaid cases is a New Hampshire federal court case in which protection from access by state auditors to private-case records was refused on the basis that federal regulations prohibit disclosure of identifiable records and there was no evidence of breach of those regulations.[35] Paradoxically, the decision emphasizes the validity of maintaining confidentiality.

Of considerable significance regarding a duty to warn, a Pennsylvania trial judge found that a psychiatrist had breached a statutorily clear confidentiality by warning without consent a patient's employer of her potential rageful outbursts. The judge found that California's *Tarasoff* criteria not only did not apply in Pennsylvania, but that Pennsylvania law clearly required the maintenance of confidentiality.[36] The patient's suit for damages was settled out of court.

Two Illinois Supreme Court cases also reflect the validity of local statutes. The state's attorney requested access to a venereal disease clinic's case records to search for women who may have been molested by a clinic employee. The lower court allowed, but the Supreme Court denied the access, on the basis that the public would use the clinic only if statutorily provided confidentiality were observed. It deemed it to the greater good of society that confidentiality prevail.[37]

In a second case, the court refused access to an abortion clinic's records by reason of doctor-patient confidentiality but recommended that, since the state's attorney had the names of the patients, he solicit informed consent from these patients to access their records for purposes of criminal prosecution against the physician.[38]

Compared to the strength of regressive forces that erode privacy and personal rights by means of government intrusions and secrecy, the forces that support the right to lead a private life in a democracy are not impressive. Yet it becomes apparent that an informed electorate is still a reality and that the democratic judicial process is still viable. The price of continued liberty is still eternal vigilance.

Practical applications regarding certification and accreditation

Now, how does all this apply in practical terms to certification and accreditation?

The impact of the *Pireno* case has been discussed above: Peer-review committees are not immune to antitrust litigation, state confidentiality statutes can be preempted in federal jurisdictions, and malpractice and liability insurance provides only limited protection in antitrust litigation.[6]

The next issue is the matter of public access to board test questions and challenges to the validity of the board examination process. Consumer groups have demanded access to test questions and answers; this would be counterproductive to the board-examination enterprise; the problem is evolving in the courts and legislatures. One result is that board examiners no longer are informed whether a candidate has taken the examination before. This fosters uniformity of examiner attitudes toward the candidates.

Challenges to the validity of the examination itself also have occurred. A candidate failed a board oral examination several times and sued to be certified by the board on the basis the examination was unfair and that he was being discriminated against, thus depriving him of income and status. The trial endured for two weeks resulting in vindication of the board's judgment. The judge also validated the assessment of candidate competence by means of an oral examination by experts.

The publication of examination results also merits discussion. Not publishing a list of failed candidates is obviously to be observed as a matter of protecting privacy and reputation. But some candidates (estimated at less than one percent) take exception to having their names published even as successful candidates. A rational explanation would be the avoidance of mailing lists or even a wish not to be identified with a given specialty. In any case, publication even of a success warrants informed consent.

Requests for information about the certification of individual physicians for the purposes of assessing competence, referral, or the research of a malpractice case are common. Such information is sensitive and warrants protection. Inquiries can be tactfully and skillfully resisted when appropriate, and most subpoenas can be quashed. The collection of such sensitive material imposes a duty to prevent its unconsented distribution.

Tape recorders at oral examinations also constitute a problem, especially when patients are involved. Boards do instruct candidates not to bring recorders on the basis that patient privacy would be breached and that the examination process itself would be impaired. Nevertheless there have been instances of candidate complaints so detailed regarding cited questions and answers as to raise suspicion. Yet reasonable preventive measures are limited.

The matter of license applications is also of interest. Most states include in their applications to practice medicine a specific question regarding a history of psychiatric illness or treatment. There have been objections that answering the question truthfully exposes the applicant to rejection or prejudice which is unfair, especially when the treatment may have consisted only of psychoanalysis undertaken for training purposes; to answer the question untruthfully exposes the applicant to inner disquiet and the hazard of future accountability. Some jurisdictions have resolved the problem by asking a general question regarding the presence of *any* disability that would interfere with practice, but most states still include the specific psychiatric question and then interview the applicant for more precise evaluation. The stigma of psychiatric experience persists.

Summary

After defining basic terms, we have discussed the antitrust aspects of confidentiality relevant to peer review. Also discussed was the fact that erosion of personal privacy is occurring in two areas: encroachments enabled by increased computer efficiency and the use of medical information for law-enforcement purposes. Accompanying the erosion of privacy is an increasing government intrusiveness and an increasing secrecy of government activities, which threaten the democratic foundation of our society. There are small evidences of countervailing legislative and judicial developments reflecting the viability of the democratic process. The practices regarding the disclosure of confidential information constitute a sensitive criterion of the political health of our nation. The paper closes with a discussion of practical applications of confidentiality issues regarding certification and accreditation.

References

1. Appelbaum, P. S., Confidentiality in psychiatric treatment. Chapter 21 in Grinspoon, L.(Ed.): *Psychiatry 1982, APA Annual Review.* Washington, D.C. American Psychiatric Press. 1982, pp. 327-34.
2. Beigler, J.S., Psychiatric confidentiality and the American legal system: an ethical conflict. In: Bloch, S., and Chodoff, P. (Ed.): *Psychiatric Ethics.* Oxford. Oxford University Press, 1981, pp. 220-34.
3. *Griswold v. Connecticut,* 381 U.S. 479, 14 L. Ed. 2d 510, 85 S. Ct. 1678. Grossman, M.: Confidentiality: The right to privacy *versus* the

right to know. In: Boston, W. E., and Sanborn, C. J. (Eds.): *Law and the Mental Health Professions*. New York, International Universities Press, 1978, pp. 178–80.
4. *Whalen v. Roe*, 429 U.S. 589, pp. 599–600 (1977).
5. *Hawaii Psychiatric Society v. George R. Ariyoshi*. CV 79-0113. U.S. District Court, District of Hawaii, Dec. 27, 1982.
6. Antitrust laws and peer review revisited. In *Peer Review Letter*. Office of Peer Review. American Psychiatric Association. Vol 2, No. 2, September 1982. Washington, D.C., p. 2. *Union Labor Life v. Pireno*. U.S. Supreme Court.
7. *Memorial Hospital for McHenry County v. The Honorable Milton I. Shadur*, U.S. District Judge, U.S. Court of Appeals, 7th Circuit, No. 80-2815, November 16, 1981.
8. Beigler, J. S., Privacy and confidentiality. In: Hofling, C. K. (Ed.): *Law and Ethics in the Practice of Psychiatry*. New York. Brunner/Mazel, 1981.
9. Computerizing suspects Okd. Chicago Sun-Times, 26 December 1982, p. 34.
10. Beigler, J. S., Psychiatry and Confidentiality. *Amer. J. Forensic Psychiatry*, 1:7–19, 1978. Also in *Hearings before the Subcommittee on the Constitution of the Committee on the Judiciary*, United States Senate, Ninety-fifth Congress, Second Session, on S. 3162. A Bill to Secure and Protect the Freedom of Individuals from Unwarranted Intrusions by Persons Acting under Color of Law. Washington, D.C., U.S. Govt. Printing Office, 1979, pp. 254–61.
11. Squeal Rule Sophistry, Editorial. New York Times, 16 February 1983, p. 24; Miniclier, K.: Clinics may squeal on teenagers. U.S. seeks to end birth-curb confidentiality. *Chicago Sun-Times*, 18 Jan. 82, p. 20; Chambers, M.: Youth-Court Secrecy, an end urged to the confidentiality of criminal records in juvenile cases. *New York Times*, 28 Jan. 82, p. 8.
12. Wise, T. P., Where the public peril begins. A survey of psychotherapists to determine the effects of *Tarasoff*. *Stanford Law Review*, 31:165–190, 1978. G.E. Dix: *Tarasoff* and the duty to warn potential victims. In: Hofling, C. K. (Ed.): *Law and Ethics in the Practice of Psychiatry*. New York. Brunner/Mazel, 1981
13. Wascher, J., Fiduccia, D., Kohn, E., *History of Third-Party Search Incidents*. Stanford University News Service, Sept. 10, 1981.
14. Confidentiality: guidelines on privacy, confidentiality and dealing with warrants. American Board of Medical Specialties "Record," May 1982, pp. 1–3.

15. *Confidentiality. The Insurance Information and Privacy Protection Model Act of the NAIC.* State Update. Division of Government Relations. Amer. Psychiatric Assn. March-April, 1981, pp. 1–3.
15a. Taylor, S., ABA's decision: lawyer confidentiality over disclosure of crimes-to-be. *New York Times*, 14 Feb. 83, p. 10. Freedman, M.H.: . . . Wrong? silence is right. Ibid., p. 19.
16. Kolata, G. B., Cryptography: A new clash between academic freedom and national security. *Science*, Vol. 209, 29 Aug. 80, pp. 995–6. Hines, W.: Computer fight: liberty vs. security. *Chicago Sunday Sun-Times*, 28 Sept. 80, p. 62.
17. Kolata, G. B., NSA asks to review papers before publication. *Science*, Vol. 215:19 March 82, p. 1485.
18. Kolata, G. B., Reagan signs order on classification. *Science*, Vol. 216: 16 April 82.
19. Taylor, S., Information act gets new fee rule. *New York Times*, 12 Jan. 82, p. 10.
20. Pear, R., Intelligence groups seek power to gain data on U.S. Citizens. *New York Times*, 10 March 81, pp. 1,9.
21. Porter, Sylvia, SEC can get personal records without citizen's knowledge. *Chicago Sun-Times*, 26 June 81, p. 53.
22. Secrecy v. Security. *Scientific American*, Dec. 82, pp. 74–75.
23. Kolata, G. B., Export control threat disrupts meeting. *Science*, Vol. 217, 24 Sept. 1982, p. 1233; Yaver, J.: Letter. Exchange of technical information. *Science*, Vol. 218, 12 Nov. 82, p. 636.
23a. Carey, W. D., 1984: Science's multicolored coat. Editorial. *Science*, Vol. 220, April 15, 1983.
24. Pear, R., F.B.I. permitted wider latitude in investigations. *New York Times*. 8 March 83, pp. 1,9.
24a. Nicodemus, C., Alter rules on spying, U.S. judge orders FBI. *Chicago Sunday Sun-Times*, April 17, 1983, p. 40.
25. Pear, R., Reagan order on classified data gives U.S. agencies wide review power. *New York Times*, 14 March 83, p. 11; Lewis, A.: Aboard at home. Reagan vs. Madison. *New York Times*, 17 March 83, p. 27.
26. Greenhouse, L., Supreme Court urged to change rule on evidence. *New York Times*, 2 March 83, p. 9; Denniston, L.: Illinois case hits a snag as test of evidence rule. *Chicago Sun-Times*, 2 March 83, p. 32; Gardus, M.: Excluding justice. *New York Times*, 4 April 83, p. 19.
27. Editorial. The O.M.B. bomb-throwers. *New York Times*, 15 March 83, p. 28. Wattleton, F.: Letter. How O.M.B.'s defunding plan misfired. Ibid., 5 April 83, p. 26.

28. Cited by: Lewis, A.: Aboard at home. Men of Zeal. *New York Times*, 31 March 82, p. 31.
29. High court upholds privacy of census address list. *New York Times*, 25 Feb. 81, pp. 1, 12. *Baldridge v. Shapiro*, No. 80-1436. *Ms Nichols v. Baldridge*, No. 80-1781.
30. Cook, R. C., Law office searches—A dilemma Illinois must resolve. *Ill. Bar Journal*, Nov. 1981, pp. 170-75.
31. News Release. Hawaii Psychiatric Society. Honolulu. 27 Dec. 82.
32. Broad, W. J., Court upholds privacy of unpublished data. University of Wisconsin successfully fights off attempt by Dow Chemical to review data of controversial study. *Science*. Vol. 216:34-35, 2 April 82. U.S. Court of Appeals, 7th Cir., 80-2013, Feb. 22, 1982.
33. *Morse v. Gerity*, 520 F. Supp. 470 (D.C. Conn., June 4, 1981), *American Med. News*, February 26, 1982, p. 13.
34. *Washington Report on Medicine and Health*. Perspectives. Medical confidentiality: whose right? 23 Nov. 1981.
35. *Joseph O'Hare, et al v. Harris et al*. U.S. District Court, District of New Hampshire, Cir. No. 80-457-D, March 12, 1981.
36. *Hopewell v. Adebimpe*, et al. No. G.D. 78-28-756. Court of Common Pleas of Alleghany County, Civil Division, June 1, 1981.
37. *People ex rel. et al v. Calvo*, Ill. Supreme Court, No. 55436, Jan. 21, 1982.
38. *People State of Ill. v. Bickham*, Ill. Supreme Court, No. 54500, Jan. 21, 1982.

Challenges to Licensing Boards—1983

Henry G. Cramblett, M.D.

Medical licensing boards

The licensure of physicians in this country is the responsibility of 62 licensing authorities in the 50 states and territories. The authority to issue licenses in the medical care field is a statutory one, and the requirements for licensure are those determined by the legislative authority of the various jurisdictions. The responsibility of a state licensing board is to serve the high purpose of protecting the public by ensuring that its licensees are competent. With statutory authority, the individual boards establish prerequisites and certain standards to assure the public that each of the individuals whom it licenses possesses qualifications meeting at least minimal standards.

Although there is still a diversity in the qualifications required for licensure in the 62 jurisdictions, there are three general prerequisites that are required of any individual seeking a license for the independent practice of medicine. Namely, the individual (1) must be of good moral and ethical character, (2) must have successfully completed the medical curriculum of an approved medical school and (3) must have obtained a passing grade on a medical licensing examination.

The pathway to licensure of recent medical graduates has become increasingly complex in the last decade. Indeed, the diversity in character, training, and experience of today's recent medical graduate requires that state medical boards continously evaluate the adequacy and integrity of our medical licensing system. For purposes of this presentation, I will categorize the recent medical graduate into three groups; namely, (1) the graduate from U.S. schools accredited by the Liaison Committee on Medical Education (LCME); (2) the graduate from foreign medical schools established to train physicians for practice in the country in which the schools are located; and (3) the U.S. citizen graduate from foreign medical schools recently established for the purpose of training physicians for medical practice in the United States. I will discuss each of these groups from the perspective of a state licensing board member, subsequently address some issues and concerns common to all three groups and, finally, indicate the difficulty in applying in an equal fashion the three general prerequisites for licensure to candidates from these groups.

Challenges to "prerequisites" to medical licensure

Personal attributes of candidate. The criterion "of good moral and ethical character" is often criticized because of its subjectivity. It is a requirement, however, that reaches to the very core of the integrity of medical profession in this country. It is the responsibility of the faculty of medical schools to determine appropriate moral, ethical, and behavioral attributes of the students who matriculate into their programs. Moreover, faculty members have the opportunity to evaluate these qualities of their students during their medical undergraduate education years. Additionally, as one of the three general prerequisites for licensure required by all state medical boards, an individual's personal attributes must also be evaluated by the licensing body. This evaluation must necessarily rely to a great extent on the observations of the medical faculty and other members of the profession who have had frequent contact with the candidate. The subjectivity inherent in attempting to evaluate a candidate's moral and ethical character has been the cause of much criticism for state licensing boards. Critics have suggested that there is inadequate accountability to the public in this regard, such that licensing boards are free to develop their own respective definitions of "good moral and ethical character" and apply these definitions in an arbitrary fashion so long as their regulated profession realizes some form of benefit. In fact, it has been an extension of similar arguments that has placed medical boards in a defensive position when critics have suggested that they engage in anticompetitive and monopolistic behavior relative to the professionals they regulate. State licensing boards remain aware of these criticisms and have pro-actively responded with numerous initiatives, including more uniformly developed and applied subjective definitions and increasing consumer participation and representation on their boards.

It is disquieting to those of us in the licensing community to note the apparent upsurge in cheating and/or dishonest conduct relating to examinations in medical schools. This in itself may be an early indicator of questionable moral and ethical character. As a matter of fact, the integrity of the National Board Examination and its derivative examinations is of increasing concern because of breaches in security. One can peruse many journals that contain advertisements purporting to have available for sale actual questions from the National Board of Medical Examiners' test-item library.

Although the faculty of a college of medicine confronted with such a situation may act decisively and may even expel a student from their college for a time, the state licensing board has no way to ascertain these dishonest deeds. If the student is readmitted and given "another chance," this information would not be among that received by the medical board.

Comparable evaluation of the personal attributes of graduates of non-LCME schools is very difficult. Often the number of faculty in proportion to the size of the student body in foreign schools is disparate to the degree that actual knowledge of the personal attributes of the student may be lacking. Moreover, the complexities of the licensing application process tend to cause difficulties in obtaining reliable information on an individual candidate for licensure. The problem is important enough to the Federation of State Medical Boards that a committee to study the personal attributes of candidates for licensure has been established. It is anticipated that a more uniform approach can be designed for collection of sufficient personal data to meet the statutory requirements of knowledge of good moral and ethical character. If, indeed, state licensing boards are remiss in fulfilling these responsibilities, might they not be inviting encroachment on their respective rights by the federal government or even their own state governments?

Requirement that candidate be a graduate of an approved and/or accredited school. The faculties of U.S. medical schools have the responsibility for development of their school's medical curriculum as well as for conferring the Doctor of Medicine degree on students who are judged to have successfully completed their academic program. Assisting the faculty in the development and maintenance of their medical program is the LCME, the accrediting body that performs periodic and thorough surveys of medical schools within its jurisdiction to ensure that each school continues to possess the capabilities and facilities essential for adequately training competent and knowledgeable new physicians and preparing them to enter graduate training programs. Vigorously reviewing the individual schools for their organization, administration, faculty growth and development, faculty-student ratio, didactic and clinical teaching facilities, basic and clinical science curriculum content, research capabilities, clinical rotation opportunities for students, and numerous other components of a medical undergraduate program deemed necessary for accreditation permits the LCME to ensure a level of consistency in necessary instruction afforded all medical students. Accordingly, state medical boards rely on the U.S. medical school faculties to provide adequate educational training programs that enable individuals to develop the knowledge, skills, and abilities necessary for the general practice of medicine. Additionally, state boards rely on the LCME's accreditation process to ensure continuing adequacy of such programs and in verifying that a candidate for licensure has successfully completed the curriculum of an approved medical school.

Prior to the last decade or so, graduates of foreign medical schools who came to this country for their graduate medical training and/or to practice medicine were primarily graduates of long-established schools. Requiring the same basic prerequisites for licensure of these students posed no special problems, since they came from schools generally well known and about which appropriate information was readily available to state medical boards. Similar to the situation with graduates of LCME-accredited schools, the prerequisite of successful completion of the curriculum of an approved medical school was met. Obviously, the word "approved" here had a somewhat different meaning for graduates of these foreign schools than for graduates of LCME-accredited schools, but the comparability of many foreign programs with the programs offered to students at the U.S. schools permitted this rather flexible interpretation. In respect to foreign graduates from long-standing and highly regarded foreign medical schools, state medical boards are presently at no less a disadvantage than they have been for years. Familiarity with these schools' faculties, facilities, and capabilities is common, and, since graduates have been coming from many of these schools for so many years, there is essentially a "track record" on which medical boards can depend in determining if the graduate has successfully completed the curriculum of an approved medical school. Important to our consideration here is the fact that these graduates were deemed to have received a medical education of sufficient quality to permit them to practice in the country of origin.

The recent development of foreign schools in the Caribbean and other areas—which are training U.S. citizens for the purpose of returning to the United States to practice medicine—has been accompanied by a unique set of problems for state medical boards. Firsthand information about the faculty, facilities, and medical education programs at these schools is often difficult to obtain. Unlike the case in U.S. schools, there is basically no external evaluation of the adequacy of the medical education available to medical boards. Although these schools are listed by the World Health Organization (WHO), the WHO itself proclaims in the preface to its 1979 directory (fifth edition) that "the World Health Organization has no authority to grant any form of recognition or accreditation to schools of medicine or to endorse their training programmes." Consequently, state licensing boards are at a distinct disadvantage in attempting to assess whether a recent graduate of one of these newer schools has met the prerequisites for licensure. Necessarily, a state board must have knowledge of the adequacy of the medical program that a candidate for licensure has completed, if the board is to consider a program to be "approved." For this reason, in an attempt to assist state boards in gathering information about these schools, The Federation of State Medical Boards established the Commission to Evaluate Foreign Medical Schools. This body after in-depth deliberation developed a questionnaire that was sent to foreign schools at the request of individual state medical boards beginning in October 1981. The questionnaire requests that the given school provide information that a state board would need to determine the adequacy of a medical education program. For instance, information is requested about a school's legal authority to operate, admission requirements of students, administration, faculty, financial resources, clinical teaching facilities, basic science and clinical science curriculum content, research programs, graduate medical education programs, and continuing medical education efforts. Once the data have been reviewed, a site visit team is dispatched for a firsthand inspection. Quite frankly, if a medical board is willing to consider a medical program to be adequate without access to this information, then perhaps it is time that state medical boards completely relinquish their responsibility for having knowledge about the medical school from which a candidate for licensure has graduated. Otherwise, one might well argue that state boards are misleading the public and breaching their legal obligations and duties to the medical care consumer. Further, if state medical boards do not have available some reasonably similar external assessment mechanism for these foreign schools as they do for LCME-accredited schools, they may continue to find themselves barraged with allegations of denial of equal protection and due proces. It is the hope of the FSMB that this questionnaire/site visit approach will assist in alleviating such allegations. To date, one school has completed the questionnaire and a site visit has been concluded, utilizing faculty from LCME-approved medical schools for the site-visit team. The report of that visit is available to state licensing boards on request. It will be the responsibility of the individual boards to determine whether the school in question meets their requirements. At least one state, i.e., Ohio, has "provisionally" approved that school.

Requirement that candidate pass a licensing examination. Currently, there are two examination pathways to licensure in this country. Graduates of LCME-accredited U.S. and Canadian schools may take Parts I, II, and III of the National Board of Medical Examiners' (NBME) examination. Successful completion of the three parts of the NBME examination and one year of approved postgraduate training lead to NBME certification which can be recognized by individual licensing boards for endorsement. This pathway is open to candidates for licensure in all states except Louisiana and Texas and the Virgin Islands. The other pathway to licensure is the FLEX examination sponsored by The Federation of State Medical Boards. This examination, given over a period of three days each June and December, is taken by some graduates of LCME-accredited schools, but most of those sitting for the examination are graduates of non-LCME accredited schools.

There continue to be criticisms of the present dual pathway to licensure. Both pathways permit medical graduates to provide direct patient care under supervision during postgraduate training without having undergone a formal assessment of their cognitive qualifications to practice medicine. Second, the National Board of Medical Examiners' examination sequence is being utilized both for evaluating academic achievement of medical students as well as by state licensing boards for the purposes of licensure. Use of this examination for purposes of academic evaluation and/or promotion has been continually criticized as being an inappropriate use of the examination.

Further, The Federation of State Medical Boards and the National Board of Medical Examiners are in agreement that it is possible to develop a better examination for the specific purpose of licensure. They are continuing to cooperate in their attempts to achieve this goal.

A third consideration that indicates the need for modifying the present examination system relates to the alleged discrimination involved in utilizing more than one means to attain one goal. Specifically, licensing boards have been criticized for administering a different licensing examination to graduates of foreign schools than to graduates of U.S. schools, all of whom are seeking the same type of license. It has been suggested further by critics that differences in timing and grading of the FLEX exam versus the NBME sequence results in different standards of licensure. Obviously, a single standardized pathway applied to all candidates would quickly dispel such criticism.

Challenges relating to scope of practice of limited practitioners

During the past 10 years, there has been a proliferation in the number and type of nonphysician health care workers. For instance, physician-assistants are licensed in many states to provide medical care under the "direct supervision of physicians." Certain other categories such as "nurse practitioners" have been trained in many areas throughout the country but are not widely licensed to participate in medical care. Rather, they are often subject to the statutes, rules, and regulations of nursing licensing boards.

As these new "practitioners" have proliferated, they have increasingly sought recognition and expanded "scope of practice." The statutes defining the practice of medicine in most states are very specific, and, although physicians have from the beginning been able to delegate certain responsibilities, nonphysicians have not been permitted to deliver medical care without appropriate supervision.

However, with increasing recognition and numbers, there are requests to increase the scope of practice to the point of permitting independent practice and authorizing such "practitioners" to charge a fee for service.

There are many legal issues involved in this situation, and I am sure that the critics of organized medicine and state regulatory boards might raise the question of conflict of interest, monopoly, and restraint of trade. While, from the legal point of view, these may be very legitimate concerns, as a physician, as an educator and as a member of a state medical board, I have yet another concern, i.e., whether there should be one standard of medical care in this country, or whether by default we permit two standards of medical care to evolve; that is, one level of care delivered by physicians and another level delivered by nonphysicians.

In addition to the levels of practice of medical care in this country being affected, there is another question as to whether such a development would be helpful to the current efforts to achieve cost containment in health care. Physician-assistants particularly were visualized as expanding medical care in under-served areas and also as having a beneficial effect on reducing "health care costs." From my personal experience as a member of a licensing board, I have not witnessed either of these two phenomena coming into play with the utilization of physician-assistants.

Challenges to disciplinary actions of licensing boards

In most states, members of the state licensing boards serve as hearing members for disciplinary matters involving its licensees under authority of the Administrative Procedures Act. Although not trained in legal matters, physicians and other members of medical boards have become aware of the importance of due process and certain legal procedural matters necessary for "fairness." Accordingly, it is now routine that the hearing member for a potential disciplinary matter is absent from the room when the board members consider a possible citation, so that he has no information prior to the formal hearing. Prior to the hearing, the member receives the appropriate instructions relating to his own conduct and to certain rules of evidence. Following the completion of the hearing, the hearing member studies the transcript and translates the appropriate information from the testimony and the evidence to form the conclusions, the findings of fact, and the proposed order. At a formal meeting of the licensing board, the individual members of the board—after also having read the complete transcript, the hearing member's report, and objections from the licensee's counsel—either approve and confirm the order of the hearing member or alter it according to their own beliefs based upon the evidence presented.

After this very laborious and expensive procedure, individual licensing boards are often frustrated by what happens in the court system. Often an injunction against the medical board is obtained, permitting the physician to practice for months or, in some cases, years. During this time, medical boards are often unfairly criticized by the press for their lack of action. To our frustration and disappointment, only too often the order of the medical board is reversed on legal procedural or technical matters not necessarily germane to the actual infractions of the licensee.

Challenges to licensing boards of ensuring continuing competence of its licensees

One of the most complex and difficult situations facing licensing boards today is to guarantee to the public in some manner that its licensees are as competent to practice medicine years after issue of a license as they were at the time of the initial issue. State medical boards are often criticized for permitting previously licensed, incompetent practitioners to continue to practice. It is certainly possible to test by examination for certain cognitive information that helps determine whether a licensee has sufficient basic medical information necessary for the initial practice of medicine. After the physician enters into practice, however, he quickly gains practical experience, intuition, and knowledge that is not easy to measure. To ensure continuing competence of physicians, many approaches have been suggested, including recertification, re-examination, mandatory continuing education, audit of office and hospital records, and, most recently, encounters with a computer on which simulated cases are presented to the physician.

Although we can discuss competence, it is almost impossible at present to devise an approach that will ensure that all of our licensees remain competent during their entire professional careers. Some have suggested that litigation involving malpractice or other allegations of subminimal practice may be a test of a physician's competence. I do not believe that this is necessarily true because, in dealing with some of the more severe disciplinary cases before our licensing board, we find quite commonly that the physician has never been sued. On the other hand, quite competent physicians are often sued, which may relate to the perceived quality of the interaction between the physician and the patient and/or the family.

In conclusion, state licensing boards as regulatory bodies serve as an important check and balance to the public to ensure that those who are licensed are qualified. Although there are shortcomings, problems, legal complexities, and challenges, as a physician, medical educator, and a member of a medical board, I believe that regulatory bodies perform a function essential to the public good. Nothing has been proposed, in my opinion, that would better serve the public interest.

Recertification

John A. Benson Jr., M.D.

Concept and goals

Logic and accountability have obliged certifying boards to adopt recertification for a very straightforward reason. Certification cannot have meaning for an indefinite period, and its meaning has eroded and needs enhancement. As with a university degree, the certificate in a given specialty recognizes competence as of a certain date. How well that competence is used in clinical performance and maintained over the years has been beyond the control of certifying boards. Very few certificates have been revoked, sometimes only temporarily, and these because of egregious public behavior rather than because of failed clinical skills.

In 1973 the membership of the American Board of Medical Specialties endorsed the principle of recertification with the policy that voluntary, periodic recertification of medical specialists become an integral part of all national medical specialties' certification programs. The policy was reaffirmed in 1978. ABMS recognized that there might be significant differences in recertification strategies, both among different specialties and within a specialty from the method used in its initial certification process. Ten years later only 8 of the 23 boards have mounted recertification processes (Table 1). Of these only the American Board of Family Practice has conducted a mandatory recertification examination. But eight boards will grant certification for only a limited period of time, usually ten years (Table 2).

Table 1. First recertification examinations.

Allergy and Immunology	1977
Family Practice	1976
Internal Medicine	1974
Obstetrics and Gynecology	1978
Pediatrics	1980
Plastic Surgery	1977
Surgery	1980
Pediatric Surgery	1982
Urology	1981

Presumably outdated certificates will either be recalled by the board or considered invalid. Whether the names of diplomats who fail to comply will be removed from the *Directory of Medical Specialists*, the reference compendium of all certified specialists, remains to be seen. How hospital staffs handle privileges for those who fail to maintain certification over a career will necessitate major accommodation.

The goals of the boards in recertification have generally been the promotion of continuing scholarship and avoidance of obsolescence. As Doctor Pisacano of the American Board of Family Practice writes, "The true professional perpetually forges ahead and never rests content on the cognitive laurels of yesterday." Although all boards recognize that cognitive skill does not guarantee good clinical care, most would agree with the boards that it is difficult to provide good clinical care without a sound, modern knowledge base. In general, most who have sought voluntary recertification have tried to prove only to themselves that they still were capable of doing a good job. So far recertification has not conveyed substantial privilege, and lack of recertification has hardly been noticed. For that matter, the public remains woefully uninformed about the significance of certification itself. Those who have studied long and hard and subjected themselves to the threat of failure of a voluntary recertification examination have mostly been the ones who least needed either the stimulus or the recognition by peers.

A new concept of the goal of recertification is emerging. It derives from two prevalent attitudes among practicing specialists:

The first is that an easy recertification test which nearly everyone passes is not a sufficiently satisfying challenge to be worth the time-consuming preparation.

Table 2. Time-limited certificates.

	Duration	Beginning
Critical Care Medicine	10 years	1984
Emergency Medicine	10	1980*
Family Practice	7	1969*
Plastic Surgery	10	1985
Surgery	10	1976
Pediatric Surgery	10	1975*
Thoracic Surgery	10	1976
Urology	10	1985

*Date of first exam given by the new board.

The second results from fear of the unknown. Physicians are concerned that some third party, perhaps the government, malpractice courts, insurers, or competitive hospital staff will utilize failure of recertification in some unpredictable manner that will remove privileges. Members of certain boards have been subjected to considerable acrimony and have even lost national standing, for example, in specialty societies in their disciplines because they advocated recertification in their specialties. This fear is buttressed by the wide differentiation of practices within a specialty and by the recognized difficulty of assesing either quality of medical care or of clinical performance. It seems as though every physician and surgeon knows some knowledgeable but disorganized or inept colleague without compassion and feels sure that that person would succeed with recertification's current test instruments. Therefore, only a small percentage of eligible diplomates have undertaken certification so far. They appear to prefer to see what is going to happen to those who fail or to postpone the matter until participation is literally required or prudent for practical reasons.

With the initial goal of certification in mind and the experience its three recertification examinations since 1974, the American Board of Internal Medicine has embarked on a new approach. It wishes to provide an accolade or honor to those who demonstrate to its satisfaction "advanced achievement in internal medicine." It will tailor its examination to the practice modes of applicants to some extent, permit repetition of modules of content that were failed, and set a higher standard for passing. ABIM's previous standard for recertification was lower and provided an advantage to its diplomates, a kind of quasi-"grandfathering." The new premise is that a reward for achievement may be more attractive and beneficial than the threat of failure and risk of withdrawal of some undetermined privilege. ABIM will offer a carrot and withdraw its stick. The stick was pretty wimpy anyway. The board is fortified in this decision by the remarkable success of the Medical Knowledge Self-Assessment Program of the American College of Physicians, the educational society of practicing internists, which every three years attracts over 40,000 subscribers to this program of continuing medical education. By contrast, only about 2,000 souls have dared to apply for each recertification exam. One could argue that the college's educational program is enough, but it offers no challenge exam and no credential that can reassure the public. The ABIM will learn in 1985 whether its premise was correct.

Recertification thus far has not conveyed privilege. It does not bring premium pay in the armed forces, fortify expert testimony, reduce malpractice insurance premiums, or enable special status on hospital staffs or in professional societies—all of which are enhanced by initial certification. But history is likely to repeat itself. In the forties and fifties, certification was undertaken by less than half of practicing specialists and didn't catch on until the last fifteen years. Today certification is no longer an option. It is my prediction that the abundance of physicians in competition with each other, rapid advances in technology (including knowledge), and need for credentialing in an age of increasing regulation will make recertification just as indispensable.

Experience of ABMS boards with recertification

In 1969 the brand-new American Board of Family Practice mandated the recertification of its diplomates after seven or eight years. At the same time the American Board of Internal Medicine independently adopted recertification in principle. Internal Medicine offered the first recertification examination in 1974. Since then eight boards have provided recertification examinations in nine areas. Although other boards have announced their intent to recertify, two have later retracted that announcement because of extreme pressure from peers, often in related specialty societies. Another reflection of this unrest is the indefinite date of the next recertification examination in at least three specialties.

The numbers recertified will disappoint idealists. In recent years, the 23 specialty boards within ABMS have issued certificates to about 17,000 new diplomats each year. In the past ten years, 155,000 initial certificates have been granted in the 23 primary specialties. In contrast, relatively few

Table 3. Recertification among the specialties.

	1974	1975	1976	1977	1978	1979	1980	1981	1982
Allergy and Immunology	—	—	—	182	—	—	88	—	—
Family Practice	—	—	1,374	1,415	1,126	1,013	920	1,037	1,652
Internal Medicine	3,212	—	—	2,153	—	—	1,948	—	940
Obstetrics/Gynecology	—	—	—	—	1,351	1,552	562	315	332
Pediatrics	—	—	—	—	—	—	—	558	115
Plastic Surgery	—	—	—	269	—	24	—	—	—
Surgery	—	—	—	—	—	—	476	134	55
Pediatric Surgery	—	—	—	—	—	—	—	—	112

have become recertified (Table 3.). For example, in its three recertification examinations, the American Board of Internal Medicine recertified 3,212 in 1974, 2,153 in 1977, and 1,948 in 1980. This represents a total of 7,313 recertified internists, a small proportion of those eligible. Some reasons for this poor turnout have been suggested already. Other reasons include the strong trend in internal medicine for subspecialization (and ABIM does not yet offer recertification in the nine subspecialties), lack of confidence in the test instrument, the large number of older practicing internists, and the differentiation of practices in such a broad primary-care specialty.

In its first year, 1970, the American Board of Family Practice certified 1,690 diplomates. Of these, 1,374 were recertified in 1976. Compliance has not been so satisfactory since; for example in 1980 only 920 were recertified in the mandatory program of Family Practice even though about 1,200 were being certified each year in the early seventies. Still Family Practice can be extremely proud of its record. In 1982 some of its recertified diplomates applied for recertification for the second time. While 1,652 of its diplomates were recertified six to eight years after their initial certification, 940 more succeeded in a second recertification.

At the present time about half the boards have received approval of recertification processes from their peers in ABMS. A thirteenth recertification process, the first in a subspecialty, namely Pediatric Surgery, has also been approved. In addition to those boards already indicated, Emergency Medicine, Orthopaedic Surgery, Pathology, and Thoracic Surgery have successfully submitted programs. Although others have announced an intent to recertify, their processes have not been formulated for approval by the other boards in ABMS.

The processes used in recertification vary. ABMS has adopted the principle that a challenge examination provides the only credible approach, and to such a proctored exam have been added other requirements. Pathology will recertify those of its diplomates who pass the current initial certifying examination as one pathway, and Family Practice asked its diplomates in 1982 to undertake the first half of its certifying examination as part of its recertification process. Licensure is required by most boards for recertification, presumably to provide evidence of continuing moral and ethical standing in the profession. Continuing medical education is also frequently required, and is always encouraged in the preparation for recertification. In some instances, the type or number of hours is left unspecified, and in others it must be approved by the authority within the specialty which accredits institutions offering continuing medical education. Since people learn in different ways, and since it has some doubts as to the effectiveness of learning from most postgraduate courses, the American Board of Internal Medicine has not required CME credits.

Family Practice includes a review of selected records from the doctor's office practice. Trained reviewers ensure that these records include key information and actions in patients with certain diseases, as identified by a panel of board experts.

ABMS has promulgated guidelines to assist its member boards in preparing recertification processes. Recertification should seek to ensure, through periodic evaluations, the physician's continuing competence in the chosen area of specialty practice. It should also encourage certified physicians to continue those educational activities essential to the maintenance of competence, either in a primary specialty or in its subspecialties. An appropriate interval for recertification has been suggested to be six to ten years. While an individual board may offer voluntary or mandatory recertification, a specialty board may not rescind its initial certificates by recertification unless the date of expiration was a condition of the original certification. So-called time-limited certificates have been established in eight disciplines, but thus far only Family Practice has had experience with TLC.

Boards are encouraged to develop procedures for recertification that are most appropriate to the characteristics for their specialty practice. In addition to cognitive examinations, performance evaluations, practice audits, and ratings by local peers should be considered.

ABMS feels strongly that the determination of the policies, procedures, and standards of a recertification process must remain the responsibility of each board and not be relinquished to specialty societies or others with potential conflicts of interests.

Qualification resulting from recertification

The use by others of the credential of recertification does not permit generalizations. The process is too new, and it has emerged during an era of skepticism about the predictive validity of testing in general. Society has challenged various national, objective tests for admission to educational processes, trades, and civil service. The medical profession has protested that tests of cognitive skills fall far short of distinguishing good from poor clinical performers. In fact the first controlled study of the predictive validity of certification done by an agency outside the certification community will be started next summer by investigators at the University of Washington. In funding this project, the American Board of Internal Medicine may display more temerity than good sense. Many guess that prevailing tests of knowledge and problem-solving ability will fail to identify the good practitioner.

Many professional organizations, particularly specialty societies whose principal mission is continuing education and state and county medical associations, require a certain number of credit hours of formal approved continuing medical education as a condition of membership. It started in 1970 with the Oregon Medical Association.

State licensing bodies followed suit. Public concern appears to have stemmed from the rise of consumerism in the sixties along with the advent of huge public reimbursements of the expenditures for health care through Medicare and Medicaid. The 1964 report of the President's Commission on Heart Disease, Cancer and Stroke, which led to the establishment of Regional Medical Programs, stated that "continuing education is a categorical imperative of contemporary medicine." The federal government was urged to play a leading role. The license to practice medicine is a privilege bestowed by the public, which saw an opportunity to slow the obsolescence of its practitioners through state requirements for reregistration. Because the effectiveness of continuing medical education has never been established, certain states such as Colorado have eliminated CME requirements for reregistration of licensure.

Recertification's role in this arena has been as a substitute for arbitrary requirements for continuing medical education. Ten states permit a recertified specialist to reregister for the privilege of practicing general medicine and surgery by virtue of recertification in their specialties instead of continuing medical education. Those states are Alaska, Arizona, Hawaii, Illinois, Kansas, Massachusetts, New Hampshire, New Mexico, Utah, and Washington.

Federal regulations often qualify specialists through certification or equivalent credentials. The boards had not intended this and, as I shall indicate later, really would prefer that other criteria be added. But a certificate issued by a national body through objective testing appeals to administrators and bureaucrats, unfortunately often for purposes of exclusivity. In drafts of federal regulations in the eighties, the the term "recertification" appears frequently, even though there is no evidence that such a credential qualifies a specialist for a given task. The temptation is obvious, but the promise cannot yet be delivered. Unlike airline pilots, physicians face the infinite permutations of complex clinical encounters. The notion has obvious face validity but to date not much else.

Thus far, recertification has presented few advantages to the physician in the practice of medicine. Hospital staff and other clincial and economic privileges do not accrue to recertified specialists. They probably are too few. But one estimates that the public, insurers, the courts, the federal government, and even the profession will find the need for some acceptable record of continuing competence. It is up to the certifying boards to lead the way in developing better measures of the complex skills required for good clinical performance—so as to prepare for these needs for documenting continuing competence.

The public remains woefully uneducated about the significance of recertification. Indeed, most do not understand the advantage of certification itself. Certification's function of peer recognition does not exclude a concern for the public welfare, and the public is well served if the quality of physicians is high. The effect on candidates of the additional training and preparation for the boards' examinations benefits the public; criteria for care are established and reviewed, personal skills of physicians are enhanced, better methods for the valid attestation of knowledge and performance are developed, and standards in medical science and education in general are fostered. In this context, certification serves the public. But self-perpetuating boards cannot claim to represent the public. And few patients seek out the certified specialist, check the certificates framed on the wall, or abandon their doctors because they are not certified or recertified.

The American Board of Medical Specialties is in a difficult position to publicize the value of certification and recertification. In the first place, the validity of certification as a predictor of excellence in performance remains unestablished. In the second place, the Internal Revenue Service interprets such advocacy as fostering the business interests of certified specialists, much as a business association or trade union might do. Such crass motives trouble idealists on boards who view themselves as standard setters developing educational programs ultimately for the public good. It is too bad that the IRS Commissioner has ruled that boards authorize certified physicians to hold themselves out to the public as specialists, certainly not the original intent of certification. That such authorization is not the mission of certification today is easier for me to say than to prove.

Effects on standards of recertification

Certifying boards have great autonomy in setting standards for their clinical disciplines. Until recently these arbitrary but never capricious standards went unchallenged. But now formal recognition, perhaps always a basic human need, has almost become essential in medical practice. Certification simply means too much, and virtually all residents completing training today seek certification. This is documented by the fact that the proportion of practicing specialists who were certified rose from about 50 percent to 78 percent in the decade ending in 1981. Board eligibility, and even failure, has become an illegitimate but coveted status. Boards cannot escape total responsibility by disclaiming intent or control. Any respectable external reveiw process should not remain satisfied with the standards of yesterday. Therefore it is my view that the standards of certification and recertification should gradually rise with the intent of steadily improving patient care.

The current standard of certification is in true jeopardy. The current demand for the "right" of certification, the possible use of certification for licensure by specialty, and the difficulty in demonstrating that success on the certifying examination reliably predicts the quality of performance in practice over the years—all threaten aspirations of excellence. The cost and harassment of legal challenge, the lack of agreement among American specialty boards as to standards, and the effects of a lack of certification can only conspire to steadily erode this standard.

What is the risk of a lesser standard, such as acceptable competence or "safe drivers"?

First, if the states license by specialty and accept certification as the major criterion, *and* if the certifying board's standard is one of minimally acceptable competence, what happens to those trained candidates who fail? Their loss of license would amount to professional death, and the boards will hear their agonized screams in court. Can the validity of our tests survive that? A board maintaining a standard of excellence can rise out of that morass since its standard exceeds that of the basic requirement for professional activity, licensure.

Second, a minimal standard for certification could lead to certified specialists who are unsuitable for the public or for those using certification for credentialing. I saw an analogy in the discussions surrounding the recommendation by the National Collegiate Athletic Association that admission standards for college athletes be higher. Their goal is fewer, unprepared dropouts or graduates, unsuccessful at entering professional sports and without sufficient skills to land jobs. Black college presidents and coaches have argued that an admission standard exceeding an SAT score of 700 and a GPA of 2.0 could be discriminatory. The current system unfairly disadvantages the unsuccessful athlete. By the same token, a cheapened certificate in medicine is no better than a meaningless "college education."

In Internal Medicine 88 percent of candidates who are graduates of U.S. medical schools become certified by their third attempt. If that is the case, and particularly if the standard of certification is not high and therefore attractive, why shouldn't the training institution provide the functional credential? Institutions could be made responsible for qualifying specialists through diplomas attesting to satisfactorily completed training.

Then, if either licensure by specialty or fee for service adopts the credential of certification—certainly logical and probably mandatory if the standard is to be minimal competence—there would be little need for expensive certification paraphernalia merely to reaffirm the satisfactory completion of training.

The linkage of recertification to reregistration of license seems benign enough. Since the current standard of licensure is low, that of minimally acceptable general skills, it is argued that linkage to recertification does not threaten its higher standard. While that is undoubtedly true today, particularly since few fulfill the educational requirements for relicensure that way, the certificate could become a requisite for success when a plethora of physicians compete for the privilege of spending a limited amount of public monies for health care.

The American Board of Medical Specialties encourages its member boards to require maintenance of an unlimited medical licensure for recertification. The premise is that this is one of several criteria the boards might use in satisfying themselves as to the moral character and legal standing of candidates in their respective states. As already indicated, a number of state licensing boards now accept certification by a specialty board in lieu of their own requirements for licensure. At present, four licensing boards require physicians so licensed to confine their practices to their specialties. ABMS opposes this because it is convinced that every specialist should maintain basic knowledge and skill in the broad apsects of medical care. The definition of boundaries between specialties is difficult and should not be conducted by state governments lest transgressions be punishable under the law. Licensure by specialty would impose serious handicaps upon physicians who seek interstate endorsement of licenses so obtained. Only three state licensing boards now endorse licenses obtained by specialty certification. Finally, ABMS feels that a requirement to limit practice to a specialty could increase the cost of medical care by entailing needless consultations and unnecessary repetition of tests. ABMS prefers that the private and voluntary nature of recertification, particularly its standards, not be subjected to the pressures of the marketplace and politics.

Returning to sports for an analogy, one notes the increasing disenchantment with professional basketball. This sport is dominated by tall, fast jumpers with reasonably stereotyped skills. While the 24-second rule may have increased excitement for the fan, it has not increased the standard of play. The 3-point shot has opened the door for the recognition of smaller, pure shooters. This fragile game will not survive in its present form. Its standards must be raised. Some have suggested wider courts, smaller rims, higher baskets, and stricter goal-tending rules. The purpose in altering the way this and other sports are played is to ensure that excellence remains excellence. High-quality play has become so routine that the fans' threshold for excitement has risen, and they obtain a narrower range of satisfaction and enjoy the games less. Why won't that happen in medicine as well? If its credentials are routine, the failure to meet the standard will lead to professional suicide.

I may be naive about the law, but the legal implications of the effect of external forces on the standards of recertification seem readily apparent. Meeting a minimal standard would be essential for every practitioner in each specialty. Failure to achieve that standard will, therefore, attract the same challenges as do admission tests to institutions of higher education. The boards are ill prepared to assure the public that their certificates signify lasting competence. It wouldn't matter that boards have autonomy over such standards, that professions are recognized as having the authority to set their own standards, or that consistent procedures had been carefully followed. Therefore, linkage to such influences should be assiduously avoided. Boards should stand aside from the marketplace, manpower considerations, and the provision or restriction of privilege and stick to the business of certification. And the goal of certification and recertification should be a steady improvement in standards to extract the best possible performance at any time from medical specialists. The goal should not be to qualify specialists for practice, and the standard should not be designed only to avoid exposure to liability. The most defensible goal will be to ensure from time to time that the certified specialist possesses the knowledge, skills, and attitudes essential to the provision of excellent care.

Peer recognition is better than social control in altering human nature—and probably in saving lives. Professional conduct is better governed by the individual's internal control rather than by external regulation. This self-monitoring function is the mark of a true profession, and in many ways each board is the guardian for its discipline. Better that certification and recertification reward initiative and aspiration, than that regulation be resisted and mediocrity result.

Establishing New Specialties

Peyton E. Weary, M.D.

The proliferation of new specialties, subspecialties, and special competency certification in the field of medicine in the past fifty years has been remarkable and has paralleled the exponential growth in scientific understanding and new health care technology. While there might perhaps be some reason to anticipate that the rate of growth may slow somewhat with the current de-emphasis on specialty medicine and marginal increases in funding by the National Institutes of Health, it will surely not cease. And, furthermore, as a consequence of the impending physician oversupply and the increased emphasis on competition in the health care field, there will be increased pressures from physicians and other health care providers to obtain recognition for special expertise as a method to achieve a competitive edge.

At this time, the American Medical Association acknowledges the existence of 80 specialties of which 52 correspond to specialty and subspecialty areas for which the American Board of Medical Specialties (ABMS) member boards issue certificates. There are, in addition, 25 boards or organizations outside of the ABMS that certify physicians. I will confine my remarks today only to the creation of new physician specialty credentials, recognizing that credentialing of physician extenders is a topic of major concern and interest as well, but time does not permit this topic to be discussed.

There are currently 23 member boards comprising the ABMS constellation. These boards issue a total of 32 primary or conjoint certificates and, in addition, certificates of special competency in 32 different categories.

Methods presently available to recognize new physician qualifications consist of the following:

1. *Creation of a new specialty board under the ABMS umbrella*

The creation of a new specialty certifying board is a function of the Liaison Committee for Specialty Boards (LCSB), a joint committee of The American Medical Association and The American Board of Medical Specialties. This process is a carefully structured one with submission of a formal application which includes extensive details concerning objectives, educational and certification requirements, plans for fellowship or residency training, bylaws, constitution, and grandfathering provisions. Furthermore, sponsorship by existing specialty boards is essential.

2. *Creation of a new general certificate by an existing ABMS primary or conjoint board*

Currently, four primary boards issue general certificates in multiple areas (pathology, preventive medicine, psychiatry and neurology, and cardiology). Clearly significant potential exists for other boards to issue additional general certificates.

3. *Creation of certificates of special competence*

With approval of the ABMS membership, member boards may singly or jointly issue certificates of special competence in a defined area. At this time, 32 such certificates exist of which three are jointly issued. This is the route adopted in recent years by most boards in recognizing special qualifications, but this process has also engendered much discussion and debate. Resistance to unbridled proliferation of special competency recognition is growing and has spurred efforts to look at alternative mechanisms.

4. *Creation of non-ABMS certifying boards*

As noted earlier, there are 25 independent certifying boards.

One of the major problems that must be addressed in the process of recognition of special competency is the fact that many of the areas for which recognition is now being sought are interdisciplinary. This has been a major issue with respect to certification in critical care medicine, vascular surgery, and most recently immunopathology. The interdisciplinary nature of these areas of special competency has been addressed in several instances by creation of joint certificates; but, where there are a large number of potential sponsors, logistical problems may arise. Suffice it to say that any certification that is clearly exclusionary might be subject to legal challenge on the basis of being anticompetitive.

This leads us to a discussion of the anticompetitive potential of the certifying process as it relates to new-specialty credentialing and the possible concerns of the Federal Trade Commission. In February of 1981, Lewin and Associates, under contract with the Federal Trade Commission, reported the results of an analysis of competition among health practitioners. A portion of this analysis dealt with issues of credentialing including new-specialty recognition. Key issues identified as suggesting potential for further review are as follows:

1. Recognition of new specialties is stated to have a theoretical potential to reduce competition among health care providers and thereby increase health care costs. The rationale for this belief is as follows:

   a. Increased specialization may result in subdivision of a broad field of practice into a number of narrow compartments.
   b. Some physicians who currently practice in these broad fields or who might eventually enter them, will instead enter these more specialized compartments.
   c. Because their activities are now more restricted, they cease to be competitive with physicians in other specialized compartments and also to some extent less competitive with those who practice in the broader field.
   d. In turn, this leads to reduced substitutability and the employment of more physicians to provide care for patients with a complex mixture of problems.
   e. Thus this fragmentation may be expected to result in reduced competition, increased patient care costs and the possibility also of increased education costs if the training period becomes more prolonged in the process of acquiring additional proficiency.

The report does note, however, that the enhanced quality of care may well justify increased costs.

The authors then proceed to ask the question whether such market-limiting effects should be tolerated and whether there should be more consideration of "nonmedical ramifications" (which I would interpret to mean cost considerations) in the public policy debates relating to new credentialing practices.

Elsewhere in this report, however, statements appear that imply that if recognition of bona fide certification programs were to be withheld on grounds other than doubts about the accuracy of the information conveyed to the public, antitrust problems would be raised.[1]

An important feature of the market for information is its competitiveness—that is, the availability of multiple sources or opportunities for new sources to arise. Antitrust analysis is thus usefully and appropriately applied to certification efforts of all kinds. An entity controlled by members of an industry should not be permitted to suppress bona fide new certification programs. If recognition of a new program were withheld on grounds other than doubts about the accuracy of the information it conveyed, antitrust problems would be presented.

The American Board of Medical Specialties and the National Commission for Health Certifying Agencies, both potentially able to exercise life-and-death power over new certification efforts in their respective fields, would present such problems if recognition of new specialties or occupations reflected efforts to minimize competition with existing specialties or occupations or among specialties and occupations. Likewise, judgments of a regulatory nature about the public need for new categories of providers would be out of place. The role of ABMS in recognizing nuclear medicine as a new specialty appeared to raise questions of these kinds. In general, it would generally appear that antitrust enforcement aimed at assuring the free flow of information and the freedom of competitive private groups to begin and to operate nondeceptive certification schemes would be in the public interest (pp. III #97–98).

It seems difficult to reconcile these conflicting sentiments, since on the one hand, we are admonished to avoid fragmentation and consider nonmedical ramifications, while elsewhere we are instructed to ignore issues other than factual medical consideration and to adopt a permissive posture with respect to fragmentation. One must wonder then about whether a consistent philosophy exists upon which to base our determinations.

2. Turning now to a second major issue, the report notes that the decision to create a new specialty or subspecialty and define its scope and the necessary qualifications of its candidates is a crucial step. The essentials must be crafted with scrupulous attention to fairness and due process. Furthermore, there must be reasonable assurance of the accuracy of the information conveyed and the relevance of the standards applied. While this would seem self-evident, the authors observe elsewhere that the courts might be very reluctant to delve into questions of accuracy, relevance, or value of the standards applied in new-specialty credentialing so long as fairness in administration prevailed.

A further point is that antitrust law, recognizing the possibility that private certification systems might be used by one set of competitors to disadvantage another unfairly, required procedural fairness and reasonable assurance that the information being conveyed is accurate and useful. Probably the courts would be unwilling to go very far into assessing the accuracy, relevance, or value of the standards applied in granting credentials as long as fairness prevailed in their administration. Objective evidence of discrimination and anticompetitive abuse would invite a remedy however (p. III #21).

It is furthermore observed that antitrust courts might exhibit deference in scrutinizing standards because there appears to be an innate distaste for antitrust challenges to professional activities.

In addition to the procedures followed, the substantive standards developed and used by the accreditors are also significant. Their reasonableness might be judged by an antitrust court on the basis of whether they supply information which is procompetitive in that it assists consumers' and others' decision-making processes. It remains to be seen, however, just how closely antitrust courts will scrutinize the standards employed in private certification. One possibility is that they will display substantial deference, reflecting their presumption of regularity in credentialing programs and their distaste for antitrust challenges to professional activities (p. III #92).

In reviewing what might be construed as invalid standards, particular attention was directed to the "grandfathering" provisions of a certification process and the possibility that boards might set arbitrarily high requirements or continually upgrade requirements for new entrants without requiring comparable competency requirements for incumbents. This, of course, would tend to restrict the field, favor incumbency, and potentially trigger antitrust measures. In addition, a related antitrust concept, that of the "least restrictive alternative," is raised in which it is questioned whether more restrictive covenants are necessary to protect the public when less-restrictive ones might achieve the same goal. It is reasonable thus to conclude that, while the possibility exists that the courts will be reasonably lenient, we still must examine each new-specialty credentialing process very carefully to ensure that anticompetitive bias is not introduced and that it will be administered fairly.

3. A third issue that requires careful scrutiny is that of broader participation in the decision as to whether there is a need for a new-specialty credentialing. This can be arbitrarily divided into two parts as follows:

    a. There is a preception that the process of deciding whether to create a new-specialty credentialing body is overly concentrated in the hands of incumbents who theoretically are anxious to maintain the status quo. In practice, however, this perception would appear to be incorrect when we look at the plethora of new-specialty credentialing activities implemented in the past 50 years; yet apparently it still remains an issue of concern.

Those who question the composition of the existing decision-making bodies are quick to concede that the medical profession, and, in particular those who have demonstrated concern for quality care through certification processes, are certainly the ones who can best ascertain the validity of new credentialing applications.

The decision to approve a new category of practitioner demands familiarity with medical developments in the new proposed field, and hence involvement of medical experts in the process is both inevitable and desirable (p. III #54).

On the other hand, the report strongly suggests the desirability of having more broadly constituted bodies, unaffiliated with any major professional organization, and with substantial public and nonphysician health care providers as the decision makers. To justify such a major disruption, the specter is raised that because physician organizations dominate the entire certification process, it might be characterized as "private economic government"; and the report speaks of the fact that antitrust law treats private economic government quite harshly. However, further analysis reveals that health professional credentialing is related only to standard setting and does not involve regulatory or boycott activities and thus probably does not constitute an example of private economic government. This question is left unsettled. It is clear though that the perception remains of an interlocking directorate or "a reticulate system of professional influence." It seems clear that professional societies which might be said to represent the narrow economic interests of specialists should not be involved in the decision of whether to recognize new specialties. Theoretically this should not apply to the American Medical Association which represents a broad constituency.

    b. A second and interrelated component of broader representation is the question of who should credential the credentialer. At this time there are several organizations that grant recognition to some certifying agencies. The National Commission for Health Certifying Agencies oversees certifying agencies for nonphysician health professionals. The U.S. Office of Education publishes a list of recognized accrediting agencies. The Council of Postsecondary Accreditation serves to accredit and coordinate voluntary accrediting activities.

Neither the ABMS nor the LCSB are subject to approval or control by any higher credentialing body.

4. A final major issue raised by the report for consideration by the Federal Trade Commission is the accuracy, relevance, and value of the information provided to the public by various health accrediting agencies. If we look at the bottom line of what we do by way of accreditation, it is to convey to the public information about the special qualifications of physicians. But we really have very little information about the public's perceptions of what it is that certification actually connotes. It is encouraging that the ABMS is about to undertake a public information program; but perhaps before doing this, we should attempt to assess what it is the public now perceives, what misconceptions prevail, and what it is the public wishes to know, as well as what it is we believe the public needs to know about the meaning of certification.

Perhaps nothing would be more troublesome than to design a public information campaign that would:

a. Fail to correct current misconceptions;
b. Fail to provide information which is desired or needed;
c. Create false expectations by unjustifiably overstating the significance of certification; and
d. Denigrate those who are not certified or those who are certified by non-ABMS agencies.

I am certain that ABMS leadership is aware of the serious consequences that might attend the last two actions because there is probably nothing that might more quickly bring the wrath of the Federal Trade Commission on our heads than to inadvertantly create an anticompetitive atmosphere. As noted eariler, this whole subject is discussed in depth in the Lewin Report by two legal consultants, professors Kissam and Havighurst. While I do not pretend to understand the technical details, two elements seem clear.

a. Public information about credentialing should be relevant to the needs of the consumer.
b. The intent must not be to harm competitors.

It would thus appear that, if we can assess the need for accurate information and reach agreement on the significance of certification to the public, we would provide a very useful service by a broad public information effort.

If I have focused too much perhaps on the Lewin report and the possible concerns of the Federal Trade Commission, it is because I have the perception that most of the legal issues that might arise in the process of new specialty credentialing could well be those related to potential anticompetitive aspects. I do have misgivings about using a report that makes recommendations which may never be adopted in any form by the commission, and yet the issues raised are theoretically possible options for future action. I do have one most encouraging quotation from remarks presented by Arthur Lerner, Assistant Director of the Commission's Bureau of Competition in May 1982: "Certification by medical specialty groups is an example of self-regulation that is reasonable and can be procompetitive when the certification criteria and procedures are fair and the certification decisions are made objectively on the basis of competence. The FTC has never challenged any medical specialty certification program; and absent serious abuse, I can foresee no circumstance where we would."[2]

References

1. Lazarus, W., Levine E. S. and Lewin L. S.; *Competition Among Health Practioners: The Influence of the Medical Professions on the Health Manpower Market*, Volume I: *Executive Summary and Final Report*. Issued by The Federal Trade Commission, February 1981.
2. Remarks of Arthur N. Lerner, Assistant Director, Bureau of Competition, Federal Trade Commission before the National Health Lawyers Association Seminar on Antitrust in the Health Care Field, Hyatt Regency Hotel, Crystal City, Virginia, May 17, 1982.

Appendix
Antitrust Issues in Health Care Law

Onek, Klein & Farr

Section one: Antitrust primer

This outline summarizes the basic principles of antitrust. Special attention is given to areas of particular concern to the health care industry.

I. Introduction
   A. Antitrust policy
      The antitrust laws are designed to protect competition. They rest on the premise that "the unrestrained interaction of competitive forces will yield the best allocation of our economic resources." *Northern Pacific Railway v. United States,* 356 U.S. 1, 4 (1958).
   B. Summary of principal antitrust statutes
      The principal federal antitrust statutes are the Sherman Act, the Clayton Act, the Federal Trade Commission Act, and the Robinson-Patman Act.
      1. Sherman Act
         a. Section 1 makes unlawful "every contract, combination . . . or conspiracy in restraint of trade." 15 U.S.C. § 1.
         b. Section 2 prohibits monopolizing, attempt to monopolize, and combinations or conspiracies to monopolize. 15 U.S.C. § 2.
      2. Clayton Act
         a. Section 3 prohibits exclusive dealing arrangements, tying sales, and requirements contracts where the effect "may be substan-

tially to lessen competition" in any line of commerce. 15. U.S.C. § 14.
    b. Section 7 prohibits acquisitions or mergers where the effect "may be substantially to lessen competition or to tend to create a monopoly" in any line of commerce in any section of the country." 15 U.S.C. § 18.
  3. Federal Trade Commission Act
     Section 5(a)(1) prohibits "unfair methods of competition in commerce, and unfair or deceptive acts or practices in commerce." 15 U.S.C. 45(a)(1).
  4. Robinson-Patman Act
     The Robinson-Patman Act was adopted as an amendment to the Clayton Act. It prohibits sellers from engaging in price discrimination where the discrimination may lessen competition. 15 U.S.C. § 13.
  5. *Note:* Many states have their own state antitrust acts, which are often patterned on the federal statutes.
C. Enforcement of the antitrust laws
  1. The federal antitrust laws are enforced by the Antitrust Division of the Department of Justice, the FTC, and private parties. States may sue as private parties.
  2. The Department of Justice is responsible for enforcing the Sherman Act and the Clayton Act, and may initiate civil actions and/or criminal charges.
  3. The Federal Trade Commission is responsible for enforcing the Federal Trade Commission Act and, along with the Department of Justice, has concurrent authority to enforce the Clayton Act.
     a. Commission enforcement proceedings are brought in an administrative setting, with a trial before an Administrative Law Judge, and a right of appeal to the full commission. Commission decisions adverse to the charged party may be appealed to the United States Court of Appeals. If the commission finds a practice to be illegal, it enters a cease and desist order and may also assess a civil penalty.
     b. The FTC may promulgate rules defining acts or practices that are unfair or deceptive or are unfair methods of competition. 15 U.S.C. § 45(m)(l)(A).
     c. Legislation currently before Congress would strip the FTC of its jurisdiction over the state-regulated professions. If this legislation is adopted, the FTC's activities in the health care field will be sharply curtailed.

4. Private parties may sue for equitable relief or seek "treble damages" under § 4 of the Clayton Act. 15 U.S.C. § 15.
   a. In *Illinois Brick Co. v. Illinois*, 431 U.S. 720 (1977), the Supreme Court held that in price-fixing cases, only a *direct* purchaser of the price-fixed goods may recover treble damages. The Court emphasized that there could be a serious danger of duplicate damage awards if indirect purchasers were also entitled to recover treble damages
   b. A more recent decision involving the health care industry, *Blue Shield of Virginia v. McCready*, 102 S. Ct. 2540 (1982), indicates that the Court is not willing to further restrict the availability of treble damages. A group health plan subscriber brought an antitrust class action against Blue Shield of Virginia and an organization of Virginia psychiatrists, seeking treble damages. The plan allowed reimbursement for services provided by psychiatrists but not for services provided by psychologists, unless the treatment was ordered and supervised by, and billed through, a physician. The subscriber claimed that Blue Shield and the psychiatrists had engaged in an unlawful conspiracy to exclude psychologists from receiving compensation. The Supreme Court held that the subscriber had standing to seek treble damages even though the alleged conspiracy was directed at psychologists, not subscribers. There was no danger of duplicative recovery, and the subscriber's injury was not "too remote."
D. Standards of legality: the *rule of reason* and per se violations
   1. Most restraints of trade are analyzed under the *"rule of reason."* The facts of a particular case will be examined in detail to determine the purpose of a restraint and its impact on competition. See *Chicago Board of Trade v. United States*, 246 U.S. 231, 238 (1918). Some restraints are so likely to be anticompetitive that they are deemed illegal *per se*. No case-by-case inquiry will be made. See *Northern Pacific Railway v. United States*, 356 U.S. 1, 5 (1958).
   2. In deciding whether a practice should be *per se* illegal, the court will examine the possible benefits of the practice, the frequency and magnitude of those harmful effects, and the desirability of a bright-line rule.
E. "Learned professions" exemption
   The Sherman Act applies only to activities within "trade or commerce." Before 1975, many health care professionals believed that they were exempt from the antitrust laws because activity was not

in trade or commerce. Recent Supreme Court cases clearly indicate, however, that there is no blanket exemption for the professions.

1. In *Goldfarb v. Virginia State Bar*, 421 U.S. 773 (1975), the Supreme Court held that neither the language of the Sherman Act nor its legislative history indicate that Congress intended to create a blanket exemption for the learned professions. In footnote 17, however, *Goldfarb* suggested that restraints on competition among professionals might be distinguishable from business restraints.

> The fact that a restraint operates upon a profession as distinguished from a business is, of course, relevant in determining whether that particular restraint violates the Sherman Act. It would be unrealistic to view the practice of professions as interchangeable with other business activities, and automatically to apply to the professions antitrust concepts which originated in other areas. The public service aspect, and other features of the professions, may require that a particular practice, which could properly be viewed as a violation of the Sherman Act in another context, be treated differently. We intimate no view on any other situation than the one with which we are confronted today. *Id.*, at 788 n. 17.

Footnote 17 was read by many as indicating that the learned professions would enjoy a broad exemption under the rule of reason.

2. The promise of footnote 17 was largely eliminated by *National Society of Professional Engineers v. United States*, 435 U.S. 679 (1978). In that case, the Supreme Court made clear that the professions would not always enjoy lenient treatment under the rule of reason. The Court examined an ethical rule of the National Society of Professional Engineers that prohibited members from submitting competitive bids for engineering services. It held that the rule was illegal *per se* because it was plainly anticompetitive; the rule could not be defended on the ground that it was designed to protect consumers from inferior services.

The Court did offer some solace, however. It stated:

> We adhere to the view expressed in *Goldfarb* that, by their nature, professional services may differ significantly from other business services, and, accordingly, the nature of competition in such services may vary. Ethical norms may serve to regulate and promote this competition and thus fall within the Rule of Reason. *Id.*, at 696.

3. Last term in *Arizona v. Maricopa County Medical Society*, 102 S. Ct. 2466 (1982), the Court first confronted the question of whether the *per se* approach or the rule of reason should apply

to an agreement among health care professionals. County medical society physicians had established a schedule of maximum fees for their services. A sharply divided court held, by a 4-3 vote, that the fee schedule was *per se* illegal. Justice Stevens, writing for the majority, rejected the claim that the health care professional deserved special treatment as a matter of course. Justice Powell, joined by Chief Justice Berger and Justice Rehnquist, dissented vigorously. Justices Blackmun and O'Connor did not participate in the decision.

In the course of its analysis, the majority conceded that the public service aspect of the professions may require that a particular practice be treated differently than it would be in another context. It noted, however, that the price-fixing agreement at issue was not premised on public service or ethical norms. *Id.,* at 2475.

    4. After the decision in *Arizona v. Maricopa County Medical Society,* it is clear that the health care professionals will not enjoy special treatment under the antitrust laws. If, however, the professionals can argue that a particular agreement is in the public interest and serves a legitimate professional goal—for example, that it promotes the quality of health care—the rule of reason may be applied.

II. Monopolies

Section 2 of the Sherman Act forbids monopolizing and attempts to monopolize.

  A. Monopolizing

    A firm monopolizes in violation of the Sherman Act when it possesses *monopoly power* in a *relevant market* and has taken some *deliberate act* to acquire that monopoly power. See, e.g., *United States v. Aluminum Co. of America,* 148 F.2d 466 (2d Cir. 1945).

    1. Monopoly power is the power to set prices and exclude competition. Courts frequently use market share as a measure of monopoloy power. See, e.g., *United States v. E. I. duPont,* 351 U.S. 377 (1956); *United States v. Aluminum Co. of America, Supra; United States v. United Shoe Machinery Corp.,* 110 F.Supp. 295 (D. Mass. 1953), *aff'd per curiam,* 347 U.S. 521 (1954).

    2. The relevant market is determined by considering the "product market" and the "geographic market."

      a. The product market is determined by considering the product sold by the firm and other products used by consumers

for the same purpose. See *United States v. E. I. duPont, Supra.*
   b. The geographic market is defined by considering the area in which the firm and its competition sell their products. See *United States v. Grinnell Corp.*, 236 F.Supp. 224 (D.R.I. 1964), *aff'd in part and remanded,* 384 U.S. 563 (1966).
   3. The "deliberate act" requirement is satisfied by acts which themselves violate the antitrust laws, see *Standard Oil v. United States,* 221 U.S. 1 (1911), or by any acts that constitute the willful acquisition of monopoly power, see *United States v. Grinnell,* 384 U.S. 563 (1966). Innocently acquired monopolies—natural monopolies, or monopolies achieved because of superior foresight or skill—do not violate § 2. *American Tobacco Co. v. United States,* 328 U.S. 781 (1946).
 B. Attempts to monopolize
   An attempt to monopolize is the "employment of methods, means, and practices which could, if successful, accomplish monopolization, and which, though falling short, nevertheless approach so close as to create a dangerous probability of it." *American Tobacco v. United States,* 328 U.S. 781 (1946). An attempt to monopolize requires a specific intent to acquire monopoly power. *Times-Picayune v. United States,* 345 U.S. 594 (1952).
 C. Section 2 and the health care industry
   In the health care industry, Section 2 claims arise most frequently with respect to hospitals. See e.g., *Huron Valley Hospital v. City of Pontiac,* 666 F.2d 1029 (6th Cir. 1981). They have also been made in certification, insurance, and hospital privileges cases, but with very little success.
III. Agreements among competitors
 A. Introduction
   The central concern of the antitrust laws is to promote competition among firms in the same industry. As a result, actions by two or more competitors—horizontal restraints—are particularly suspect. They may be attacked under Section 1 of the Sherman Act or under the Federal Trade Commission Act.
 B. Price agreements
   1. Agreements relating to price are *"per se"* violations. *United States v. Socony Vacuum Oil Co.,* 310 U.S. 150 (1940). This rule has been applied in the health care industry. *Arizona v. Maricopa County Medical Society,* 102 S. Ct. 2466 (1982).
   2. The courts have used an expansive interpretation of what constitutes price-fixing.

a. Minimum prices are clearly prohibited. *Goldfarb v. Virginia State Bar*, 421 U.S. 773 (1975).
b. Maximum price fixing is also illegal. *Arizona v. Maricopa County Medical Society*, 102 S. Ct. 2466 (1982).
c. Activity that stabilizes prices is illegal. *United States v. Container Corp. of America*, 393 U.S. 333 (1969).
d. Agreements to limit production or services may be viewed as an illegal price-fixing scheme.
e. Agreements that establish uniform discount policies or terms of sale are illegal. *Vandervelde v. Put & Call Brokers & Dealers Association*, 344 F Supp. 118, 136 (S.D.N.Y. 1972).
f. Agreements not to advertise prices have been treated as unlawful restraints on price competition. See e.g., *United States v. Gasoline Retailers Association*, 285 F.2d 688 (7th Cir. 1961); *American Association of Orthodontists*, 49 F.T.C. 487 (1952); see also *American Medical Association v. Federal Trade Commission*, 638 F.2d 443 (2nd Cir. 1980), *aff'd by equally divided court*, 50 U.S.L.W. 4313 (1982). For further discussion of the problems raised by advertising restrictions, see Outline Section Four.
g. Although courts are generally quick to condemn price fixing, some literal price-fixing arrangements have escaped *per se* treatment on the ground that they yield substantial efficiencies that could not otherwise have been realized. See *Broadcast Music, Inc. v. Columbia Broadcasting System, Inc.*, 441 U.S. 1 (1979).

3. The use of relative value schedules for physician specialties has been challenged by the Department of Justice and the FTC as illegal price fixing. See, e.g., *American College of Radiology* 3 CCH Trade Reg. Rep. ¶ 21,236 (FTC consent order) (1977). The courts, however, have not always agreed with this view. *United States v. American Society of Anesthesiologists*, 473 F Supp. 147 (S D N Y 1979). The problems posed by relative fee schedules are more fully discussed in Outline Section Five.

C. Division of markets
1. An agreement among actual or potential competitors that divides or allocates a market is illegal *per se*. *Timken Roller Bearing Co. v. United States*, 341 U.S. 593 (1951). No defenses are allowed. *United States v. Topco Associates, Inc.*, 405 U.S. 596 (1972).

2. The rule applies to geographic division of markets, see *Addyston Pipe & Steel Co. v. United States,* 175 U.S. 211 (1899), and division of markets along product lines, see *Hartford Empire Co. v. United States,* 323 U.S. 386 (1945).
D. Group boycotts and connected refusals to deal
  1. An agreement by a group of competitors that they will not deal with a particular person or business, or that they will deal only on unreasonable terms, is *per se* illegal under Section 1 of the Sherman Act. *Klors Inc. v. Broadway-Hale Stores, Inc.,* 359 U.S. 207 (1959). The justification for the concerted action is ordinarily not relevant. *Fashion Originators Guild of America, Inc. v. FTC,* 312 U.S. 457, 467-468 (1941).
  2. Although industry-wide self-regulation that has significant economic consequences is ordinarily struck down, see *United States v. American Medical Association,* 130 F.2d 233; *Fashion Originators Guild v. FTC,* 312 U.S. 457 (1941), some reasonable regulations are upheld.
     a. A group may expel an individual engaged in unethical or illegal conduct. *Cowen v. New York Stock Exchange,* 256 F. Supp. 462 (N.D.N.Y. 1961); *Molinas v. National Basketball Association,* 190 F. Supp. 241 (S.D.N.Y. 1961).
     b. A professional group's regulations that are designed to serve the public interest may be judged under the rule of reason. See *National Society of Professional Engineers v. United States,* 435 U.S. 679 (1978).
  3. Allegations of group boycotts have frequently been made in the health care industry, but the courts have not always upheld these claims as some of the following cases illustrate.
     a. Denial of hospital staff privileges. See, e.g., *Robinson v. Magovern,* 521 F. Supp. 842 (W.D. Pa. 1981) aff'd, No. 77-0075 (3rd Cir. 1982); see also Outline Sections Three and Four.
     b. Restrictive membership requirements for professional associations. See e.g., *Boddicker v. Arizona State Dental Association,* 549 F.2d 626 (9th Cir.), *cert. denied,* 434 U.S. 825 (1977); see also Outline Section Four.
     c. Denial of accreditation or certification. See, e.g., *Levin v. Joint Commission on Accreditation of Hospitals,* 354 F.2d 515 (D.C. Cir. 1966); see also Outline Sections Three and Four.
     d. Ethical code provisions that restrict scope of medical prac-

tice see e.g., *United States Dental Inst. v. American Association of Orthodontists*, 396 F. Supp. 565 (N.D. Ill. 1975); see also Outline Section Four.
- e. Denial of insurance. See, e.g., *Virginia Academy of Clinical Psychologists v. Blue Shield of Virginia*, 624 F.2d 476 (4th Cir. 1980); see also Outline Sections Three and Six.
- f. Boycotts of Medicare patients, see, e.g., *United States v. South Carolina Health Care Association*, 1980-2 Trade Cas. ¶ 63,316 (D.S.C. 1980), or Workmen's Compensation patients, see, e.g., *New York v. Roth*, 419 N.Y.S. 2d 85 (N.Y. City Ct. 1979); see also Outline Section Five.
- g. Refusal to deal with a health maintenance organization and its physicians. See, e.g., *Medical Service Corp. of Spokane County*, 3 CCH Trade Reg. Rep. § 21,195 (1976); see also Outline Section Four.
- h. Refusal by Blue Cross/Blue Shield to deal with class of retail druggists. See, e.g, *Medical Arts Pharmacy of Stamford, Inc. v. Blue Cross and Blue Shield of Connecticut, Inc.*, 675 F. 2d 502 (9th Cir. 1982); see also Outline Section Six.

E. Proving the existence of an agreement among competitors
  1. Direct evidence of an agreement if clearly sufficient to establish a Sherman Act violation. Problems arise, however, when the evidence of an agreement is only circumstantial. In particular, the courts have grappled with the question whether price leadership or conscious parallelism by firms in an oligopolistic industry is sufficient to prove the existence of an "agreement."
  2. In *Interstate Circuit, Inc. v. United States*, 306 U.S. 208 (1939), the Supreme Court suggested that price leadership in an oligopolistic industry would be unlawful; if a leader firm raised its prices and all other firms followed, they would do so knowing that concerted action was invited and necessary.
  3. In subsequent cases, however, the Supreme Court has indicated that conscious parallelism is not enough. "The crucial question is whether respondent's conduct . . . stemmed from an independent agreement, tacit or express. To be sure, business behavior is admissable circumstantial evidence from which the fact finder may infer agreement. But this Court has never held that proof of parallel business behavior conclusively establishes agreement." *Theatre Enterprises v. Paramount Film Distributing Corp.*, 346 U.S. 537 (1954).

4. Conscious parallelism may constitute an "unfair method of competition" within the meaning of Section 5 of the Federal Trade Commission Act.

F. Exchange of information among competitors

When competitors exchange information on prices, costs, production, and so forth, an agreement to restrain trade may be inferred. In addition, even if no agreement is inferred, the exchange of information may be regarded as creating an unacceptably high probability of anticompetitive behavior.

1. Exchange of information on prices is highly suspect. An antitrust violation is almost certain to be found where current and future prices are listed, the names of the parties are provided, and the industry is highly concentrated.

    a. In *American Column & Lumber Co. v. United States*, 257 U.S. 377 (1921), the Supreme Court reviewed the exchange of information by a group of 365 hardwood manufacturers who controlled one third of the market. The manufacturers reported the details of production, inventories, and current price lists. They also reported the details of individual sales, including the identities of buyers, and held monthly meetings at which they discussed future production and prices. After this exchange of information began, prices increased. The Court held that the exchange was unlawful.

    b. In *Maple Flooring Manufacturers Ass'n v. United States*, 268 U.S. 563 (1925), the Supreme Court upheld the activities of a trade association that disseminated information on average cost, freight rates, and the terms of past sales. Unlike the manufacturers in *American Column*, the association never disclosed the identities of individual buyers and sellers. And although meetings were held, future prices were never discussed.

    c. In *United States v. Container Corp.*, 393 U.S. 333 (1969), the Court reviewed the exchange of information by paper box manufacturers who controlled 90 percent of the market. The manufacturers reported the most recent price charged or quoted to particular customers. After observing that the exchange had stabilized prices, the Court struck it down under § 1.

2. Exchanges of information other than price are less likely to be found unlawful. They may be attacked only where designed to lessen competition. Compare *Cement Manufacturers Protective*

Association v. United States, 268 U.S. with *Eastern States Retail Lumber Dealers Association v. United States*, 234 U.S. 600 (1914).
   3. Information exchanges among health care providers have been questioned. See, e.g., *United States v. American Society of Anesthesiologists*, 473 F. Supp. 147 (S.D.N.Y. 1979).
IV. Vertical restraints
   A. Introduction
   Buyers and sellers sometimes enter into agreements that are anticompetitive. Such agreements, referred to as *vertical restraints*, may violate Sherman Act §§ 1 and 2, and Clayton Act § 3.
   B. Resale price maintenance
   Resale price maintenance occurs when a seller contractually sets the price at which his buyer can resell the product. Such agreements are *per se* illegal under Section 2. *Dr. Miles Medical Co. v. John D. Park & Sons*, 220 U.S. 373 (1911) (minimum prices); *Kiefer-Stewart v. Joseph E. Seagram & Sons*, 340 U.S. 211 (1951) (maximum prices).
      1. Sellers may announce "suggested retail prices" but may not require adherence. Compare *United States v. Colgate*, 250 U.S. 300 (1919) with *United States v. Parke-Davis*, 362 U.S. 29 (1960).
      2. Resale price maintenance cases in the health care industry have usually involved pharmaceutical manufacturers. See, e.g. *United States v. Parke-Davis*, 362 U.S. 29 (1960).
   C. Sole outlets
   When a manufacturer appoints a distributor as his sole outlet in a given region, the rule of reason applies. Such arrangements will almost always be found to be lawful, unless there is no interbrand competition. *Packard Motor Car Co. v. Webster Motor Car Co.*, 243 F.2d 418 (D.C. Cir.), *cert. denied*, 355 U.S. 822 (1957).
   D. Customer and territorial restrictions
      1. A manufacturer may decide to use an exclusive distributor. He may also seek to restrict the area in which that distributor may sell his goods or to restrict the customers to whom he may sell the goods.
      2. In *Continental TV, Inc. v. GTE Sylvania, Inc.*, 433 U.S. 36 (1977), the Supreme Court held that vertical restrictions on customers or territory should be measured under the rule of reason. This decision overruled *United States v. Arnold Schwinn & Co.*, 388 U.S. 365 (1967), in which the Court had held that such restrictions were *per se* illegal.
   E. Vertical boycotts
   Agreement between sellers and buyers to exclude other sellers and

buyers may violate the antitrust laws. The Second and Ninth Circuits have held that unless a horizontal boycott is also involved, vertical boycotts should be measured under the rule of reason. *Oreck v. Whirlpool Corp.*, 579 F.2d 126 (2nd Cir.), *cert. denied*, 439 U.S. 946 (1978); *Gough v. Rossmore Corp.*, 585 F.2d 381 (9th Cir. 1978).

F. Exclusive dealing
   1. A seller and buyer may agree that the buyer will purchase exclusively from the seller. Such agreements, which are referred to as exclusive dealing agreements, prevent the seller's competitors from selling to the buyer.
   2. The legality of an exclusive dealing agreement will ordinarily depend on the length of the contract and the size of the market foreclosed. See *Tampa Electric Co. v. Nashville Coal Co.*, 365 U.S. 320 (1961); *Standard Oil Co. v. United States*, 337 U.S. 293 (1945); *Brown Shoe Co. v. FTC*, 384 U.S. 316 (1966).

G. Tying arrangements
   1. Definition: Under a tying arrangement, the seller refuses to sell one product (the tying product) to a customer unless the customer also buys a second product (the tied product).
   2. Clayton Act § 3 specifically forbids tying agreements. The statutes makes it "unlawful for any person . . . to lease or make a sale . . . of commodities . . . or fix a price thereof . . . on the condition [or] agreement . . . that the lessee or purchaser thereof shall not use or deal in the . . . commodities of a competitor . . . of the seller or lessor, where the effect may be to substantially lessen competition or tend to create a monopoly in any line of commerce."
      a. Two distinct products must be involved. See, e.g., *Fultner Enterprises, Inc. v. United States Steel Corp.*, 394 U.S. 495 (1969).
      b. The seller must have significant market power in the tying product so that the tying arrangement will substantially lessen competition in the tied product market.
      c. The owner of a patent or copyright may not attempt to extend his monopoly to unpatented or uncopyrighted products through a tying arrangement. See *United States v. Loew's, Inc.*, 371 U.S. 38 (1962).
      d. The courts are split on the question of whether trademark tying is illegal *per se*. Compare, e.g., *Siegel v. Chicken Delight, Inc.*, 448 F.2d 43 (9th Cir. 1971), *cert. denied*, 405

U.S. 955 (1972), with *Capital Temporaries, Inc. v. Olsten Corp.*, 506 F.2d 658, 664 (2nd Cir. 1974).
3. A tying arrangement will not be covered by the Clayton Act if it does not involve a tangible "commodity." It will nonetheless be unlawful under Sherman Act § 1 if the seller has market power in the tying product and the arrangement lessens competition in the tied product market. *Times-Picayune v. United States*, 345 U.S. 594 (1953).
4. Defenses. Lower courts have permitted tying arrangements when necessary to launch a new and uncertain business. See *United States v. Jerrold Electronics*, 187 F.Supp. 545 (E.D. Pa. 1960), *aff'd per curiam* 365 U.S. 567 (1961). The courts are less likely to be persuaded by a claim that a tying arrangement is necessary to protect goodwill because substitutes for the tied product will not be compatible with the tying product. See *Standard Oil v. United States*, 337 U.S. 293 (1949).
5. Tying arrangement cases have arisen in the health care field. See, e.g., *Portland Retail Druggists Association v. Kaiser Foundation Health Plan*, 622 F.2d 641 (9th Cir. 1981); *Hyde v. Jefferson Parish Hospital District*, 686 F. 2d 286 (5th Cir. 1982), *cert. granted*, 51 U.S.L.W. 3649 (1983); 513 F. Supp. 522 (E.D. La. 1981); *Klamath Lake Pharmaceutical Association v. Klamath Medical Service Bureau*, 507 F. Supp. 980 (D. Ore. 1981); *SmithKline Corp. v. Eli Lilly and Co.*, 575 F.2d 1056 (3d Cir.) *cert. denied*, 439 U.S. 838 (1978). See also Outline Section Four.

V. Mergers
  A. Introduction
    1. Clayton Act § 7 provides that "no corporation engaged in commerce shall acquire, directly or indirectly, the whole or any part of the stock or . . . assets of another corporation engaged also in commerce, where in any line of commerce in any section of the country, the effect of such acquisition may be substantially to lessen competition, or to tend to create a monopoly."
        a. "Line of commerce" has been interpreted as requiring the court to define the relevant product market. *United States v. Greater Buffalo Press*, 402 U.S. 549 (1971).
        b. "Section of the country" has been interpreted as requiring the court to define the appropriate geographic market. *United States v. Philadelphia National Bank*, 374 U.S. 321 (1963).
        c. "May be to substantially lessen competition." Section 7 is designed to *prevent* anticompetitive activity. Thus, the

statute will apply whenever a tendency toward monopoly can be shown. *United States v. Penn-Olin Chemical*, 378 U.S. 158 (1964).
2. There are three basic types of mergers: *horizontal* mergers between competitors, *vertical* mergers between buyers and sellers, and *conglomerate* mergers between unrelated firms. As explained below, different rules apply to each type of merger.
3. Department of Justice merger guidelines. The Department of Justice issues "Merger Guidelines" which state its policies concerning acquisitions. *See Merger Guidelines of Department of Justice—1982*, 3 Trade Reg. Rep. ¶ 4500 (1982). These guidelines are a useful tool for analysis and are discussed more fully below.
4. The Hart-Scott-Rodino Antitrust Improvements Act of 1976, 15 U.S.C. § 18A, requires that certain proposed mergers, acquisitions, and tender offers be reported to the FTC and the Antitrust Division of the Justice Department. After they have been reported, a waiting period of at least thirty days is imposed. The requirement applies only if:
   a. The acquirer has net sales or total assets of at least $100 million, and the target has net sales or total assets of at least $10 million.
   b. After the acquisition, the acquirer holds either 15 percent or more of the voting securities or assets of the target or an aggregate total of voting securities or assets of the target valued in excess of $15 million.

B. Horizontal mergers
1. Test: In *United States v. Philadelphia National Bank*, 374 U.S. 321 (1963), the Supreme Court ruled that a horizontal merger "which produces a firm controlling an undue percentage share of the relevant market and results in a significant increase in the concentration of firms in that market, is so inherently likely to lessen competition substantially that it must be enjoined in the absence of any evidence clearly showing that the merger is not likely to have such anti-competitive effects."
   a. The burden of justifying a merger will fall on the parties to the merger. *United States v. General Dynamics*, 415 U.S. 486 (1974).
   b. A merger may be barred even if the firms included have only a small market share, where there is a trend towards con-

centration. *United States v. Von's Grocery*, 384 U.S. 270 (1966).
   c. Failing company defense: a merger between a failing company and a competitor may be allowed, if there are no other alternatives open to the failing company, and no other purchaser could be interested. *Citizen Publishing Co. v. United States*, 394 U.S. 131 (1969).
2. In 1982, the Department of Justice issued new guidelines on horizontal mergers. The department will focus on post-merger concentration of the market and the market shares of the merging firms. If the concentration or markets shares are low, no further analysis will be conducted. To measure market concentration, the Justice Department will use the Herfindahl-Hirschman Index (HHI), which is calculated by summing the square of the market shares of all the firms in the market. The HHI replaces the traditional four-firm concentration ratio, which had been relied on in the previous guidelines. Unlike the four-firm ratio, the HHI reflects distribution of market shares of the top four firms and the composition of the market outside those firms. It also gives greater weight to the larger firms. When the post-merger HHI exceeds 1000, a challenge may follow. When the post-merger market is "unconcentrated" with an HHI below 1000, the department would be unlikely to challenge the merger. When the post-merger market is "moderately concentrated," with an index between 1000 and 1800, a challenge is still unlikely if the merger increases the index by less than 100 points. If the merger increases the index by more than 100 points, a challenge is more likely than not. When the post-merger market is highly concentrated, with an index above 1800, challenge is unlikely if the merger produces an increase of less than 50 points. If the increase is between 50 and 100, challenge is more likely than not. If the increase is greater than 100, challenge is likely.
3. Horizontal merger problems arise in the health care industry when one hospital seeks to acquire another. See, e.g., *American Medicorp, Inc. v. Humana, Inc.*, 445 F. Supp. 589 (E.D. Pa. 1977). The cases are discussed more fully in Outline Section Two.

C. Vertical mergers

In determining the legality of vertical mergers, the courts and the Justice Department examine the relevant geographic and product market, the probable effect on the market, and the share of the market that will be foreclosed. If the market share foreclosed is

substantial, the purpose of the merger may be considered. See, e.g., *Brown Shoe Co. v. United States*, 370 U.S. 294 (1962). The Justice Department's new guidelines state that vertical mergers will be challenged only when they have horizontal effects.
  D. Conglomerate mergers
  Conglomerate mergers—mergers that are neither horizontal nor vertical—may be challenged in several situations.
   1. When a firm acquires another firm in a market that it expects to enter and therefore eliminates potential competition, the merger may be challenged. *United States v. Penn-Olin Chemical Co.*, 378 U.S. 158 (1964).
   2. When a large firm acquires a firm in a small market, and the acquired firm will be able to take advantage of the large firm's name and resources, the merger may be challenged because of the unfair advantage. *FTC v. Procter & Gamble*, 386 U.S. 568 (1967).
   3. Mergers may be challenged because of "potential reciprocity." Reciprocity problems arise when Company A acquires an unrelated Company B and then forces Company C (a supplier of Company A) to purchase materials it needs from Company B. See *FTC v. Consolidated Foods*, 380 U.S. 592 (1965).
VI. Price discrimination: the Robinson-Patman Act
  A. Description of the statute
  Under the Robinson-Patman Act (Section 2(a) of the Clayton Act), it is unlawful for any person engaged in commerce to discriminate in price: (1) between different purchasers; (2) of commodities of like grade and quality; (3) where the effect may be substantially to lessen competition in any line of commerce, or tend to create a monopoly; or (4) to injure competition with any person who benefits from the discrimination, or the customers of that person.
   1. Both the seller who offers and the buyer who receives discriminatory prices violate the statute. *FTC v. Fred Meyer, Inc.*, 390 U.S. 341 (1968).
   2. Two purchases must take place. *Bruce's Juices, Inc. v. American Can Co.*, 330 U.S. 743 (1947). There must be sales; leases and consignments are not covered.
   3. The transaction must involve a tangible commodity. The provision of services—physician services, for example—is not covered.

4. At least one of the two sales must be "in commerce." See *Gulf Oil Corp. v. Copp Paving Co.*, 419 U.S. 186 (1974).
B. Statutory defenses
   1. Cost justification: Price discrimination can be justified if it is attributable to different costs incurred by the manufacturer.
   2. Changing conditions: Sellers can meet changes in the market for their goods.
   3. Meeting competition: A seller may meet a competitor's lower price. See *United States v. Container Corp.*, 393 U.S. 333 (1969).
C. Exemption for nonprofit institutions
   1. The Non-Profit Institutions Act exempts from the Robinson-Patman Act purchases by nonprofit institutions of supplies for their own use. This exemption may prove useful to some members of the health care industry.
   2. In *Abbott Laboratories v. Portland Retail Druggist Association*, 425 U.S. 1 (1976), the Supreme Court considered whether certain pharmaceutical purchases by a nonprofit hospital were for its "own use."
      a. *Abbott* found the following drug purchases to be for the hospital's own use: inpatient use; emergency facility use; outpatient use in connection with treatment on hospital premises; home use in connection with treatment as an inpatient, outpatient or emergency facility patient use; and use by hospital employees, students, or staff physicians and their dependents.
      b. *Abbott* found the following drug purchases not to be for the hospital's use: refills for former patients; drugs obtained by a hospital employee, student, or staff physician and given to a third party, where the third party is not a dependent; and use by prescription buyers who are not patients.
      c. *Abbott* suggests that a hospital may resell pharmaceuticals to the public in emergency situations without incurring liability under the Robinson-Patman Act.
   3. The FTC has stated in an advisory opinion that a nonprofit hospital may resell, at cost, pharmaceuticals to a nonprofit nursing home without losing its exempt status. The nursing home would not lose its exempt status so long as the drugs were for its own use. FTC advisory opinion regarding St. Peter's Hospital, Albany, New York, dated May 27, 1977.

D. Exemption for government institutions
This term the Supreme Court held that pharmaceutical sales to state-run hospitals are not subject to the proscriptions of the Robinson-Patman Act. *Jefferson City Pharmaceutical Association, Inc. v. Abbott Laboratories*, 103 S. Ct. 1808 (1983) (reversing 5th Court decision). Earlier lower court decisions had held that the Robinson-Patman Act is not applicable to government purchases. See, e.g., *General Shale Products Corp. v. Struck Construction Co.*, 37 F. Supp. 598 (W.D. Ky. 1941), *aff'd on other grounds*, 132 F.2d 425 (6th Cir. 1942), *cert. denied*, 318 U.S. 780 (1945).

VII. Defenses
A number of traditional antitrust defenses may be available to health care providers. These defenses are discussed below and in later sections of the outline.

A. State action; *Parker v. Brown* immunity
   1. In *Parker v. Brown*, 317 U.S. 341 (1943), the Supreme Court held that a state marketing program for raisins that limited competition was not covered by the antitrust laws. It reasoned that the Sherman Act prohibited actions of individuals, not actions of the state.
   2. Recent decisions have limited the application of the state action doctrine
      a. In *Goldfarb v. Virginia State Bar*, 421 U.S. 773 (1975), the Court held that a bar association could not establish minimum fee schedules. It rejected the state action defense because the state had not required the bar association to fix fees. Cf. *Bates v. State Bar of Arizona*, 433 U.S. 350 (1977) (advertising restrictions were imposed by the state and therefore exempt).
      b. In *Cantor v. Detroit Edison Co.*, 428 U.S. 579 (1976), the Court found that a state had not "compelled" a private utility's practice of including lightbulb costs in electricity bills and replacing bulbs without charge, but had merely acquiesced in the practice. Because of the absence of compulsion, state action immunity was unavailable.
      c. It remains unclear whether a "compulsion" finding is necessary. In *California Retail Liquor Dealers Association v. Midcal Aluminum, Inc.*, 445 U.S. 97 (1980), the Court relied on a two-part test:

(1) Is the anticompetitive restraint "clearly articulated and affirmatively expressed as state policy"?
(2) Is the restraint "actively supervised" by the state?
    d. Political subdivisions of the state cannot take advantage of state action immunity unless the subdivision acts pursuant to a state policy. See, e.g., *Community Communication Co. v. City of Boulder*, 102 S. Ct. 835 (1982).
 3. State action immunity and the health care industry
    a. The state action immunity defense has been relied on by hospitals that have acted in conjunction with state and local planning agencies. See *Huron Valley Hospital, Inc. v. City of Pontiac*, 466 F. Supp. 1301 (E.D. Mich. 1979), *vacated and remanded on other grounds*, 666 F.2d 1029 (6th Cir. 1981). These cases are discussed in detail in Outline Section Two.
    b. The state action immunity defense has been rejected in several other health care cases. See *Virginia Academy of Clinical Psychologists v. Blue Shield*, 624 F.2d 476 (4th Cir. 1980), *cert. denied*, 450 U.S. 916 (1981) (agreement between Blue Shield plans to pay for psychotherapy services provided by clinical psychologists only if billed through a physician was held not immune because state did not compel the defendants to limit coverage for psychologists); *Health Care Equalization Committee v. Iowa Medical Society*, 501 F. Supp. 970 (S.D. Iowa 1980) (although Blue Cross enjoys *Parker* immunity from a suit by chiropractors alleging interference with their practice because a state statute prohibited the coverage of chiropractic services, the efforts of defendant state public health commissioner to undermine chiropractic were not immune because not mandated by clear state policy). *See also Sausalito Pharmacy, Inc. v. Blue Shield of California*, 677 F.2d 47 (9th Cir. 1982); *Academy of Ambulatory Foot Surgery v. American Podiatry Association*, 516 F.Supp. 378 (S.D.N.Y. 1981).
B. Noerr-Pennington doctrine
 1. The Noerr-Pennington doctrine protects concerted efforts to influence government decision making. The doctrine rests in part on the constitutional right to petition the government.
 2. Supreme Court cases developing the doctrine:

a. *Eastern Railroads Presidents Conference v. Noerr Motor Freight, Inc.*, 365 U.S. 127 (1961), held that the Sherman Act does not prohibit two or more persons from associating to persuade the legislature or the executive to take particular action with respect to an antitrust law.
b. *United Mine Workers v. Pennington*, 381 U.S. 657 (1965), held that concerted efforts directed at nonelected officials did not violate the antitrust laws.
c. *California Motor Transport Co. v. Trucking Unlimited*, 404 U.S. 508 (1972), held that the doctrine applied to joint efforts before administrative or judicial bodies.
3. Joint action before government bodies will enjoy antitrust immunity under the doctrine only if it is conducted in good faith. Where the activity is a "sham," and designed to injure a competitor, there will be no protection. *California Motor Transport Co. v. Trucking Unlimited*, 404 U.S. 508 (1977).
4. Noerr-Pennington defenses have been rejected in several health care cases.
a. *United States Dental Institute v. American Association of Orthodontists*, 396 F. Supp. 565 (N.D. Ill. 1975) (defendant association seeks to have state agency deny certification to a post graduate course in orthodontia).
b. *Feminist Women's Health Center v. Mohammed*, 586 F.2d 530 (5th Cir. 1978) (peer review organization is not public body to which Noerr-Pennington doctrine applies).
c. *Virginia Academy of Clinical Psychologists v. Blue Shield*, 624 F.2d 476 (4th Cir.), *cert. denied*, 450 U.S. 916 (1980) (insurers collaborate to defy state statute requiring insurance payments to psychologists; no Noerr-Pennington defense since action, although possibly calculated to provoke judicial resolution, was really just an agreement to continue anticompetitive activity in face of state statute).
d. *Hospital Building Co. v. Trustees of Rex Hospital*, 425 U.S. 738 (1976) (no Noerr-Pennington defense where jury finds that defendant hospital's opposition to plaintiff's certificate of need application was an abuse of adjudicatory process; opposition that was not frivolous or did not contain false information might have been protected)
5. The Noerr-Pennington defense has been accepted in several health care industry cases.

a. In *Federal Prescription Service v. American Pharmaceutical Association*, 663 F.2d 253 (D.C. Cir. 1981), *cert. denied*, 102 S. Ct. 1293 (1982), a pharmacists' association was accused of inducing a state pharmacy board to issue regulations restricting the activities of a mail-order prescription drug firm. The court found no evidence that the pharmacists had subverted the integrity of the governmental process; there was no evidence of bribery or conspiracy. Instead, the lobbying efforts were a "genuine attempt to secure governmental action." *Id.* at 262. Since the defendants had only engaged in traditional lobbying, the allegations of anticompetitive intent were not sufficient to support the conclusion that their actions should be regarded as a "sham."
b. In *Phoenix Baptist Hospital v. Samaritan Health Services*, No. 81-5848, (9th Cir. 1982), defendant hospitals were immunized from liability for appearing in opposition to plaintiff hosptial's application to government agency for permission to expand.
6. The Noerr-Pennington defense may be of assistance in health industry cases. There is some doubt about the proper application of the "sham" exception. In general, however, the defense will be successful unless the challenged action was designed solely to injure a competitor, and the defendants did not care whether the government relief sought was ever actually obtained.

C. Interstate commerce
1. Jurisdiction under the Sherman Act is coextensive with congressional power over interstate commerce. See *United States v. South-Eastern Underwriters Association*, 322 U.S. 533 (1944).
2. Early Sherman Act cases relied on a distinction between direct and substantial effects, and remote and incidental effects, on interstate commerce. In the past, this distinction had the effect of protecting health care providers from the antitrust laws. See, e.g., *Spears Free Clinic and Hospital v. Cleeve*, 197 F.2d 125 (10th Cir. 1952) (alleged medical society conspiracy against Colorado chiropractors is local in nature); see also *Riggall v. Washington County Medical Society*, 249 F.2d 266 (8th Cir. 1957), *cert. denied*, 355 U.S. 954 (1958); *Elizabeth Hospital Inc., v. Richardson*, 269 F.2d 167 (8th Cir. 1959); *Wolf v. Jane Phillips Episcopal Memorial Medical Center*, 513 F.2d 684 (10th Cir. 1975).

3. In later decisions, the Supreme Court indicated that the interstate commerce test would be more easily satisfied.
    a. In *Hospital Building Co. v. Trustees of Rex Hospital*, 425 U.S. 738 (1976), the Supreme Court found that the plaintiff could avoid a motion to dismiss by pleading that a substantial percentage of its resources were provided by out-of-state insurance companies and the federal government; that it purchased a substantial percentage of its supplies from out-of-state sources; and that it paid management fees to its out-of-state lenders. This combination of factors, if proved, established a substantial effect on interstate commerce.
    b. See also *McLain v. Real Estate Board of New Orleans, Inc.*, 444 U.S. 232 (1980). *McLain* involved a claim that local real estate firms and trade associations had engaged in a price-fixing conspiracy. The Court suggested that plaintiffs need not show that the alleged unlawful activities had a substantial effect on interstate commerce. It was enough that the defendants' activities, in general, had a substantial effect.
4. In more recent health care industry cases, the courts have seemed quite willing to find a substantial effect on interstate commerce. See, e.g., *Hyde v. Jefferson Parish Hospital District No. 2*, 513 F. Supp. 532 (E.D. La. 1981) *rev'd on other grounds*, 686 F.2d 286 (5th Cir. 1982) *cert. granted* 51 U.S.L.W. 3649 (1983), (purchase of out-of-state supplies, treatment of out-of-state patients, and receipt of Medicare benefits); *Feldman v. Jackson Memorial Hospital*, 509 F. Supp. 815 (S.D. Fla. 1981) (receipt of Medicare payments and out-of-state payments); *Robinson v. Magovern*, 521 F. Supp. 842 (W.D. Pa. 1981), *aff'd*, No. 77-7705 (3rd Cir. 1982) (supplies purchased out of state, out-of-state patients treated, out-of-state revenues received); *United States v. Hospital Affiliates International, Inc.*, 1980-81 Trade Cas. (CCH) ¶ 63,721 (E.D. La. 1980) (same). See also, e.g., *Malini v. Singleton & Assoc.*, 516 F. Supp. 440 (S.D. Tex. 1981); *Mishler v. St. Anthony's Hospital System*, 1981-2 Trade Cas. (CCH) ¶ 64,342 (10th Cir. 1981); *Hoffman v. Delta Dental Plan*, 517 F. Supp. 564 (D. Minn. 1981).
5. Some suits may still be dismissed for lack of jurisdiction, however.
    a. In *Crane v. Inter-Mountain Health Care, Inc.*, 637 F.2d 715 (10th Cir. 1980) (en banc), a pathologist claimed that he was

unlawfully denied hospital staff privileges. The court ruled that dismissal was premature, but noted that a mere allegation that the defendant's business affected interstate commerce was insufficient to satisfy the jurisdictional requirements.
- b. In *Cardio-Medical Associates, Ltd. v. Crozer-Chester Medical Center*, 1982-1 Trade Cas. (CCH) ¶ 64,614 (E.D. Pa. 1982), which also involved a denial of hospital staff privileges, the court held that mere allegations that defendants were health care providers who operated in interstate commerce, that the excluded doctors provided services to patients from out of state, and that the defendant hospital provided services to patients from out of state, were not sufficient to satisfy the jurisdictional requirement. Plaintiffs must identify a channel of interstate commerce directly and be substantially affected by the alleged activities of the defendants. Moreover, plaintiffs must show an effect on their activities as a result of the defendants' actions.
- c. See also *Nara v. American Dental Association*, 526 F. Supp. 452 (W.D. Mich. 1981); *Barr v. National Right to Life Committee, Inc.*, 1981-2 Trade Cas. (CCH) ¶ 64,315 (M.D. Fla. 1981).
6. The interstate commerce defense is not completely dead. In certain health cases—for example, those involving hospital staff privileges—a court may be willing to find that the jurisdictional prerequisites have not been satisfied.

D. Implied repeal
1. When application of the antitrust laws would conflict with some federal regulatory statutes, the courts may find an implied repeal of the antitrust laws. Repeals by implication are disfavored. See, e.g. *United States v. Philadelphia National Bank*, 374 U.S. 321, 350-351 (1963).
2. The question whether federal health planning statutes impliedly repeal the antitrust laws has been confronted by the courts. See, e.g., *National Gerimedical & Gerontology Center v. Blue Cross*, 5 452 U.S. 378 (1981). The relevant decisions are discussed in detail in Section Two.

E. McCarran-Ferguson Act
The McCarran-Ferguson Act, 15 U.S.C. §§ 1011-1015 (1976), exempts from the antitrust laws activities within the "business of insurance" to the extent that such activities are regulated by state

law and do not involve acts of boycott, intimidation or coercion, or agreements to commit such acts.
1. The "business of insurance" requirement.
   a. In *Group Life Health Insurance Co. v. Royal Drug Co.*, 440 U.S. 205 (1979), the court reviewed an antitrust challenge to a prepaid prescription drug insurance plan. The plan was implemented through agreements between Blue Shield of Texas and local pharmacies. Under the agreement, individual policyholders who patronized participating pharmacies could purchase any drug for two dollars. If they used a nonparticipating pharmacy, they were reimbursed only 75 percent of the difference between the drug's price and a two-dollar deductible. Nonparticipating pharmacies claimed that the agreement constituted a price-fixing conspiracy. The Supreme Court held that the "business of insurance" requirement was not satisfied. It relied on three criteria: whether the practice transfers or spreads a policyholder's risk; whether the practice is an integral part of the relationship between the insurer and the insured; and whether the practice is limited to entities within the insurance industry.
      (1) With respect to the first criteria, the Court reasoned that the provider agreements did not involve the underwriting of risks. Rather, they were "merely arrangements for the purchase of goods and services, similar to other arrangements made by insurance companies," to reduce costs. *Id.* at 214.
      (2) With respect to the second criteria, it reasoned that the agreements primarily affected the relationship between the insurer and providers, not the insurer and its policyholders.
      (3) With respect to the third criteria, the Court observed that the agreements involved parties wholly outside the insurance industry.
   b. Cases decided after *Royal Drug* have relied on the framework set forth in that opinion; they have focused on risk spreading and the insurer-insured relationship. The results have not been particularly consistent, however. In *Virginia Academy of Clinical Psychologists v. Blue Shield*, 624 F.2d 476 (4th Cir.), *cert. denied*, 450 U.S. 916 (1980), the plaintiffs, an organization of clinical psychologists, alleged Blue Shield had

conspired against them by refusing to pay for psychologist services provided to subscribers unless the services were billed through a physician. The court found that the plan was not within the business of insurance. "The cost savings obtained by using specific providers, even though mentioned in the subscriber contract, was not sufficiently a part of the insurer-insured relationship . . . because the subscriber received the same benefit . . . in any event." See also *St. Bernard Hospital v. Hospital Service Association*, 618 F.2d 1140 (5th Cir. 1980) (contracts between member hospital and insurance association not within exemption because they only reduced costs); *Hahn v. Oregon Physician's Service*, 689 F.2d 840 (9th Cir. 1982) (restricting reimbursement for podiatrist services is not within the business of insurance). But see e.g., *Health Care Equalization Committee v. Iowa Medical Society*, 501 F. Supp. 970 (S.D. Iowa 1980) (insurance company refusal to pay for chiropractic services is protected by statute); *Klamath Lake Pharmaceutical Service Bureau, supra; Mulhearn v. Rose-Neath Funeral Home, Inc.*, 512 F. Supp. 747 (W.D. La. 1981); *Hoffman v. Delta Dental Plan*, 517 F. Supp. 564 (D. Minn. 1981); *Liberty Glass Co. v. Allstate Insurance Co.*, 607 F.2d 135 (5th Cir. 1979); *United States v. American Society of Anesthesiologists, Inc.*, 473 F. Supp. 147 (S.D.N.Y. 1979).

c. Last term, the Supreme Court held that the use of peer review committees by insurance companies is not within the "business of insurance." *Union Labor Life Insurance Co. v. Pireno*, 102 S. Ct. 3002 (1982). Policies issued by the defendant insurance company provided reimbursement for chiropractic services only when they were necessary and the fees were reasonable. The insurance company relied on peer review committees established by the New York State Chiropractic Association to review particular claims. A chiropractor who was denied reimbursement by the insurance company on the grounds that certain services were not necessary sued, alleging a conspiracy to fix the price for chiropractic treatment. The Supreme Court held that the use of the peer review committees were not within the business of insurance. It relied on the same three criteria employed in *Royal Drug*.

(1) The arrangement played no part in the spreading of the risk; it was unconnected to the contract between the insurance company and the policyholder, which was the risk-transferring event.
(2) The use of peer review committees did not affect the relationship between the insurer and the insureds, but rather that between the insurer and third parties.
(3) The arrangement involved parties outside the insurance industry, and thus did not lie at the center of the legislative concerns underlying the McCarran-Ferguson Act.

2. The "regulated by state law" requirement.
   a. In *Barry*, the Court found that a change in its insurance policies did not meet the "regulated by state law" requirement. Although the change had been filed with the state insurance department, the defendants' conduct "occurred outside of any regulatory or cooperative arrangement established by the laws of Rhode Island."
   b. In *Union Labor Life Insurance Co. v. Pireno*, 102 S. Ct. 3002 (1982), the Supreme Court declined the opportunity to address the question whether the establishment of peer review procedures by an insurance company satisfied the "regulated by state law" requirement. The District Court had held that the requirement was satisfied, but the Second Circuit suggested that it was not. See *Pireno v. New York State Chiropractic Association*, 650 F. 2d 387, 390 n. 5 (2nd Cir. 1981).
3. The "boycott" exception. In *St. Paul Life Insurance Co. v. Barry*, 438 U.S. 531 (1978), the Supreme Court indicated that "boycott," as used in the McCarran-Ferguson Act, has roughly the same meaning as it does when used in the context of the Sherman Act. See also *Virginia Academy of Clinical Psychologists v. Blue Shield*, 624 F.2d 476 (4th Cir.,) *cert. denied*, 450 U.S. 916 (1980); *Proctor v. State Farm Mutual Automobile Insurance Co.*, 561 F.2d 262 (D.C. Cir. 1977), *vacated and remanded*, 440 U.S. 942 (1979), 1980–81 Trade Cas. (CCH) ¶ 63,591 (D.D.C. 1980) (on remand), *aff'd*, 1982–1 Trade Cas. (CCH) ¶ 64,606 (D.C. Cir. 1982), *cert. denied*, 103 S. Ct. 86 (1982); *Bartholomew v. Virginia Chiropractors Association*, 612 F.2d 812 (4th Cir. 1979), *cert. denied*, 446 U.S.

938 (1980); *Klamath Lake Pharmaceutical Association v. Klamath Medical Service Bureau, supra; Anglin v. Blue Shield*, 510 F. Supp. 75 (W.D. Va 1981); *Hoffman v. Delta Dental Plan, supra; Ratino v. Medical Service of District of Columbia*, 1981–1 Trade Cas. (CCH) ¶ 64,144 (D. Md. 1981).

Section two: Competition among hospitals or other health facilities

Recent years have seen the filing of numerous antitrust cases challenging alleged efforts to monopolize the health care markets through mergers of hospitals, efforts to exclude competitors, and other miscellaneous means. This section summarizes the theories that may be used in challenges to anticompetitive acts by competing health care facilities, as well as the available defenses.

I. Mergers and acquistions

In part because of the relative novelty of Sherman or Clayton Act challenges to mergers of hospitals and related facilities, the courts have only begun to develop an understanding of the market for health care services—the forms that competition may take, the geographical scope of particular markets, the particular "product" markets that can be discerned, and so forth. In those cases that *have* been brought so far, much of the attention of the courts has been taken up with analysis of defenses that stem from the regulated nature of the industry: "implied repeal" under the National Health Planning and Resource Development Act (NHPRDA) and "state action." As the scope of these defenses becomes clearer, the focus will turn to the elements of the antitrust claims, and how they apply to a new and unique industry. This is where creative attorneys can make a significant difference.

A. Elements of a Clayton section 7 claim

When two existing hospitals merge, the clearest basis for an antitrust challenge is, of course, section 7 of the Clayton Act. Section 7 prohibits mergers of companies that are engaged "in commerce or in any activity affecting commerce," if "in any line of commerce or any activity affecting commerce in any section of the country" the effect may be "substantially to lessen competition or to tend to create a monopoly." Recent cases illustrate the application of this provision to the hospital industry.

1. Standing

Anyone may sue to enjoin a merger under section 7 on a showing of a threatened injury that would justify relief under normal equitable principles. 15 U.S.C. § 26.[1] Generally, this presents no problem, because it is the government or a competitor who is suing to prevent a merger.[2] Some complications may, however, arise when the interest of the plaintiff is somewhat more tangential than that of a competitor. Thus, in *City of Fairfax v. Fairfax Hospital Association*, 562 F.2d 280

(4th Cir. 1977), *vacated on other grounds*, 435 U.S. 999 (1978), the proposed lease of a hospital to its only competitor was challenged by a group of physicians and by the city in which the facilities were located. The district court had dismissed the case, in part on grounds of lack of standing. *Id.* at 282. The Fourth Circuit reversed, holding that allegations that the merger would indirectly injure the doctors and the city were sufficient, if proved, to create standing.[3] *Id.* at 283.[4]

2. Interstate commerce

Until 1980, the Clayton Act was limited to mergers of companies that were "in commerce." This requirement was more strict than the Sherman Act requirement that a challenged action have a "substantial effect" on interstate commerce[5] and could have provided a potent defense in a lawsuit involving local hospitals.[6] In 1980, however, Congress amended section 7 to apply to companies engaged in "any activity affecting commerce," thus seemingly equating the Clayton Act with the Sherman Act, which reaches to the furthest extent of Congress's power under the Commerce Clause.[7] In view of the Supreme Court's broad reading of the Sherman Act commerce requirement in *Hospital Building Co. v. Trustees of Rex Hospital*, 425 U.S. 738 (1976), it seems likely that any merging hospital or health facility is in an "activity affecting [interstate] commerce." After all, any change in the level of services provided at the hospital will affect numerous suppliers in other states.[8] As a result, the commerce element should not be a significant battleground in the future.

3. Effect on competition

No merger is illegal under the Clayton Act unless its effect "may be substantially to lessen the competition, or to tend to create a monopoly." 15 U.S.C. § 18. As a result, in hospital merger cases, plaintiffs must be prepared to rebut a claim that the hospital market is not competitive—or competitive only in undesirable ways—so that the challenged merger cannot be illegal.

This defense is presently being pressed by the Hospital Corporation of America (HCA) in a pending FTC enforcement action challenging HCA's acquisition of a second chain of proprietary hospitals. (FTC Docket No. 9161, filed July 30, 1982). Relying on economic studies, HCA claims that the usual rules for assessing market shares under the Clayton Act should not apply to hospitals.⁹ Asserting that hospitals compete on quality, not price, HCA argues that there is much less reason to fear oligopolies in that industry. Even in an oligopolistic situation, cost-based reimbursement will continue the incentives favoring continued qualitative improvements.

4. Product markets
Any section 7 plaintiff must be able to prove a product market in which the defendant has sufficient market power to cause a lessening of competition. Obviously, market power, based on market shares, can be debated through the use of competing definitions of the product market. For example, in *American Medicorp, Inc. v. Humana, Inc.*, 445 F. Supp. 589 (E.D. Pa. 1977), involving a takeover of one proprietary hospital chain by another, the plaintiff sought to prove the existence of a market in "development of hospitals." *Id.* at 597. It claimed that the proprietary chains compete for the approval of community groups that is essential to winning a certificate-of-need for a new hospital. *Id.* at 599. But the court failed to see the basis for this creative market definition and demanded more proof. *Id.* at 602. In its analysis of the preliminary injunction issue, the court looked instead to the market in "operation and management of short-term acute-care community hospitals."

In *United States v. Hospital Affiliates International, Inc.*, 1980-81 Trade Cas. ¶ 63,721 (E.D. La. 1980), involving another merger of chains, the government convinced the court to look at the market in "in-patient psychiatric care by private psychiatric hospitals and non-governmental general acute care hospitals." *Id.* at 77,852. The court excluded state psychiatric hospitals because of their generally lower quality and the differing populations they serve. As this case suggests, psychiatric hospitals present a particularly fertile area for battles over product markets, because of the differing but overlapping functions of private long- and short-term residential facilities, state residential facilities, general hospital psychiatric wards, day-care centers, and so forth.¹⁰ Even in cases involving general, acute-care hospitals, there may be disputes about specialized facilities, as well as outpatient services that may "compete" with hospital services.

5. Geographical markets
Because of the nature of the services provided, hospitals'

relevant geographic markets tend to be local. Even where chains operate nationally, their percentages of the entire industry will generally be small.[11] But a merger of chains may be significant in one or more local areas where the chains happen to overlap. Thus, in *American Medicorp, supra*, the court found that a merger of two large chains would substantially lessen competition in only one geographic market: Bluefield, West Virginia. 445 F. Supp. at 605.[12]

On the local level, there may be disputes about how far patients are willing to go. In the pending HCA case, for example, the government suggested three geographic markets centered in the Chattanooga area: the county, the standard metropolitan statistical area (SMSA), and the health service area (HSA). The defendant is suggesting other market boundaries that lessen its apparent market power.

There may, of course, be regional or even national competition among specialized facilities. For example, there may well be a separate national market for long-term, private psychiatric hospitals.

B. Defenses
   1. Implied Repeal

   Often a merger or acquisition (or other challenged action) will have been approved by state health planning authorities created at the urging of Congress in the National Health Planning and Resource Development Act (NHPRDA), 42 U.S.C. §§ 300k *et seq*. Where this occurs, it may be argued that the antitrust laws no longer apply because Congress intended to exempt activities approved under the NHPRDA.

   This argument appears most prominently in *National Gerimedical Hospital v. Blue Cross*, 452 U.W. 378 (1981), a case that did not involve a merger. In *Gerimedical*, Blue Cross was sued because it had denied participating status to a new hospital in Missouri that was built against the recommendation of the local advisory body in the health planning apparatus: the health systems agency (HSA). Unlike most other states, Missouri did not at that time require regulatory approval of new construction through a "certificate of need." Nevertheless, Blue Cross defended the antitrust suit with the argument that actions undertaken in concert with an HSA policy are exempt.

   In making this argument, Blue Cross could point to the basic finding underlying the NHPRDA: Competition either does not exist in the hospital industry or is undesirable because it leads to overinvestment.[13] It could also point to the important planning function delegated to local HSAs. These factors were enough to convince two lower courts to find a blanket repeal of the antitrust laws in areas subject to the health planning process, but the Supreme Court reversed. It held that there is no *blanket* repeal of antitrust laws in the health field. It then held that there was no clear inconsistency between health planning and antitrust laws on the particular facts before it, since the Blue Cross action was a spontaneous one, not required or approved by any regulatory body. However, in a footnote, the Court left open the possibility of future claims to exemptions, where those may be necessary to let the NHPRDA work. 101 S. Ct. at 2423 n. 18.

When similar arguments have been raised in later cases, they have met with mixed results. In *Huron Valley Hospital v. City of Pontiac*, 666 F.2d 1029 (1981), involving a monopolization claim, the Sixth Circuit reversed a finding of blanket repeal of the antitrust laws by the NHPRDA, and remanded with instructions to stay the antitrust suit until parallel state proceedings were concluded. The court made it clear that a narrow exemption from antitrust liability might still be established after the state regulatory process was complete. In *North Carolina v. P.I.A. Asheville, Inc.*, 1982–1 Trade Cas. ¶ 64,764 (W.D.N.C. 1981), the court dismissed a Clayton Act challenge to a hospital acquisition that had been approved through a certificate of need, relying in part on an implied repeal theory.[14]

2. State action

A closely related defense is derived from the decision in *Parker v. Brown*, 317 U.S. 341 (1943). That decision and its progeny exempt from antitrust scrutiny any anticompetitive actions taken pursuant to a deliberate state policy. To qualify for an exemption, "the challenged restraint must be 'one clearly articulated and affirmatively expressed as state policy'; [and] . . . must be 'actively supervised' by the State itself." *California Retail Liquor Dealers Ass'n v. Midcal Aluminum, Inc.*, 445 U.S. 97, 105 (1980), quoting *City of Lafayette v. Louisiana Power & Light Co.*, 435 U.S. 389, 418 (1978).

Because the certificate of need in *P.I.A. Asheville, supra*, was issued by a state regulatory body, pursuant to a state law requiring regulation approval of hospital acquisitions, the district court held, in the alternative, that the hospital merger was a form of exempt state action. In *City of Fairfax v. Fairfax Hospital*, 562 F.2d 280 (4th Cir. 1977), the district court had granted summary judgment on the state action question, relying on the fact that the acquiring hospital was built on public land, had its budgets approved by the county, and also had to submit important contracts to the county for comment, *id.* at 282. The Fourth Circuit vacated this ruling, finding such facts insufficient to show the required state policy and state supervision, but remanded for a full hearing, *id.* at 284.[15] Finally, in an unpublished opinion, *Phoenix Baptist Hospital v. Samaritan Health Services*, No. 81-5848 (Aug. 25, 1982), the Ninth Circuit held that *Parker v. Brown* exempted at least some of the actions of two hospital subsidiaries that formed a joint venture and applied for a certificate of need for a new hospital.

C. Other challenges to mergers

In a number of cases, challengers of hospital mergers add conspiracy claims under Sherman Act § 1 or monopolization claims under Sherman Act § 2. E.g., *American Medicorp, Inc. v. Humana, Inc.*, 445 F. Supp. 589, 590 (E.D. Pa. 1977). These additional claims add very little, except to the extent that plaintiffs can successfully broaden the scope of their complaints beyond a particular merger to a larger conspiracy or monopolization effort. See, e.g., *Phoenix Baptist Hospital, supra* (allegations of larger conspiracy by parent hospitals not dismissed).

II. Other forms of anticompetitive conduct

Even where no merger or acquisition occurs, hospitals may be sued under the Sherman Act for other actions alleged to be part of an effort to be anticompetitive.

A. Preventing entry—claims

Most often, such suits involve alleged efforts to monopolize the hospital market by preventing the entry of a new competitor. For example, in *Phoenix Baptist, supra*, the defendant hospitals were sued not only for building a new hospital as a joint venture, but also for later opposing the plaintiff's application for permission to expand. In *Huron Valley, supra*, the claim was that an existing hospital conspired with health planning agencies and others to prevent construction of a new competitor. 666 F.2d at 1030-31. Recently, in *Hospital Building Co. v. Trustees of Rex Hospital*, No. 81-1134 (4th Cir. Oct. 19, 1982), the court reversed a jury verdict for a plaintiff who claimed a conspiracy to prevent entry in a local hospital market. Based on the NHPRDA, the court created a limited "rule of reason," allowing the defendants to show that their activities in the planning process were aimed only at preventing "needless duplication" of health facilities. Op. at 15. The case was remanded for a new trial. In *Denver v. Santa Barbara Commun. Dialysis Center*, 1981-1 Trade Cas. ¶ 63,946 (C.D. Cal. 1981), the plaintiffs alleged that a number of actions were part of the defendants' efforts to prevent the survival and expansion of competing outpatient renal dialysis services. A large number of cases have involved alleged hospital efforts to suppress development of HMOs through denial of staff privileges to the doctors involved, or through other discriminatory practices.[16]

B. Preventing entry—defenses

Like merger claims, these monopolization claims are subject to a variety of legal defenses. The state action[17] and implied repeal arguments[18] discussed above may also apply here. It may also be argued that the anticompetitive conduct is too local to have the effect on interstate commerce required under the Sherman Act.[19] But there are at least two further defenses that were not discussed in reference to mergers.

1. Noerr-Pennington

The Supreme Court decisions in *Eastern R.R. Presidents Conf. v. Noerr Motor Freight, Inc.*, 365 U.S. 127 (1961), and *United Mine Workers v. Pennington*, 381 U.S. 657 (1965), immunize the actions of persons who participate in administrative or adjudicative processes, even where that participation may have anticompetitive effects. Grounded in the First Amendment, this immunity applies unless the participation is a "sham"—a bad-faith effort solely aimed at harassment of a competitor. *California Motor Transport Co. v. Trucking Unlimited*, 404 U.S. 508, 515 (1978). When an alleged monopolization effort takes the form of opposing a competitor's application for a certificate of need, the *Noerr-Pennington* defense comes into play. Thus, in *Phoenix Baptist, supra*, the defendants were immunized from liability for appearing in opposition to the plaintiff's application for permission to expand. The Ninth Circuit found

that this effort was not a "sham" because it was not groundless—indeed, it succeeded. See also *Hospital Building Co. v. Trustees of Rex Hospital*, No. 91-1134 (4th Cir. Oct. 19, 1982) (discussing sham exception in a similar context).
2. Tenth Amendment
State defendants who are sued for the participation in creating a monopoly may also have another defense: the Tenth Amendment. Under *National League of Cities v. Usery*, 426 U.S. 833 (1976), certain integral functions of state government are constitutionally shielded from federal regulation. In *Gold Cross Ambulance v. City of Kansas City*, No. 80-1131-cv-w-7 (W.D. Mo. 1982), aff'd on other grounds,—F.2d—(8th Cir. 1983), such an argument was successfully used in defense of a city-created ambulance monopoly.
C. Group purchasing agreements
One recent monopoly case did not involve a hospital's effort to suppress its own competition. In *White and White, Inc. v. American Hospital Supply Co.*, 1982-1 Trade Cas. ¶ 64,722 (W.D. Mich. 1982), 29 hospitals, through a voluntary association, had signed a group purchasing agreement with the nation's largest distributor of hospital supplies. In return for purchases of a certain volume, these hospitals received discounts. Four smaller distributors sued, claiming a conspiracy between the hospitals and the defendant supply company. After a lengthy analysis of the industry and the challenged agreement, the court found a conspiracy in restraint of trade in violation of Sherman Act § 1, as well as attempted monopolization of the hospital supply industry in violation of Sherman Act § 2.

References

1. Standing for a treble-damages claim is somewhat more restricted; an injury in one's "business or property" is required. 15 U.S.C. ¶ 15.
2. See, e.g., *United States v. Hospital Affiliates International, Inc.*, 1980-81 Trade Cas. ¶ 63,721 (E.D. La. 1980) (U.S. as plaintiff); *American Medical International, Inc.*, 1981 Trade Cas. ¶ 21,851 (July 30, 1981) (FTC enforcement action); *North Carolina v. P.I.A. Asheville, Inc.*, 1982-1 Trade Cas. ¶ 64,764 (W.D.N.C. 1981) (state as plaintiff); *Phoenix Baptist Hospital v. Samaritan Health Services*, No. 89-5848 (9th Cir. Aug. 25, 1982) (competing hospital as plaintiff); *American Medicorp, Inc. v. Humana, Inc.*, 445 F. Supp. 589 (E.D. Pa. 1977) (takeover target as plaintiff).

3. Unlike states, cities do not enjoy automatic standing under a *parens patriae theory*. *City of Rohner Park v. Harris*, 601 F.2d 1040, 1044-45 (9th Cir. 1979).
4. See also *Oleksy v. Sisters of Mercy*, 1980-1 Trade Cas. ¶ 63,066 (Mich. Ct. App. 1979) (under Michigan antitrust statute, group that wished to purchase a hospital that was sold to another group suffered no injury, but could sue as a private attorney general).
5. See *Hospital Bldg. Co. v. Trustees of Rex Hospital*, 425 U.S. 738 (1976).
6. Cf. *United States v. American Bldg. Maintenance Industries*, 425 U.S. 271 (1975) (local janitorial service company not "in commerce").
7. See *United States v. South-Eastern Underwriters Ass'n*, 322 U.S. 533 (1944).
8. In *Hospital Building Co.*, the Court held that the Sherman Act was satisfied because the plaintiff hospital was supplied and reimbursed from out of state, paid a management fee to an out-of-state parent company, and planned to borrow money for expansion from out of state. 425 U.S. at 741–47.
9. See also *Oleksy v. Sisters of Mercy*, 1980-1 Trade Cas. ¶ 63,066, at 77,304 (Mich. Ct. App. 1979) (under Michigan law, antitrust challenge to hospital acquisition rejected in part because of highly regulated nature of hospital industry).
10. Compare the complaint in the FTC's action against HCA (No. 9161, filed July 30, 1982), alleging a market in "inpatient psychiatric treatment services excluding substance abuse treatment services and long-term treatment of chronic mental illness."
11. See *American Medicorp, Inc. v. Humana, Inc.*, 445 F. Supp. 589, 602 (E.D. Pa. 1977).
12. The court refused to enjoin the takeover, finding this market too insignificant. 445 F.Supp. at 606.
13. See S. Rep. No. 93-1285, at 39 (1974). In the 1979 amendments to the NHPRDA, Congress required planners to rely on competition where possible, but repeated the finding that in "inpatient health services and other institutional health services . . . competition does not or will not appropriately allocate supply." 42 U.S.C. § 300k-3(b)(2).
14. See also *Save Our Samaritan v. Bay Medical Center*, Civ. No. 79-10297 (E.D. Mich. Jan. 13, 1981) (hospital merger found exempt under NHPRDA), *remanded for reconsideration* [in light of *National Gerimedical, supra,* and *Huron Valley, supra*], No. 81-1093, *vacated and remanded* (6th Cir. 1982).
15. The Supreme Court then vacated and remanded this ruling in light

of *City of Lafayette v. Louisiana Light & Power Co.*, 435 U.S. 389 (1978). 435 U.S. 992 (1978). *City of Lafayette* held that municipalities themselves may be subject to the antitrust laws.
16. E.g., *United States v. Halifax Hospital Medical Center*, 1981-1 Trade Cas. ¶ 64,151 (M.D. Fla. 1981) (consent decree); *American Medical International, Inc.*, 3 Trade Reg. Rep. (CCH) ¶ 21,851 (pending FTC action, docket no. 9158).
17. E.g., *Phoenix Baptist Hospital, supra; Gold Cross Ambulance v. City of Kansas City*, No. 80-1131-cv-w-7 (W.D. Mo. May 7, 1982) (city-created ambulance monopoly).
18. In *Huron Valley, supra*, and *Denver v. Santa Barbara Commun. Dialysis Center, supra*, implied repeal arguments were made. In both cases, the courts chose not to dismiss the claims, but to await the outcome of health planning proceedings and appeals.
19. See *Denver v. Santa Barbara Commun. Dialysis Center, supra*.

Section three: Physicians and nonphysicians

Physicians compete only with other physicians, but also with nonphysicians who provide alternatives to medical treatment—for example, psychologists, chiropractors, and podiatrists. A variety of actions taken by physicians, hospitals, insurance companies, and other members of the health care industry may have the effect of reducing competition between physicians and nonphysicians. This section of the materials discusses the antitrust consequences of practices that reduce competition between physicians and nonphysicians. Although many lawsuits have been filed, most of these cases have not yet resulted in a decision on the merits. Instead, the cases have focused on the availability of various antitrust defenses.

I. Agreements involving insurance companies
  A. Types of cases
    1. Limitations in health insurance coverage
      Health insurance policies frequently provide only limited coverage for treatment provided by nonmedical practitioners. Such limitations in coverage, which affect competition, have spawned several lawsuits. In *Virginia Academy of Clinical Psychologists v. Blue Shield of Virginia*, 624 F.2d 476 (4th Cir. 1980), Virginia psychologists sued Blue Shield of Virginia, Blue Shield of Southwestern Virginia, and the Neuropsychiatric Society of Virginia. They challenged Blue Shield insurance policies which refused to pay for services provided by clinical psychologists unless the services were ordered, supervised, and billed by physicians. The psychologists claimed that the Blue Shield plans were controlled by physicians and that the physicians had conspired with the Neuropsychiatric Society to reduce competition by psychologists, in violation of the Sherman Act.

      In *Hahn v. Oregon Physicians Services*, 689 F.2d 840 (9th Cir. 1982), Oregon podiatrists sued providers of prepaid health insurance, health maintenance organizations, and an individual practice association, alleging that they had conspired to boycott podiatrists in favor of other physicians, in violation of the Clayton and Sherman Acts. The plaintiffs challenged several of defendants' practices. They objected to defendant insurers' health insurance policies, which required subscribers to obtain certain podiatric services solely from medical doctors. They also complained that they were not allowed to be members of the HMOs or the individual associations, and that as a result of this practice they were reimbursed for their services at a lower rate than members of the medical organizations.

In *Ballard v. Blue Shield of Southern West Virginia, Inc.* 543 F.2d 1075 (4th Cir. 1976), West Virginia chiropractors sued six corporations that sold Blue Cross-Blue Shield health insurance, the doctors who were directors of the corporations, and the West Virginia State Medical Association. They claimed that the defendants conspired to refuse health insurance coverage for chiropractic services. According to the chiropractors, this conspiracy violated the Sherman Act because it made chiropractic services financially unattractive to consumers and thus had the effect of eliminating competition. See also *Health Care Equalization Committee v. Iowa Medical Society*, 501 F. Supp. 970 (S.D. Iowa 1980) (similar claim).

Each of the above suits was brought by nonmedical practitioners who claimed that their business was harmed by limits on insurance coverage. Consumers who wish to use alternative health services but whose insurance policies provide only limited coverage for such services have also brought suits. *Blue Shield of Virginia v. McCready*, 102 S. Ct. 2450 (1982) involved a challenge to the same coverage limitation at issue in *Virginia Academy of Clinical Psychologists*—the limitation providing that policyholders would be reimbursed for psychologists' services only if they billed through a physician. In *McCready*, however, unlike *Virginia Academy of Clinical Psychologists*, the plaintiff was not a psychologist but a consumer who wished to use psychologists' services. See also *Health Care Equalization Committee, supra.*

2. Denial of medical malpractice insurance

At least one physician-nonphysician suit involves a denial of medical malpractice insurance. In *Nurse Midwifery Associates v. B. K. Hibbet*, 549 F. Supp. 1185, (M.D. Tenn. 1982), two nurse-midwives and an obstetrician sought to establish a maternity practice in Nashville, Tennessee.[1] The obstetrician was subsequently denied medical malpractice insurance. The midwives and the obstetrician filed suit against the insurance company and several Nashville obstetricians who participated in the operations of the insurance company. The plaintiffs claimed that the defendant obstetricians and the insurance company conspired to deny malpractice insurance in order to eliminate competition by midwives.

B. Defenses

The defendants in the cases involving limitations in health insurance policies have attempted to use a wide variety of traditional antitrust defenses.

1. McCarran-Ferguson Act

In most of the insurance cases, defendants have claimed exemption from the antitrust laws under the McCarran-Ferguson Act, 15 U.S.C. § 1101 *et seq.* The Act extends immunity to insurance company activities that are: (1) part of the "business of insurance"; (2) "regulated by state law"; and (3) do not take the form of coercion, intimidation, or boycott. 15 U.S.C. §§ 1012(b) and 1013(b). In general, the McCarran-Ferguson Act defense has met with little success.

The "business of insurance" requirement: The "business of insurance" has been narrowly defined by the Supreme Court. In *Group Life & Health Ins. Co. v. Royal Drug Co.*, 440 U.S. 205 (1979) and *Union Labor Life Insurance Co. v. Pireno*, 102 S. Ct. 3002 (1982), the Court identified three criteria for determining whether a business practice is part of the business of insurance. First, it must be determined whether the practice has the effect of transferring or spreading a policyholder's risk. If an arrangement does not spread the risk, but merely reduces the insurer's costs, it is not part of the business of insurance. Second, it must be determined whether the contract is an integral part of the relationship between insurer and insured. Finally, it must be determined whether the practice is limited to entities within the insurance industry. If the primary impact of a particular practice is on markets other than that for insurance, the McCarran-Ferguson exemption does not apply.

Most courts applying these criteria have concluded that an insurance company's decision not to pay for services provided by nonphysicians is not part of the "business of insurance." In *Virginia Academy of Clinical Psychologists v. Blue Shield of Virginia, supra,* the Fourth Circuit observed that the decision not to reimburse insureds for services provided by clinical psychologists was not a decision "whether to underwrite the risk of those disorders or even the need for psychotherapy;

rather, it was a question of who they would pay for such services." *Id.* at 484. The defendants' actions were not part of the risk-spreading function; rather, they were related to the cost of carrying out their contractual obligation.[2] Similarly, in *Hahn v. Oregon Physicians' Services, supra,* the Ninth Circuit found that the decision not to pay for podiatrist services was not part of the business of insurance because there were no bona fide risk-related reasons for an insurer to distinguish between the services of M.D.s and podiatrists. The court further noted that the practice affected entities outside the insurance industry; its primary impact was on competition in markets other than that for insurance.[3] See also *Nurse Midwifery Assoc. v. Hibbet, supra* (denial of medical malpractice insurance is not part of the business of insurance because it was directed at activity in a noninsurance market).

In *Health Care Equalization Committee v. Iowa Medical Society, supra,* the district court found that an insurance company decision not to provide coverage for chiropractic services was within the "business of insurance." The court reasoned that this decision directly concerned the relationship between the insurer and the insured. Moreover, the decision was part of the insurance company's risk-spreading function. The decision in *Health Care Equalization Committee* is clearly inconsistent with the decisions in *Virginia Academy of Clinical Psychology Nurse Midwifery Associates, Inc.,* and *Hahn.* In the future, it seems likely that courts will follow the approach adopted by the latter cases, and conclude that a decision to deny insurance coverage to nonphysician services is not part of the business of insurance.

The "boycott" requirement: Even if a particular practice is part of the "business of insurance," the McCarran-Ferguson Act exemption will not be available if the practice constitutes a boycott. In *St. Paul Fire & Marine Ins. Co. v. Barry,* 438 U.S. 531 (1978), the Supreme Court stated that the "boycott" requirement does not apply only to boycotts by insurance companies; it also covers boycotts by other groups. The Court further stated that the word "boycott" has roughly the same meaning that it does when used in the Sherman Act context. McCarran-Ferguson Act boycotts would include any methods by which a group of individuals pressures a party with whom it has a dispute by withholding patronage or services from that party.

Several physician-nonphysician cases have relied on the McCarran-Ferguson Act's boycott exception. In *Nurse Midwifery Associates v. Hibbet*, the District Court reviewed *Barry* and then concluded that the insurance company's decision to deny medical malpractice insurance to the obstetrician who wished to establish a practice with midwives was a boycott. Thus, the McCarran-Ferguson exemption did not apply. See also *Ballard v. Blue Shield of Southern West Virginia, supra* (combination by insurers and physicians to deny insurance coverage to chiropractors was a boycott within meaning of Sherman Act, and thus also within meaning of McCarran-Ferguson Act).

The "regulated by state law" requirement: The question whether a particular insurance practice is "regulated by state law" need be addressed only if the practice is part of the business of insurance, and is not a boycott. Assuming these hurdles can be crossed, the "regulated by state law" requirement may be easily satisfied. Many insurance company activities are extensively regulated. See *Health Care Equalization Committee v. Iowa Medical Society, supra,* at 995 (Blue Cross and Blue Shield activities heavily regulated under the state law).[4]

2. Interstate commerce

Several of the insurance company cases have involved claims that plaintiffs failed to satisfy the Sherman Act's interstate commerce requirement. This defense ordinarily fails. In *Ballard v. Blue Shield at Southern West Virginia, Inc., supra,* the plaintiff chiropractors had argued that the restrictions in insurance coverage adversely affected interstate commerce by reducing the sale of therapeutic devices and equipment manufactured outside West Virginia, by increasing the cost of health care to patients who traveled in interstate commerce for chiropractic treatment, and by injuring interstate insurance companies that were willing to pay chiropractic claims. The district court dismissed the case, finding that these allegations were insufficient to satisfy the jurisdictional requirement. However, the Fourth Circuit reversed and remanded. The court reasoned that it was quite possible that "the alleged reduction or elimination of the chiropractors' business throughout the entire state of West Virginia may adversely affect interstate commerce." *Id.* at 1078.

In *Hahn v. Oregon Physicians' Services,* the plaintiff podiatrists pointed to their own contacts with interstate commerce: out-of-state purchase of medical supplies and equipment, treatment of patients from out of state, the receipt of payments from out-of-state insurers, and participation in Medicare. The district court concluded that the jurisdictional prerequisites were not satisfied since plaintiffs' interstate contacts were insubstantial. The Ninth Circuit remanded for further proceedings, noting that jurisdiction could be established simply by showing that defendants' activities had a substantial impact on interstate commerce, even if plaintiffs' interstate contacts were insubstantial.

3. State action immunity

Defenses based on the state action doctrine have met with mixed success in these cases. In *Ballard v. Blue Shield of Southern West Virginia, Inc., supra*, a chiropractors case, the Fourth Circuit refused to apply the defense. It stated that the McCarran-Ferguson Act expresses congressional intent to subject boycotts by insurance companies to the Sherman Act. Thus, the state action doctrine should not be used to impute a contrary intent to Congress. The court also observed that the defendant insurance companies were not compelled by state law to exclude chiropractors from their insurance plans. In fact, West Virginia law specifically authorized the defendants to insure chiropractic treatment.

In *Health Care Equalization Committee v. Iowa Medical Society, supra*, however, the district court found that state action doctrine protected an insurance company decision to deny coverage for chiropractic services. It reasoned that the Iowa insurance statute clearly expressed a policy excluding chiropractic services from coverage by health care service corporations. The legislature repeatedly identified the particular services for which coverage was provided, but never included chiropractic services. State regulatory officials had issued opinions stating that the statute prevented coverage for chiropractic services. Under the circumstances, it would be unfair to subject the insurance companies to antitrust liability. In effect, their decision not to provide coverage was compelled by state law.

4. Consumer standing

In *McCready v. Blue Shield of Virginia*, 102 S. Ct. 2540 (1982), the defendant insurance companies argued that a consumer of psychologists' services who alleged a conspiracy to limit reimbursement for psychologists' services did not have standing to seek treble damages for psychologists' services. According to the defendants, only the psychologists who were directly harmed by the alleged conspiracy had standing. The Supreme Court rejected this argument, holding that the consumers did have standing. See Outline Section One. Thus, in the future, suits may be brought by both nonphysician practitioners and consumers of their services.

C. The merits

In *Virginia Academy of Clinical Psychologists v. Blue Shield of Virginia*, the Fourth Circuit addressed the merits of the psychologists' claims that the Virginia Neuropsychiatric Society and two Blue Shield plans had violated the antitrust laws by refusing to reimburse insureds for psychologists' services unless the services were billed through a physician. The court began by finding that the Blue Shield plans had participated in a "combination or conspiracy" within the meaning of the Sherman Act.[5] Both Blue Shield plans were combinations of physicians, operating under the direction of their physician members. In addition, the Blue Shield plans had collaborated with each other in deciding to limit coverage for psychologists' service. The court decided, however, that the Neuropsychiatric Society of Virginia was not involved in this combination. In response to the Blue Shield plan's request for proposals, it had recommended that they limit reimbursement for psychologists' services. However, it had no control over the Blue Shield plan's decisions. The court stated that the insurance companies, acting independently, were free to solicit proposals from providers. And the Neuropsychiatric Society, as a seller of services, could make recommendations, absent some form of coercion.

After rejecting various defenses raised by the Blue Shield plans,[6] the Fourth Circuit found that the Blue Shield combination could be characterized as a boycott.[7] It further decided that the rule of reason should apply. Because of the special considerations involved in the delivery of health services, it was not prepared to apply a *per se* rule of illegality to medical plans which refuse a condition payment to competing or potentially competing providers.

Relying on the rule of reason, the court concluded that the Blue Shield plans had violated the Sherman Act. Psychiatrists and psychologists were ordinarily competitors. However, particularly because Blue Shield plans were the dominant source of health care coverage in Virginia, the requirement that the psychologist's fees be billed through a physician substantially diminished this competition. The billing requirement could not be justified simply on grounds of "good medical practice." The policy was not designed to ensure that a physician supervised the psychologist to ensure the quality of the therapy. Psychologist services were covered if billed through *any* physician—not just physicians who regularly treat mental disorders.

The Fourth Circuit conceded that an insurance company rule requiring referral and supervision by a physician might serve as a cost control measure. "[R]equiring examination and consultation by a physician would assure that therapy was not needlessly performed to treat a problem with physical etiology." *Id.* at 485. According to the Fourth Circuit, however, this goal could be achieved only in a manner that did not limit the economic independence of psychologists.

Virginia Academy of Clinical Psychologists was decided before *Arizona v. Maricopa County Medical Society*, 102 S. Ct. 2466 (1982), in which the Supreme Court held that a maximum fee schedule was illegal *per se*. It rejected the notion that physicians would always enjoy a safe harbor under the rule of reason. This decision casts some doubt on the continuing validity of the Fourth Circuit's conclusion that the Blue Shield boycott should be tested under the rule of reason. However, *Maricopa* does suggest that if an agreement involving health care providers serves a legitimate medical goal, the rule of reason will apply. Thus, the physician-insurance company agreements described in this section may continue to be measured under the rule of reason, provided the physicians and insurance companies can supply a reasonable professional justification for the agreement.

Even if the rule of reason does still apply, it seems likely that billing arrangements that are similar to those in issue in *Virginia Academy of Psychologists* and that cannot be justified on quality or cost-control grounds will be struck down. However, other physician-insurance company agreements that do serve quality or cost-control goals may be acceptable. For example, an agreement providing that nonphysician services will be covered only if actively supervised by a physician qualified to undertake such supervision might be upheld. Similarly, an agreement providing that nonphysician services will be covered only if the services have been recommended by a physician who concluded that such services were necessary might be upheld. Agreements refusing to provide coverage for nonphysician services in *any* circumstances will be more difficult to justify. The outcome may depend on a careful analysis of the appropriate market. Any state statutes governing the coverage of such services will also be relevant.

It is important to remember that Sherman Act § 1 requires a combination or conspiracy—that is, group action. Thus, a decision by an insurance company to deny insurance coverage for nonphysician services will not run afoul of the Sherman Act, provided that the insurance company acted independently. Of course, if the insurance company is controlled by physicians, the group action requirement may be satisfied. See *Virginia Academy of Clinical Psychologists, supra.*

II. Suits involving hospitals

Physicians, hospitals, or other members of the health care industry may take actions that restrict nonphysicians' access to hospital facilities. Such actions, which affect the nonphysician's ability to compete, have been challenged under the antitrust laws. As was true in the insurance cases, most of these challenges have not yet resulted in a decision on the merits.

A. Description of problem
 1. Denial of staff privileges by hospitals
 Several cases have involved claims that physicians and hospitals conspired to deny hospital staff privileges to nonmedical health practitioners. In *Feldman v. Jackson Memorial Hospital* 509 F. Supp. 815 (S.D. Fla. 1981), a podiatrist filed a suit against physicians, hospitals, and medical administrators located in southern Florida, claiming that they had conspired in violation of the antitrust law by refusing to grant him membership on the medical staff of public and private hospitals. Similarly, in *Nurse Midwifery Associates v. Hibbett, supra,* which also involved an insurance claim, the nurse midwives claimed that physicians and hospitals had sought to bar them from obtaining hospital privileges.

 Suits have also been filed alleging that the American Hospital Association, along with a number of other hospital and physician organizations, has sought to limit or eliminate chiropractic practice by refusing to give chiropractors access to hospital facilities. See *New York v. American Medical Association,* Civ. No. 79C1732 (E.D.N.Y. 1980); *Health Care Equalization Committee v. Iowa Medical Society, supra; Wilk v. American Medical Association,* Civ. No. 76-3777 (N.D. Ill.) (complaint filed Oct. 20, 1976); *Slavek v. American Medical Association*, Civ. No. 77-1726 (E.D. Pa.) (complaint filed in 1977).[8]

2. JCAH involvement

Several cases have challenged actions taken by the Joint Commission on Accreditation of Hospitals (JCAH). The JCAH is an independent body which certifies hospitals. Its member organizations include the major national medical and hospital associations. Nonphysicians have complained that hospitals will be denied JCAH accreditation if they extend staff privileges to nonphysician practitioners.

In *Ohio ex rel. Brown v. JCAH*, Civ. No. C-2-79-1158 (S.D. Ohio,) Ohio challenged a JCAH standard providing that psychologists could provide hospital services only if supervised by a physician. Ohio sued JCAH, its member organizations, and several Ohio medical societies, claiming that, by promulgating and enforcing this standard, they had sought to reduce competition by psychologists. In effect, they had organized a boycott of psychologists. Similar claims have been made by podiatrists. See, e.g., *Levin v. JCAH*, 354 F.2d 515 (D.C. Cir. 1966) (podiatrists attempt to sue a Virginia hospital corporation and the JCAH, claiming that they had sought to deprive podiatrists of access to hospital facilities). The JCAH has also been sued by chiropractors. *New York v. AMA, supra* (JCAH alleged to have participated in boycott of chiropractors by refusing to accredit hospitals that give staff privileges to chiropractors); *Wilk v. AMA, supra* (same); *Health Care Equalization Committee v. Iowa Medical Society, supra* (same).

B. Defenses

1. Interstate Commerce

In *Feldman v. Jackson Memorial Hospital, supra*, in which a podiatrist claimed that physicians and hospitals conspired to deny staff privileges, the defendants moved to dismiss on the ground that there was an insufficient nexus to interstate commerce. Plaintiff had alleged that the interstate commerce requirement was satisfied because the defendant hospitals received reimbursement from out-of-state insurance companies; the plaintiff and defendant doctors and hospitals treated patients covered by Medicare and Medicaid; the defendant doctors and hospitals purchased supplies and equipment from out of state; the rules being challenged were based on rules developed by a

Massachusetts hospital; and out-of-state podiatrists would be unable to receive surgical training at the defendant hospitals.

The District Court refused to dismiss the case. It reasoned that the plaintiff need only show that the medical services supplied by the defendants have an effect on interstate commerce; he need not show that the defendants' alleged unlawful action have an effect on interstate commerce. Under the circumstances, particularly in light of the specificity of plaintiff's allegations, dismissal was not warranted.

In general, it seems very unlikely that a defense based on the interstate commerce requirement will be successful in the hospital cases. The defendants' activities will almost always have a sufficient impact on interstate commerce. See also *Hospital Building Co. v. Trustees of Rex Hospital*, 425 U.S. 738 (1976); *McLain v. Real Estate Board of New Orleans*, 444 U.S. 232 (1980). But see *Cardio-Medical Associates, Ltd. v. Crozer-Chester Medical Center*, (E.D. Pa. 1982) (discussing interstate commerce requirement in case involving denial of staff privileges to physician); *Crane v. Intermountain Health Care, Inc.*, 637 F.2d 715 (10th Cir. 1980) (en banc) (same).

2. JCAH and the implied immunity defense

In *Ohio ex rel. Brown v. JCAH, supra*, the JCAH has filed a motion for summary judgment claiming that it is immune from antitrust liability under the doctrine of implied immunity. It observes that the Medicare Act provides that a hospital will not be eligible for Medicare if psychologists are permitted to admit and treat patients without the participation or supervision of a physician. In other words, the JCAH standards are virtually identical to federal law. Thus, if the JCAH standard violates the antitrust laws, there is a clear repugnancy between the Medicare statute and the antitrust laws. But Congress would have wanted the Medicare statute to prevail over the antitrust laws. Thus, the JCAH standards are impliedly immune from the antitrust laws.

The plaintiff has responded by arguing that Congress did not intend the Medicare Act to prevail over the antitrust laws, and that the doctrine of implied immunity depends on the existence of a regulatory authority that controls the actions of the JCAH. The District Court has not yet decided this motion.

C. Merits

Decisions on the merits have been reached in relatively few of these cases. A jury verdict in favor of the defendants has been returned in *Wilk v. AMA, supra.* That case included a claim that the AHA and the JCAH had conspired to boycott chiropractic services by encouraging hospitals to deny staff privileges to chiropractors. The decision in the case, which is unreported, is now on appeal in the Seventh Circuit.

In *New York v. AMA,* another chiropractic boycott case, the American Hospital Association has entered into a consent decree with the state of New York. In this decree, it agrees not to adopt or support any policy that would limit or eliminate lawful chiropractic practice. In particular, the AHA agrees not to advise any hospital member that the association objects to chiropractors having access to hospitals for the purpose of administering treatment and furthering their training. In addition, it agrees that it will communicate to its members that it will not censure any hospital that gives a chiropractor access to its facilities. See also p. 20 *infra.*

The likely outcome of future nonphysician staff privileges cases is unclear. Hospitals, physicians, and the JCAH may claim that there are legitimate professional concerns related to quality care that justify access restrictions. Such arguments may help ensure that the boycotts are not treated as per se illegal. However, depending on the specific restriction involved and the nature of the relevant market, such arguments may not be sufficient to avoid a finding of liability under the rule of reason.

As was suggested earlier, it is important to distinguish between actions by a group and those by a single individual or entity. Only the former violates Sherman Act § 1. Thus, for example, a hospital acting on its own could decide to deny staff privileges to nonphysicians. The denial of staff privileges raises antitrust problems only if the hospital is controlled by physicians or acts in concert with physicians.[9]

III. Physician referrals

A. Description of problem

Physicians may refuse to refer patients to nonphysicians or may refuse to accept referrals from nonphysicians. Such practices, which have anticompetitive consequences, have been challenged. Several lawsuits have focused on AMA ethical rules which provide that physicians should not aid any treatment that lacks a scientific basis.

Chiropractors claim that physicians have interpreted this rule as preventing them from making referrals. These lawsuits typically also name as defendants local medical societies and various national physician organizations, for example, the American College of Surgeons, the American College of Physicians, and the American College of Orthopedic Surgeons. The chiropractors allege that these groups have engaged in the conspiracy to boycott chiropractors, and that this goal is in part achieved by refusing to accept or make referrals. See *New York v. AMA, supra; Wilk v. AMA, supra; Slavek v. Pennsylvania, supra; Health Care Equalization Committee v. Iowa Medical Society, supra.*

B. Merits

A jury verdict has been returned in favor of the AMA and various other physician organizations in *Wilk v. AMA.* The AMA had defended on the ground that, despite its ethical rules, there was no evidence that physicians actually did refuse to refer patients to chiropractors. In *New York v. AMA,* the AMA entered into a consent decree, under which it agreed to inform its members that they were free to decide whether to refer patients to chiropractors or accept patients from chiropractors. The AMA entered into a similar consent decree in *Slavek v. AMA, supra.*

Agreements to boycott nonphysicians by refusing to make or accept referrals are likely to be struck down under the antitrust laws. Where there is evidence of such an agreement, the physicians may be hard pressed to show that their actions serve legitimate professionals or procompetitive goals.

IV. Access to radiology services

A. Description of problem

A final problem is of particular concern to chiropractors. Chiropractors sometimes use radiology to diagnose health problems. In several suits, they have claimed that radiologists, as well as hospitals that provide radiological services, have agreed that they will not provide diagnostic x-rays to consumers referred by chiropractors and to release x-rays to the chiropractors. In *New Jersey Chiropractic Society v. Radiological Society of New Jersey,* 156 N.J. Super. 365, 383 A.2d 1182 (1978), an association of chiropractors and consumers of chiropractic services sued the New Jersey Radiological Society and several professional corporations and hospitals providing radiological services. Similar claims were made against providers of radiological services in *Wilk v. AMA, supra; Slavek v. AMA,* supra; *New York v. AMA, supra;* and *Health Care Equalization Committee, supra.*

B. Merits

In *Wilk v. AMA*, the jury returned a verdict in favor of the defendants who provided radiological services, including the American College of Radiology. In its consent decree in *New York v. AMA*, the American Hospital Association agreed that it would not object if member hospitals were to decide to give access to chiropractors for the purpose of obtaining and interpreting diagnostic x-rays.

References

1. Under Tennessee law, nurse-midwives may practice only if supervised by a physician; the obstetrician agreed to provide this supervision.
2. The district court had found that the defendant's actions were within the business of insurance. *Virginia Academy of Clinical Psychologists v. Blue Shield of Virginia*, 469 F. Supp. 552 (E.D. Va. 1979).
3. In this case also, the district court had concluded that the McCarran-Ferguson Act exemption did apply. See *Hahn v. Oregon Physicians' Service*, 508 F. Sup. 970 (D. Ore. 1981).
4. Decisions may turn on whether there is a specific statute contemplating or compelling the particular practice that has been challenged.
5. Defendants had argued that there was no combination because the Blue Shield plans had not collaborated, and because they could not conspire with themselves.
6. In addition to their McCarran-Ferguson Act claim, see p. 5 *supra*, defendants argued that their collaboration was protected by the Noerr-Pennington doctrine. They claimed that their decision to limit coverage was part of an effort to challenge a new Virginia statute requiring direct payment to health care providers. The Fourth Circuit rejected this defense, reasoning that the plans' action was really just an agreement to continue anticompetitive behavior in defiance of a procompetitive state statute.
7. It relied in part on *Ballard v. Blue Shield of Southern West Virginia*, which found that a denial of insurance coverage for chiropractic services was a boycott for McCarran-Ferguson Act purposes. See p. 7 *supra*.
8. *Health Care Equalization Committee* and *Wilk* both list a number of medical organizations as defendants, including the AMA, the AHA, the JCAH, various national physician organizations, and local

medical societies. These cases allege that defendants, through a variety of practices, have engaged in a far-reaching boycott of chiropractic. See also pp. 19-20 *infra*. *Health Care Equalization Committee* included insurance company defendants.

9. Presumably, a hospital could ask a physicians' association for advice concerning whether it should grant staff privileges to nonphysicians, provided that its final decision is independent.

Section four: Competition among physicians

In recent years restrictions imposed on a physician's practice by other physicians have been challenged under the antitrust laws. Discussed below are antitrust challenges that have been made to (1) exclusive arrangements between hospitals and hospital-based physician groups and other exclusions from hospital staff privileges, and (2) the potentially restrictive activities of professional associations and other organizations of physicians.

I. Antitrust challenges to the denial of hospital staff privileges

In the past ten years, there has been a substantial increase in the number of cases challenging the denial of hospital staff privileges on antitrust grounds. In part this has been a result of changes in the competitive situations of hospitals and physicians: Greater numbers of physicians have entered the job market, there has been a decline in the number of hospitals, and exclusive staff arrangements have become increasingly common. Litigation has also been encouraged by the recent willingness of courts to judge professionals by the same standards that are applied in other lines of business. See *Goldfarb v. Virginia State Bar*, 421 U.S. 773 (1975), reh'g denied 423 U.S. 679 (1975), *National Society of Professional Engineers v. United States*, 435 U.S. 679 (1978), *Arizona v. Maricopa County Medical Society*, 102 S. Ct. 2466 (1982). Nevertheless, it is only in the last two years that there have been a significant number of decisions on the merits.[1]

Exclusions from hospitals staffs take three forms: (1) exclusions from open staffs, based on the physician in question, (2) exclusions from closed staffs, justified by high occupancy rates and pressure on facilities; and (3) exclusions from specific departments that are closed as a result of exclusive contracts between hospitals and a group of physicians. The restraints involved are of different types, thus triggering potentially different antitrust analyses. However, as discussed below, because of the standards courts have almost uniformly applied, the analyses and the results have been very similar. In almost all of the cases, exclusions have been upheld. There is some risk of liability, however. This risk may have increased as a result of the recent decision in *Arizona v. Maricopa County Medical Society, supra*, which rejected the claim that health care professionals deserve special treatment under the antitrust laws.[2]

  A. Establishing interstate commerce jurisdiction

    Jurisdiction under the Sherman Act extends both to activities that are in interstate commerce and to activities that, though purely intrastate in character, substantially affect interstate commerce.[3]

Although early antitrust staff privilege cases foundered on this requirement, it has been a barrier very infrequently since *Hospital Building Co. v. Trustees of Rex Hospital*, 425 U.S. 738 (1976) and *McLain v. Real Estate Board of New Orleans*, 444 U.S. 232 (1980).

In the first of these cases, the Court found the jurisdictional requirement satisfied by a small hospital's allegations that defendant's activities had prevented construction of a new facility which would have entailed the interstate flow of goods. In *McLain*, the Court reinstated a complaint alleging price fixing among real estate brokers, stating it was "sufficient for petitioners to demonstrate a substantial effect on interstate commerce generated by respondents brokerage activity."

The requisite effect has been found in almost all subsequent staff privilege cases. *Robinson v. Magovern*, supra, (out-of-state purchases of supplies, drugs, and equipment); *Zamiri v. William Beaumont Hospital*, 430 F. Supp. 875 (E.D. Mich. 1977) (revenue from Medicare, Medicaid, and out-of-state third-party payors). *McElhinney v. Medical Protective Company*, supra, (Medicare payments, out-of-state patients, staff physician practice out of state).

However, there is one remaining source of uncertainty; the reach of *McLain*. A number of courts have read it broadly, as holding that interstate commerce need only be affected by defendants' general business rather than by the activity that has been challenged.[4] But many courts have struggled to find the opinion consistent with earlier cases and interpreted it as still requiring a nexus between the challenged activity and interstate commerce.[5]

A restrictive reading of *McLain* will not necessarily result in dismissal. *Malini v. Singleton and Associates*, Civ. No. H-&8-1870 (S.D. Tex. opinion filed May 29, 1981). However, it has had that effect in staff privilege cases. *Cardio-Medical Associates v. Crozer-Chester Medical Center*, 1982-1 Trade Cas., ¶ 64,614 (E.D. Pa. 1982) (complaint dismissed without prejudice because plaintiff who had been denied cardiology privileges, did not demonstrate any logical connection between hospital's exclusive contract with cardiologists and interstate commerce).

B. Definition of relevant market

Like other antitrust claims, staff privilege claims must be considered in the context of relevant geographic and product markets. As these cases have begun to survive jurisdictional challenges and other pretrial motions to dismiss, courts have started to focus on defining the relevant markets in which the alleged restraint is to be analyzed.[6] As in other cases, it is clear that the court's choice of market may be dispositive. See *Hyde v. Jefferson Parish Hospital District No. 2, supra; Robinson v. Magovern.*

Although courts are no longer reluctant to apply traditional tests developed in a commercial setting to define markets in the health care area, their definitions have also recognized that the nature of the industry may require some modification of traditional analyses. For example, a number of courts have recognized that because of the prevalence of third-party payment, quality of care rather than price is the primary competitive variable. *Robinson v. Magovern, supra. SmithKline Corp. v. Eli Lilly & Co.*, 575 F. 2d. 1056 (3d Cir. 1978). In redefining the relevant market in *Hyde v. Jefferson, supra,* the court noted that the district court's traditional analysis was inappropriate because third-party payment and the lack of complete information about quality which made patient quality comparisons unrealistic. See also *Santos v. Columbus-Cuneo-Cabrini Medical Center, supra.*

1. Product market definition

    The product market should include all products that consumers consider to be reasonable substitutes for each other. *United States v. E. I. du Pont de Nemours & Co.*, 351 U.S. 377 (1956). These are often stated to be those products that have a high cross-elasticity of demand *Times-Picayune Publishing Co. v. United States*, 345 U.S. 594, 612 (1953).

    Robinson v. Magovern illustrates the process of defining the relevant product market in a staff privilege case. After being denied staff privileges in cardiothoracic surgery at Allegheny General Hospital, Doctor Robinson brought a §§ 1 and 2 Sherman Act case against the hospital, individual trustees, Chief of the Division of Thoracic Surgery, and a five-physician corporation which performed about 95 percent of the open-heart surgery at the hospital. Applying its rule that the product market should "encompass all products—both items that are presently available and potential entrants—that have a significant, positive cross-elasticity of demand," the court held the market to be adult open-heart surgery. Because such surgery is usually recommended as a last resort, there are no real substitutes for it, and the required training, equipment, and team deter lateral entry from other surgical fields. These factors—lack of substitutes and high entry barriers—are likely to combine in many cases to make the excluded physician's area of specialization or practice the relevant product market. See also *Weiss v. York Hospital, supra.*

2. Geographic market definition

The relevant geographic market is the "area of effective competition in the known line of commerce [which] must be chartered by careful selection of the market in which the seller operates, *and to which the purchaser can reasonably turn for suppliers."* United States v. Philadelphia National Bank, 374 U.S. 321 (1963); *Tampa Electric Company v. Nashville Coal Co.,* 365 U.S. 320 (1961). Thus, the court must determine the geographic market in which the consumer has the ability to seek alternatives if the supplier changed one of the competitive variables to his disadvantage.

In defining the relevant market, courts have traditionally looked at a considerable number of factors including the supplier's geographic ability to sell (considering transportation costs and delivery limitations), the industry's perception of the market, whether or not outsiders sell in the region, and responsiveness of price and quality in region to changes elsewhere. See L. Sullivan, *Handbook of the Law of Antitrust,* 68 (1977).

The analysis of the court in *Robinson v. Magovern* illustrates the process of defining a geographic market in a staff privilege case. Finding that the prospect of separation from family or high travel and lodging costs limited the willingness of even open-heart candidates to travel, the court rejected the national market proposed by defendants. The court also rejected plaintiff's proposed two-county market, finding subdivisions and/or groupings of counties by governmental units, planning agencies and the hospital necessarily irrelevant because of disparities in geographic service areas among a hospital's various medical specialities. The court also found the high percentage of the residents of the two counties who had their open-heart operations in the area and the hospital to be irrelevant, stressing that actual sales patterns may be "virtually meaningless" if there are other choices available. The court ultimately defined the market as a sixteen-county area.

Two exclusive contract cases, *Santos v. Columbus-Cuneo-Cabrini Medical Center, supra,* and *Hyde v. Jefferson Parish*

Hospital District No. 2, supra, also illustrate the impact that special features of the health care market may have on the process of defining geographic markets. The district court in *Santos* had defined the market as the hospital in question (which together with two others treated about 3 percent of all surgical patients treated in Cook County hospitals). Lifting the district court's preliminary injunction, the Court of Appeals expressed doubt that a market could be "sliced so small." It instructed the court below to consider whether the hospital rather than the patient was the real purchaser of anesthesia services in light of third-party payment. It also instructed the court to consider the fact that the patient took no part in the selection of the anesthesiologist, the hospital's responsibility for assuring the availability of anesthesiology services, its incentive to maximize use of its facilities, and its potential liability. If the hospital were the purchaser of anesthetic services, the relevant market would be the areas in which the hospital could turn for the alternative provision of anesthesia services.

In *Hyde*, the court concluded that the district court's inappropriate application of traditional analysis had resulted in a market that was too broad. Because third-party payment eliminated the incentive to compare costs and patients were incapable of comparing quality, patients chose hospitals by location, usually the one closest to home. Therefore, the relevant market was much smaller than the district court had found.

C. Challenges to denials of staff privileges under the Sherman Act
  1. Section 1
    Denials of staff privileges have been challenged under § 1 of the Sherman Act as unlawful exclusive contracts (sometimes called vertical boycotts), group boycotts or concerted refusals to deal, and illegal tying arrangements.
    a. Challenges to exclusive contracts
      Exclusive contracts are vertical arrangements—agreements between a buyer and a supplier that the supplier will provide services on the condition the buyer does business with no other supplier. Except when they have been challenged as a tying arrangement (See *Hyde v. Jefferson Parish Hospital District No. 2*), they have been analyzed by courts under the rule of reason. Efforts of plaintiffs to trigger a *per se* rule by calling them "vertical boycotts" have not been successful

to date. The Second and Ninth Circuits have addressed the issue squarely, holding that all vertical boycotts are to be judged by the rule of reason unless they have horizontal elements. *Oreck Corp. v. Whirlpool Corp.*, 579 F. 2d 126 (2d Cir. 1978), *cert. denied* 439 U.S. 946 (1978), *reh. denied*, 439 U.S. 1104 (1978). *Gough v. Rossmore Corp.*, 585 F.2d 381 (9th Cir. 1978). In *Santos v. Columbus-Cuneo-Cabrini Medical Center, supra,* the Seventh Circuit also held that the rule of reason was applicable to vertical arrangements, noting that all parties had conceded its applicability.

Under the rule to reason, the court must consider all the circumstances, including the nature of the service, the nature of the restraint, the restraint's probable effect, and the reason for its adoption in deciding whether an allegedly restrictive practice should be prohibited. *Chicago Board of Trade v. United States*, 246 U.S. 231 (1918). "The true test of legality is whether the restraint imposed is such as merely regulates and perhaps thereby promotes competition or whether it is such as may suppress or even destroy competition." *National Society of Professional Engineers v. United States*, 435 U.S. 679 (1978).

When challenging an activity under the rule of reason, a plaintiff must prove: (1) that defendants conspired or agreed; (2) that the conspiracy had an adverse anticompetitive effect within the relevant markets; (3) that the objects of and conduct pursuant to the agreement were illegal; and (4) that plaintiff was injured as a proximate result of the agreement. *Martin B. Glauser Dodge Co. v. Chrysler Corp.*, 570 F.3d 72 (3d Cir. 1977), *cert. denied,* 436 U.S. 913 (1979).

Plaintiffs in staff privilege cases have found it particularly difficult to establish an adverse effect on competition and the necessary anticompetitive purpose. Defendants have often been able to undercut plaintiffs' arguments by pointing to the procompetitive effects or benefits of the exclusive arrangement. Commonly cited benefits include: guaranteed twenty-four-hour coverage; assurance of competent staff; better equipment monitoring and supervision of staff; scheduling to maximize facility use; better teamwork and work routines because of frequent joint work; greater competence because of increased specialization; and lower operating costs because of greater control and standardization of procedure.

To date, these benefits have always been found adequate to justify any anticompetitive effects of the arrangement. Several recent decisions illustrate this form of analysis. In *Smith v. Northern Michigan Hospital, Inc.*, 518 F. Supp. 644 (W.D. Mich. 1981), the court considered defendants' summary judgment motion in a case arising from the loss of an exlusive contract by one group of emergency room physicians to another after a hospital merger. The court concluded that the contract did not restrain trade and granted summary judgment. The court emphasized that the record supported the merged hospital's claim that it had a legitimate medical and financial purpose for consolidating the emergency room operations. The hospital was motivated by "the desire to provide effective, efficient medical care and not by any malevolent intent toward plaintiffs." The court noted that the physicians who received the contract were better qualified than plaintiffs and stressed that an exclusive contract permits more control over standards, personnel, and procedures, which is desirable for the hospital because of its potential liability.

In *Powsner v. St. Joseph Mercy Hospital of Detroit*, No. 77-5279 (Mich. Cir. Ct. 1977), a state antitrust law case, the court upheld an exclusive contract with a group of cardiologists. The court identified extensive benefits, similar to those in *Smith*. It found that the restraint was a product of the hospital's concern about high-quality patient care and concluded that any incidental restraint was reasonable when weighed against such benefits.

In the future, physician plaintiffs may follow the lead of *Hyde v. Jefferson Parish Hospital District No. 2, supra,* and challenge exclusive contracts as tying arrangements in the hopes of avoiding the barriers created by the rule of reason. In *Hyde*, an anesthesiologist who had been denied staff privileges because of the hospital's exclusive contract for anesthesia service sued, alleging that the contract was a tying arrangement in which users of the hospital's operating room (the tying product) were compelled to purchase the anesthesia service chosen by the hospital (tied product) and was illegal *per se*.

The court stated that tying arrangements were forbidden by the Sherman Act when: (1) they involve two separate products; (2) the defendant has sufficient market power in tying market to coerce the purchase of the tied product; (3) a not insubstantial amount of interstate commerce in the tied market is involved, and (4) there are anticompetitive effects in the tied market.

After concluding that the defendants had the requisite market power, the court considered the anticompetitive effects of the arrangement. These included preventing anesthesiologists from entering the part of the market controlled by the hospital and, thus, reducing incentives for improvement and ultimately lowering quality; diluting professional coverage (the corporation used a large proportion of nurse anesthetists); and limiting the surgeon's and patient's choice of anesthesiologists.

The court then considered defendants' arguments that business justifications should insulate them from liability. It stated that such justifications will never excuse an illegal tying arrangement if there is a less restrictive way of accomplishing the same ends and concluded that all justifications offered by defendant could be so accomplished.

Finally, the court considered defendants' argument that the usual *per se* rule applicable to a tying arrangement should be rejected because of the judiciary's inexperience in the health care antitrust area and because of the professional nature of the services. The court concluded that *Maricopa County, supra*, foreclosed both arguments as well as defendants' contention that they should be immune from *per se* liability because of the procompetitive justifications for the contract.

The decision in *Hyde v. Jefferson Parish Hospital District No. 2* is troubling. Virtually any exclusive contracts could be characterized as tying arrangements, and thus struck down as illegal *per se*. The court seems to have been heavily influenced by the fact that the hospital was primarily concerned with increasing its profits. The court also suggested that a hospital might legitimately limit its staff size to prevent overcrowding and a decline in the quality of patient care. The Supreme Court will review the decision in this case next term.

b. Challenges to horizontal refusals to deal

When an exclusive contract is not involved, denials of staff privileges have been challenged as horizontal concerted refusals to deal or group boycotts.

There is some confusion about the standard by which these agreements are to be tested. The Supreme Court has repeatedly held concerted refusals to deal or group boycotts to be *per se* violations. *Radiant Burners, Inc. v. Peoples Gas and Light Co.*, 364 U.S. 656 (1961); *Klor's, Inc. v. Broadway-Hale Stores, Inc.*, 359 U.S. 202 (1959). However, the *per se* rule has never been applied to denials of staff privileges caused by horizontal refusals to deal. Some courts had struggled to justify this result by finding that the activity is not a group boycott. They have also reasoned that the question whether an arrangement is a group boycott depends on the effect of the arrangement and that a rule of reason analysis must be used to determine the effect (See, *McElhinney v. Medical Protective Company*, supra [refusal to deal not group boycott because it does not smack of "monopolistic tendency;" even if it is a boycott]). The *per se* rule should not apply because the arrangement is not "pernicious and without plausible redeeming virtues." More often, courts, and even parties, have merely assumed that a rule of reason analysis was required. For example, *Williams v. Kleaveland*, supra; *Hoffman v. Garden City Hospital Osteopathic*, supra.

Courts may be willing to examine this issue more closely after *Arizona v. Maricopa County Medical Society*, supra. See *Hyde*, supra. But see *McElhinney v. Medical Protective Company*, supra, in which the court undertook an extensive analysis of the applicability of *per se* or rule of reason standards and interpreted *Maricopa County* as permitting a rule of reason analysis even when restraints or a commercial nature are involved if the restraints are premised on public service or ethical norms. The court concluded that the rule of reason should be applied because the restraint was not commercial but was primarily a disciplinary proceeding with at most a thin economic overlay.

Under the rule of reason, the plaintiff in a refusal-to-deal case must establish the same factors as a plaintiff challenging an exclusive contract: that there was a contract or conspiracy, that it had an anticompetitive effect, that the objects of and conduct pursuant to the agreement were illegal, and that the plaintiff was injured as a proximate result of the conspiracy. The first two elements have been the major stumbling blocks for the physician plaintiff.

To satisfy the conspiracy requirement, the plaintiff must establish that two or more persons agreed to accomplish by concerted action either some unlawful purpose or a lawful purpose by unlawful means. Defendants in horizontal staff-privilege cases occasionally allege that the threshold requirements of at least two people or separate entities has not been satisfied. In *Robinson v. Magovern, supra,* and *Williams v. Kleaveland, supra,* defendants argued that there could be no conspiracy because the defendants were all members of the same economic entity. Although recognizing this is to be the general rule, the courts rejected the "intracorporate conspiracy" argument. Both courts stated the rule was to be modified when the officer, agent, or employee has an independent personal stake in achieving the object of the conspiracy. They both found a possibility of such a stake. *Contra Sokol v. University Hospital,* 402 F. Supp. 1029 (D. Mass. 1979).

The requisite conspiracy or agreement may be established by showing conscious interdependent parallel acts coupled with other "plus factors," such as indications of traditional conspiracy motives, actions contrary to economic self-interest, or poor economic performance. *Theater Enterprises, Inc. v. Paramount Film Distributing Corp.,* 346 U.S. 537 (1954). For example, in *McElhinney v. Medical Protective Company, supra,* the court concluded that plaintiff had satisfied the conspiracy requirement by establishing conscious parallel acts and threats of individual defendants to leave the hospital if it did not get rid of plaintiff.

The conspiracy requirement has not been satisfied by the plaintiff in a number of refusal to deal staff privilege cases. See *Robinson v. Magovern, supra* (no concerted activity because hospital had not denied the plaintiff's application for staff privileges in response to a request by the head or members of the thoracic surgery group.); *Stella v. Mercy Hospital, supra; Sokol v. University Hospital, Inc., supra.*

After establishing a conspiracy, a physician plaintiff must establish an unlawful purpose and an anticompetitive effect within the relevant product and geographic markets. *United States v. U.S. Gypsum Co.*, 483 U.S. 422 (1978). Unlawful purposes under the antitrust laws include an intent to influence market prices, *United States v. Container Corp.*, 393 U.S. 333 (1969); an intent to affect the quality or quantity of goods or services, *Sitkin Smelting and Refining Co. v. FMC Corp.*, 575 F.2d 440 (3d Cir. 1978); or an intent to exclude a person or group from the market, *American Motor Inns, Inc. v. Holiday Inns, Inc.*, 521 F.2d 1230 (3d Cir. 1975). Courts have focused on this element in a number of staff-privilege cases to the detriment of the plaintiff's case. *Stella v. Mercy Hospital, supra* ("Overwhelming documentation supporting contention that suspension based solely on irreconcilable differences of opinion on what constitutes appropriate or even standard medical treatment; such considerations cannot be basis of antitrust conspiracy").

The anticompetitive impact must be on general competitive conditions in the market, not just on the plaintiff. *Brunswick Corp. v. Pueblo Bowl-O-Matic, Inc.*, 429 U.S. 477 (1977). Courts have repeatedly found either that the plaintiffs have not established any anticompetitive effect or that, on balance, defendant's actions in denying staff privileges have been pro- rather than anticompetitive. In *Robinson v. Magovern, supra*, the court decided that the criteria the hospital used when evaluating Doctor Robinson's application were reasonably related to its institution objectives and concluded that the restraint on trade created by the hospital's policy and competitive strategy was not unreasonable.

The court first considered the procompetitive effects of the staff-privilege policy. "By rejecting the concept of an open staff and, instead, by building a high-quality staff that takes an integrated approach to the delivery of medical services,

Allegheny General has improved its ability to compete with other regional hospitals. Vigorous competition among these hospitals should raise the prevailing level of care, thus benefiting the public."

It found the offsetting anticompetitive effect not to be severe. Because Doctor Robinson could accommodate any patient who wanted him to perform surgery at another hospital, the hospital's staff policy "does not unduly impair a patient's ability to obtain the services of the physician of his choice."

In *Weiss v. York Hospital, supra,* the jury found that although defendants conspired to deny the plaintiff staff privileges because he was an osteopathic rather than an allopathic physician, the conspiracy did not constitute an unreasonable restraint upon interstate commerce. See also *McElhinney v. Medical Protective Company, supra.*

2. Section 2

Denials of staff privileges have also been challenged under § 2 of the Sherman Act as involving monopolization, attempts to monopolize, and conspiracies to monopolize. Such challenges are generally joined to challenge under § 1.

a. Monopolization

Monopolization requires:

> (1) the possession of monopoly power in the relevant market and (2) the willful acquisition or maintenance of that power as distinguished from growth or development as a consequence of a superior product business acumen or historic accident. *United States v. Grinnel Corp.*, 384 U.S. 563, 570–571 (1966).

After establishing the relevant product and geographic markets, the plaintiff must establish the defendant's monopoly power in those markets. A defendant has monopoly power if it has the ability to change the competitive variables (price, quality) of a product to the consumers' disadvantage without causing competitors to enter the market. *American Tobacco Co. v. United States,* 328 U.S. 781 (1946).

b. Attempt to monopolize

In support of a monopolization attempt case, plaintiff must establish (1) a specific intent to monopolize the relevant markets; (2) predatory or anticompetitive conduct directed toward accomplishing the purpose; and (3) a dangerous probability of success.

c. Conspiracy to monopolize

To establish a conspiracy to monopolize, plaintiff must demonstrate (1) an agreement between two or more persons or entities, (2) specific intent to monopolize; and (3) the commission of an overt act in furtherance of the purpose of the conspiracy. Most courts hold that a plaintiff need not establish dangerous probability of success, but the absence of any likelihood of success may negate specific intent. On the other hand, specific intent may be inferred from predatory conduct. See discussion in *Robinson v. Magovern*.

3. Staff privilege cases under section 2

Until very recently, challenges to privilege denials under § 2 have not met with success. *Robinson v. Magovern, supra,* illustrates the difficulties that physician plaintiffs have had. The plaintiff there alleged monopolization, attempt, and conspiracy by the hospital and the group that dominated open-heart surgery at the hospital. The court first concluded there was no monopolization. It held that the hospital with 30 percent of the market and at least five viable competitors did not possess monopoly power. All testifying physicians had stated that they would refer to surgeons on competing staffs if quality of care at the hospital declined. The group's similar inability to lower quality without losing volume establishes that it did not have monopoly power.

The court next concluded that the defendants had not attempted to monopolize. It said that their market power was insufficient to establish dangerous probability of success of monopolization. Specific intent was also absent. Recruiting all open-heart surgeons in the market would have been more consistent with eliminating competition.

Finally, the court concluded that the defendants had not conspired to monopolize. It found no evidence that they had agreed to work together and concluded that the defendants did not have the requisite specific intent: An attempt would have been futile, there were justifications for the defendant's opposition, and there were possible lawful explanations for the conduct questioned.

In *Powsner v. St. Joseph Mercy Hospital of Detroit,* the court found no monopoly and little probability of one and concluded after considering the exclusive arrangement's benefits that defendant had acted to provide quality patient care.

However, an osteopathic surgeon in *Weiss v. York Hospital, supra*, prevailed against a hospital after a jury trial on claims of monopolization, attempted monopolization, and conspiracy to monopolize arising out of his exclusion and the exclusion of the class of osteopathic surgeons from staff privileges. The fact that the policy applied to a class of providers may have been the key factor.

D. Remedies

Because few courts have reached the merits of staff-privilege cases, there has been little consideration of remedies, specifically the availability of injunctive relief. However, the issue has been considered in several recent cases.

A preliminary injunction was found to have been wrongly issued in *Santos v. Columbus-Cuneo-Cabrini, supra,* on the grounds that: (1) temporary loss of income was not an irreparable injury; (2) the balance of hardships rested with defendants and their employees because of the disruption of the hospital and careers that would follow termination of the challenged exclusive arrangements; and (3) likelihood of success was small.

The court in *Weiss v. York Hospital, supra,* considered injunctive relief appropriate because there was no adequate legal remedy. The public was harmed by the practice; it would be difficult to establish monetary damages for the class; and an award of only damages might not deter future illegal conduct.

II. Practice restrictions resulting from activities of physicians' organizations

A number of antitrust challenges have been made to activities of professional associations and other organizations or groups of physicians that have restricted the practice or the ability to compete of physicians. Although consent decrees have been entered in a number of these cases, few have been decided on the merits. Courts that have reached the merits have focused on whether the restrictions have interfered with the market's ability to determine fees or access to the market and whether they interfere with innovations taking place within the profession. The following have been challenged most frequently.

A. Restrictions on professional advertising

Restrictions on advertising are generally considered to be anticompetitive in effect because they increase the difficulty of finding the lowest cost seller of acceptable quality; isolate sellers from competition, thus reducing the incentive to price competitively; and make it more difficult for new competitors to enter the market.

1. Challenges under the Sherman Act
   Challenges to restrictions on advertising by attorneys have often not been successful under the Sherman Act because the proscriptions have been adopted by state governments. Thus, courts have held the claims to be barred by the exemption for state action because of the roles of state supreme courts in developing and/or enforcing the restrictions. *Bates v. State Bar of Arizona*, 435 U.S. 350 (1977); *Princeton Community Phone Book, Inc. v. Bates*, 582 F.2d 706 (3d Cir. 1978). However, the courts did overturn the restrictions on First Amendment grounds. In addition, where private associations seek to restrict member advertising, it is clear that the state action exemption will not apply.
2. Challenges under the Federal Trade Commission Act
   In *American Medical Association v. Federal Trade Commission*, 638 F.2d 443 (2d. Cir. 1980) *aff'd by equally divided court*, 50 U.S.L.W. 4313 (1982), the FTC had alleged that an agreement by the AMA and state and local medical associations to prevent member advertising through ethical canons constituted unfair methods of competition and unfair practices in violation of § 5 of the Federal Trade Commission Act. The Court upheld the FTC's conclusion that the restrictions severely inhibited competition and that the associations had acted in concert. The AMA was ordered to desist from prohibiting advertising. However, it was permitted to adopt and enforce reasonable ethical guidelines governing false or deceptive advertising or in-person solicitation of those vulnerable to undue influence.

   Several similar consent orders have been finalized. *Broward County Medical Association*, 3 CCH Trade Req. Rep. ¶ 21,913 (1982) (restriction arising from association's code of ethics and "unwritten code"); *American Dental Association*, 3 CCH Trade Reg. Rep. ¶ 21,953 (1982); *Association of Independent Dentists*, 3 CCH Trade Reg. Rep. ¶ 21,952 (1982) (association's bylaws prevented member advertising without prior approval).

B. Restrictions inhibiting innovations in the delivery of health care
   A number of cases under the Sherman and Federal Trade Commission Acts have challenged efforts by one group of doctors to deter other doctors from instituting innovations in the financing and delivery of services. The restrictions have generally been enforced by disciplinary action, withdrawal of referrals or other cooperation,

peer pressure, pressure from the state licensing board, or denial of hospital staff privileges.

1. Efforts to discourage development of HMOs

    United States v. Halifax Hospital Medical Center and Volusia County Medical Society, 1981-1 Trade Cas. ¶ 64,152 (M.D. Fla.) is illustrative of challenges to efforts to discourage HMO development. Suit was brought under § 1 of the Sherman Act, alleging that the county's largest hospital, the county medical society, and others had conspired to hinder the development of an HMO by excluding physicians contemplating HMO affiliations from staffs, establishing a committee to deter such physicians from relocating in the area, and adopting and distributing resolutions opposing the HMO. A consent decree was entering enjoining these and similar acts.

    In *Blue Cross of Washington and Alaska v. Kitsap Physician Services*, 1982-1 Trade Cas. ¶ 64,588 (W.D. Wash. 1981), the court preliminarily enjoined, under § 1 of the Sherman Act, the dominant, physician-controlled insurer from enforcing a bylaw denying plan membership to physicians who contracted with a closed-panel HMO. The court stated that such restrictions should be judged by the rule of reason, citing recent Ninth Circuit cases testing alleged group boycotts by the rule and emphasizing the desirability of applying the rule where courts lack experience.

    For similar reasons, the FTC challenged under § 5 of the Federal Trade Commission Act, the AMA's ethical opinion forbidding physicians to provide services to a hospital or lay body under conditions that would permit the body to sell the services for a fee. The FTC's conclusion that this violated § 5 was sustained. *AMA v. FTC, supra.*

    FTC challenges of restrictions with allegedly similar effect have resulted in consent decrees in several cases. *Forbes Health System Medical Staff*, Docket C-2994, 3 Trade Reg. Rep. ¶ 21,674 (1979) (hospital medical staff prohibited from discriminating against physicians with HMO affiliation or who practice on other than fee-for-service basis); *Medical Services Corp. of Spokane County*, Docket C-2853, 3 CCH Trade Reg. Rep. ¶ 21,195 (1976) (Blue Shield prohibited from excluding HMO-affiliated physicians from becoming participating physicians).

2. Restraints imposed by specialist groups

   One of the earliest cases challenging restrictions imposed by physicians involved a §§ 1 and 2 challenge to attempts by an association of pathologists to prevent pathologists from working for the developing commercial medical laboratory business and to inhibit the development of the industry. The consent decree prohibited the association and those acting with it from restricting or preventing anyone from organizing or operating a laboratory, referring specimens or patients to a laboratory, affiliating with any laboratory, or being employed by any laboratory, and from boycotting or penalizing a person because he does business with or is employed by a laboratory. *United States v. College of American Pathologists*, 1969 Trade Cas. ¶ 72,825 (N.D. Ill. 1969).

   In *Arizona ex rel. Corbin v. Arizona Radiological Society*, 1979-1 Trade Cas. ¶ 62,683 (Super. Ct. Ariz. 1979) and *American Society of Anesthesiologists, Inc.*, Docket C-2952, 3 CCH Trade Reg. Rep. ¶ 21,475 (1979), consent decrees enjoined professional societies from restricting their members to a fee-for-service practice through rules, ethical principles, or coercion.

3. Restrictions on other innovations in providing health care

   In *Feminist Women's Health Center v. Mohammed*, 586 F.2d. 530 (5th Cir. 1978), *cert. denied*, 444 U.S. 924 (1979), a non-profit abortion clinic alleged that individual doctors of the OB/GYN department of the only hospital in the county with complete OB/GYN facilities and the director of the state medical licensing board had conspired to restrain trade in and monopolize the market for abortion services in Tallahassee in violation of §§ 1 and 2 of the Sherman Act. Conduct cited in furtherance of this conspiracy, allegedly designed to shut down the clinic, included adverse department discussions of the center; conclusions that practitioners at the center were guilty of ethical violations; a department letter to private organizations of physicians expressing the view that physicians should not associate with organizations that were guilty of these ethical violations; a letter informing the state licensing board that the clinic was using out-of-town doctors to perform abortions without adequate provision for aftercare; advice by the director of the state board to an out-of-town resident physician not to get involved with the clinic; and a letter designed to cut off services to the clinic by out-of-town resident physicians.

The Court of Appeals addressed only the applicability of two traditional antitrust defenses to the alleged conspiracy. Reversing the district court's conclusion about the applicability of *Noerr-Pennington* as to all communications except the complaint to the state board, the court held that the doctrine did not apply to communications within peer groups (OB/GYN department). The court also reversed the district court's grant of summary judgment as to the director of the licensing board on state action grounds, finding that the director was not authorized by statute to use pressure or persuasion to cause physicians to stop doing what had never been adjudicated illegal or improper.

C. Restrictions limiting specialty practice or professional advancement

A number of challenges have been brought under §§ 1 and 2 of the Sherman Act to membership, certification, or ethical restrictions of professional organizations that are alleged to improperly limit specialty practice or advancement.

1. Membership requirements

Restrictive membership requirements of professional organizations in which membership is to a physician's economic advantage have been challenged both as unlawful tying arrangements and as concerted refusals to deal. In *Boddicker v. Arizona State Dental Association,* 549 F. 2d 626 (9th Cir. 1982), *cert. denied,* 434 U.S. 825 (1977), dentists challenged a requirement that members of state and local dental associations (from which dentists were alleged to derive substantial benefits) also be members in the American Dental Association as a *per se* illegal tying arrangement. In affirming dismissal, the Court of Appeals determined that necessary elements of a tying arrangement—market power in tied product, two distinct products, economic benefits to seller of tying product—were not present and that the dentists had not proven an adverse effect on competition between dentists.

To date, plaintiff in *Kreuzer v. American Academy of Periodontology and American Dental Association,* 516 F. Supp. 1034 (D.D.C. 1981) has been similarly unsuccessful. He alleged that the membership requirements and ethical rules of two professional organizations acting in concert and the concerted actions of individuals within the specialty organization prevented him from practicing a specialty for which he was fully qualified and licensed. Active membership in the specialty organization, allegedly critical for patient referrals in the specialty, was foreclosed to anyone who did not restrict his practice to the specialty. The court dismissed the case as to the American Dental Association, after extensive discovery, finding no proof of the necessary agreement in that the communications between the two organizations amounted only to the exchange of information. The case as to the remaining defendants continues, however.

2. Certificate activities

In *United States Dental Institute v. American Association of Orthodontists*, 396 F. Supp. 565 (N.D. Ill. 1975), a school offering nonstandard orthodontia training to dentists licensed to perform such services charged an illegal boycott of the school by the AAO and its officials, carried out by activities such as opposing state certification, refusing to grant AAO certification, and declaring it unethical to teach in a noncertified program. The anticompetitive effect identified was the limitation of the practice of orthodontia to fully certified orthodontist specialists. The court has refused to grant defendant's motion to dismiss. It ruled that plaintiffs have stated a cause of action under the Sherman Act.

In an action involving rival associations of podiatrists, plaintiffs charged that the American Podiatric Society and a state affiliate had taken certain anticompetitive acts (particularly the refusal to accept the certification of plaintiff organization of podiatrists to perform certain podiatric procedures) that were designed to injure the organizations. Blue Cross and Blue Shield were sued because of their alleged refusal to use podiatrists not certified by the defendant. *Academy of Ambulatory Foot Surgery v. The American Podiatric Association*, 1981-1 Trade Cas. ¶ 64,022 (S.D. NY 1981) (dismissed without prejudice on venue grounds).

D. Defenses

Traditional antitrust defenses have been of little use to defendants in this area. McCarran-Ferguson was rejected by the court in *Blue Cross of Washington and Alaska v. Kitsap Physician Service, supra*, the court concluding that the bylaw excluding HMO-affiliated physicians from insurance plan membership did not relate to the business of insurance because it did not relate to the spreading of risk.

The "learned profession" exemption was rejected by the courts in *United States Dental Institute, Inc. v. American Association of Orthodontists, supra* (not applicable to defendant's active steps to prevent practitioners from securing training, thus preserving special commercial interest of members) and *Boddicker v. Arizona State Dental Association, supra* (agreement between national, state, and local associations not obviously designed to improve dental services). See also discussion above of court's rejection of *Noerr-Pennington* and state action defenses in *Feminist Women's Health Center v. Mohammed, supra*.

References

1. *Smith v. Northern Michigan Hospital, Inc.* 518 F. Supp. 644 (W.D. Mich. 1981), *Robinson v. Magovern*, 521 F. Supp. 842 (W.D. Pa. 1981), aff'd, No. 77-0075 (3d Cir. 1982); *McElhinney v. Medical Protective Company*, No. 78-8 (E.D. Ky. Sept. 21 1982), *Hoffman v. Garden City Hospital-Osteopathic*, No. 52334 (Mich. Ct. App., May 4, 1982); *Stella v. Mercy Hospital*, No. 80-3003 (E.D. Mich., April 5, 1982); *Weiss v. York Hospital*, No. 80-0134 (M.D. Pa., Oct. 21, 1982); *Hyde v. Jefferson Parish Hospital District No. 2*, 686 F. 2d 286 (5th Cir. 1982), cert. granted, 51 U.S.L.W. 3649 (1983).
2. Physicians who have been denied staff privileges have claimed not only that the denial violated the antitrust laws, but also that it violated their right to procedural due process. See, e.g., *Sosa v. Board of Manager*, 437 F.2d 173 (5th Cir. 1971). This outline focuses on the antitrust claims. In general, due process claims are unlikely to succeed if the physician was given adequate notice and the hospital adhered to its usual hearing procedures. Of course, in any procedural due process case, the state action requirement must be satisfied. This requirement will ordinarily be satisfied if the hospital is a public entity.
3. *McLain v. Real Estate Board of New Orleans*, 444 U.S. 232 (1980); *Hospital Building Co. v. Trustees of Rex Hospital*, 425 U.S. 738 (1976), *Atlantic Cleaners and Dyers, Inc. v. United States*, 286 U.S. 427 (1932).

4. *Community Builders, Inc. v. City of Phoenix*, 652 F.2d 823 (9th Cir. 1981); *McElhinney v. Medical Protective Company, supra; Williams v. Kleaveland*, 1982-2 Trade Cas., ¶ 64,919 (W.D. Mich. 1981).
5. *Crane v. International Health Care, Inc.*, 637 F.2d 715 (10th Cir. 1980), *Cordova and Simonpietri Insurance Agency v. Chase Manhattan Bank, N.A.*, 649 F.2d 35 (1st Cir. 1981), *Malini v. Singleton and Associates*, 516 F. Supp. 440 (S.D. Tex. 1981); *Heille v. City of St. Paul, Minn.*, 512 F.Supp. 810 (D. Minn. 1981); *Cardio-Medical Associates v. Crozer-Chester Medical Center*, 1982-1 Trade Cas. ¶ 64,614.
6. *Robinson v. Magovern, supra; Hyde v. Jefferson Parish Hospital District No. 2, supra; Santos v. Columbus-Cuneo-Cabrini Medical Center*, No. 81-2628, (7th Cir. 1982); *Williams v. Kleaveland, supra; Weiss v. York Hospital, supra.*

256 Legal Aspects of Certification and Accreditation

Section five: Pricing in the health care industry

Health care providers may take joint action that, either directly or indirectly, affects the price for their services. Because one of the central concerns of the antitrust laws is to preserve price competition, such action has been carefully scrutinized by the courts. This section discusses some of the relevant cases.

I. Actions that directly affect price
   A. Price-fixing by physicians: *Arizona v. Maricopa County Medical Society*
   In *Arizona v. Maricopa County Medical Society*, 102 S. Ct. 2466 (1982), the Supreme Court held that maximum price-fixing by physicians was illegal *per se*. The Court had previously held that maximum price-fixing in other industries was illegal *per se*. However, until *Maricopa*, it had been unclear whether the same rule would be applied in the health care profession.
      1. *Description of the decision in Maricopa County*
      The Maricopa County Medical Society established the Maricopa Foundation for Medical Foundation Care to promote fee-for-service medical practice. Approximately 70 percent of the doctors in Maricopa County belong to the foundation. The foundation entered into contracts with health insurers under which the insurers agreed to reimburse the foundation's members for health services provided to their policyholders according to a maximum fee schedule established by the foundation. In return, the foundation's members agreed to accept such reimbursment as payment in full for their services. The foundation periodically revised upward the maximum fee schedule.
      The State of Arizona sued to enjoin the maximum fee agreements on the ground that they constituted price-fixing in violation of the Sherman Act § 1. Arizona argued that the fee schedule was *per se* illegal. According to the state, the schedule stabilized and enhanced the level of physician fees and increased health insurance premiums. The foundation claimed that the rule of reason should apply. It argued that the schedule actually limited physician fees and helped insurers to limit the risks they underwrote. The Ninth Circuit decided that the maximum price agreement should be measured under the rule of reason. It reasoned that *per se* treatment was inappropriate because professionals were involved and because the economics of the health

care industry were not well understood.[1]

The Supreme Court reversed in a 4-3 decision. Justice Stevens, joined by Justices Brennan, Marshall, and White, wrote the opinion for the majority. Justice Powell, joined by Chief Justice Berger and Justice Rehnquist, dissented. Justices Blackmun and O'Connor did not participate in the decision. Relying on a long line of price-fixing cases, the majority found that the maximum fee agreements were illegal *per se*. Maximum price-fixing would provide the same economic rewards to all practitioners regardless of their skill, experience, or willingness to employ difficult procedures. The restraint would discourage entry into the market and deter new developments. The fact that doctors rather than nonprofessionals were involved did not preclude application of the *per se* rule: Respondents had not claimed that the quality of the services their members provide was enhanced by the use of maximum fees. The majority also rejected the claim that it should not apply the *per se* rule because it had little antitrust experience in the health care industry.

The majority was not persuaded that the agreements could be justified as procompetitive. The foundation had contended that the fee schedules enhanced competition because they made it possible to provide consumers of health care with a particularly attractive form of insurance coverage: The consumer could choose doctors and obtain complete coverage at fairly low premiums. The majority conceded that a binding assurance of complete coverage could be obtained only if the insurer and doctor agreed in advance on maximum fees. The majority pointed out, however, that doctors need not do the price-fixing. The insurance company itself would be quite capable of fixing maximum reimbursable prices and making agreements with physicians guaranteeing full reimbursement.

Justice Powell dissented vigorously. He began by observing that the arrangement did not foreclose competition among physicians, since they were free to associate with other medical insurance plans or to serve other patients. He also observed that insurers represent consumer interests: They have an incentive to restrain medical costs and keep premiums low. In fact, a strong argument could be made that the agreements were procompetitive. Justice Powell then argued that a practice should be deemed *per se* illegal only after carefully considering substantial benefits and procompetitive justifications. Caution is particularly important when the agreement under attack is novel. According to Justice Powell, the majority had failed to exercise such caution here. Although this case did involve literal price-fixing, the agreement among physicians was not so plainly anticompetitive that it should be condemned as *per se* illegal before careful study.

2. *Implications of the decision in Maricopa County*

Maricopa County seems to foreclose special treatment for physicians and other health care professionals in future price-fixing cases. Minimum price-fixing arrangements or other arrangements that tend to stabilize prices will probably be characterized as *per se* illegal. Although *Maricopa County* does suggest that rule of reason treatment will be available if a restraint is "premised on public service or ethical norms," *id.* at 2475, such a justification will ordinarily not be available in the case of simple price restraints. It is more uncertain whether rule of reason treatment will be available for various other types of trade restraints, such as boycotts or concerted refusals to deal. If a refusal to deal can be justified on the ground that it ensures quality medical care, for example, the rule of reason may be applied.[2]

Although the Court rejected the physicians' argument that their maximum fee schedule would enhance efficiency and help contain medical costs, *Maricopa County* does not suggest that all price-related efforts to reduce costs will be struck down. The opinion indicates that unilateral attempts by health insurance carriers to set and enforce maximum reimbursement rates for physicians and hospitals will not necessarily be struck down under the antitrust laws. Such efforts, which are designed to contain costs, may be procompetitive in effect. See generally Outline Section Six, which discusses the antitrust implications of cost-containment activities by insurance companies. In addition, it appears that a physician or other health care provider may provide information that an insurance company needs to set maximum prices. However, if providers collaborate in providing information to insurance companies, they run some risk of antitrust liability. See pp. 7-12 *infra;* but see *Virginia Academy of Clinical Psychologists v. Blue Shield of Virginia,*

676 F.2d 476 (4th Cir. 1980) (refusing to hold Neuropsychiatric Society of Virginia liable for recommending that Blue Shield adopt certain reimbursement policies, at least in the absence of coercion); *United States v. American Society of Anesthesiologists,* 473 F. Supp. 197 (S.D.N.Y. 1979). The risk increases if they attempt to coerce the company into accepting their fee schedule, see Section 5B, *infra.* The risk also increases if they control the insurance company. See *Virginia Academy of Clinical Psychologists v. Blue Shield, supra* (Blue Shield found to be an agent of physicians).

B. Price-fixing by nurses

Price-fixing arrangements by nurses have been challenged under state antitrust laws. In *New Jersey v. Nurses Private Duty Registry,* New Jersey filed a complaint against a registry of registered and licensed practical nurses, claiming that it had engaged in price-fixing. The registry entered into a consent decree in which it agreed that it would not become involved in any agreement to fix prices for private-duty nursing services in New Jersey, and that it would not generate fee schedules, rate cards, or other devices that might enable the fixing of such prices by the registry or its members. *New Jersey v. Nurses Private Duty Registry,* 1977-2 Trade Cas. ¶ 61,809 (N.J. Sup. Ct. 1977). After *Maricopa,* such activity would probably be *per se* illegal.

C. Price-fixing by pharmacists

Price-fixing by pharmacists is very likely to be found *per se* illegal under the antitrust laws. See *Zazzali v. New Jersey Pharmaceutical Ass'n,* 1981-2 Trade Cas. ¶ 64,376 (N.J. Sup. Ct. 1981) (New Jersey attorney general files suit claiming state pharmaceutical association had violated New Jersey antitrust statute by price-fixing; association enters into consent decree in which it agrees that it will not fix prescription drug prices, disseminate price information, establish fee schedules, and induce adherence to specific fees).

Attempts to restrict price advertising by pharmacists may also violate the antitrust laws. See *United States v. American Pharmaceutical Ass'n and Michigan Pharmaceutical Ass'n,* 1981-2 Trade Cas. ¶ 64,168 (W.D. Mich. 1981) (national and statewide pharmaceutical associations enter into consent decree providing that they will not attempt to impose restrictions or price advertising; associations still free to urge pharmacists to limit advertising that might induce the use of medically acceptable requirements).

D. Relative value scales

The preparation and dissemination of relative value schedules by medical specialty groups, and their use by specialist practitioners, have been attacked by the FTC, the Department of Justice, and several states as price-fixing devices tending to standardize fees. Relative value schedules are numerical guides used to classify different medical procedures on the basis of relative degree of difficulty, risk, skill, and the time involved in performing the procedure. A number known as the "unit value" is assigned to each procedure. The guides were originally developed to assist persons who buy, sell, or administer health insurance. Physicians may use the relative value guide to establish fees for each of the services they provide: The physician multiplies the unit value assigned to each procedure by his customary dollar per unit charge to arrive at a fee for that procedure.

1. *Consent decrees*

The FTC has obtained consent decrees in relative value guide cases involving radiologists, orthopedists, obstetricians and gynecologists, and physicians in California and Minnesota. See *California Medical Ass'n*, Docket C-2867, 3 Trade Reg. Rep. ¶ 21,403 (1979); *Minnesota State Medical Ass'n*, Docket C-2909, 3 Trade Reg. Rep. ¶ 21,293 (1977); *American College of Radiology*, Docket C-2871 3 Trade Reg. Rep. ¶ 21,236 (1977); *American Academy of Orthopaedic Surgeons*, Docket C-2856, 3 Trade Reg. Rep. ¶ 21,171 (1976); *American College of Obstetricians and Gynecologists*, Docket C-2865, 3 Trade Reg. Rep. ¶ 21,171 (1976). In these consent decrees, the defendant organizations typically agree to cease developing, publishing, or circulating the value scales to their members.

A consent decree has been entered in a Justice Department action, *United States v. Illinois Podiatry Society, Inc.*, 1977-2 Trade Cas. ¶ 61,767 (N.D. Ill. 1977). In that case, the Illinois Podiatry Society agreed that it would stop developing, publishing, or circulating relative value guides; that it would stop recommending that its members rely on the guide; and that it would stop using the guide to settle fee disputes between podiatrists and their patients, podiatrists and insurers, or podiatrists and governmental agencies who provide reimbursement for services.

Finally, several consent decrees have been entered in actions brought by the states. In *Hawaii v. Hawaii Society of Anesthesiologists, Inc.,* 1981-2 Trade Cas. ¶ 64,164 (Hawaii Cir. Ct. 1981), the Hawaii Society of Anesthesiologists agreed that its members would not conspire to use a relative value guide to set fees, or attempt to coerce third-party payers to use a relative value guide in determining payments to be made to insureds or to anesthesiologists. See also *Arizona v. Maricopa County Medical Society,* 1979-1 Trade Cas. ¶ 62,694 (D. Ariz. 1978); *New Jersey v. Nurses Private Duty Registry,* 1977-2 Trade Cas. ¶ 61,809 (N.J. Sup. Ct. 1977).

2. *The decision in United States v. American Society of Anesthesiologists*

Although enforcement agencies have obtained a number of consent decrees, the attack on relative value guides has not been uniformly successful. In *United States v. American Society of Anesthesiologists,* 473 F. Supp. 147 (S.D.N.Y. 1979), the District Court found that the use of relative value guides by the American Society of Anesthesiologists did not violate the Sherman Act. The District Court began by briefly reviewing the history of the practice of anesthesiology, and the society's development of relative value guides. The court then considered the merits of the government's challenge.[3] The court recognized that members of the American Society of Anesthesiology had agreed to adopt, publish, and disseminate a relative value guide. However, there was no agreement that the guide would be used in pricing anesthesiologist services in order to curtail competition. It concluded that use of the guide was neither illegal *per se,* nor illegal under the rule of reason. Although many anesthesiologists employed the guides in their individual practices, there was no evidence that the guides were intended as anything other than a suggested methodology for arriving at fees. The court emphasized that, unless all physicians used the same conversion factor, the use of the relative value guide would not fix prices. And, in fact, use of the guide did not seem to have stabilized fees.

In the course of reaching its decisions, the court observed that the guide was not used in fee negotiations with patients. Anesthesiologists rarely have contact with patients prior to the surgery, and fees are almost never discussed. In fact, the guides were used primarily to negotiate acceptable fees with third-party insurers. But this use of the guide did not violate the antitrust laws. The insurance carriers actively sought input from anesthesiologists and had even urged that a uniform pricing system be established. The anesthesiologists had never attempted to coerce insurance carriers to accept the relative value guide or any particular conversion factor in determining what reimbursement they would allow. The relative value guides simply gave anesthesiologists a starting point in negotiations.

3. Implications of the relative value guide cases

Because the decision in *American Society of Anesthesiology* involves a unique specialty, it may be of limited precedential value. Nonetheless, the decision does suggest that use of relative value guides will not always run afoul of the antitrust laws. A medical society may be able to prepare and distribute a guide, provided that it does not recommend that its members use the guide to establish fees. The outcome of a particular case may depend on analysis of the relevant facts. Is there any evidence of an agreement to use the guide to fix prices? Is there any evidence that the use of the guide stabilized the prices received by members of a specialty? Is there any evidence that most physicians used the guide to set prices? Is there any evidence that physicians used the same conversion factor in computing fees? If the answer to any of these questions is affirmative, a court is likely to find price-fixing.

Health care providers may be able to provide pricing information—including a relative value guide—to insurance companies without running afoul of the antitrust laws. *American Society of Anesthesiologists, supra;* see also *Virginia Academy of Clinical Psychologists, supra.* But see *Illinois Podiatry Society, supra* (consent decree provides that podiatrists may furnish testimony to third-party insurers and government agencies regarding prices, but only so long as they limit the testimony to their own experience and do not refer to a relative value schedule).

Similarly, the providers may be able to provide relative fee schedules to government officials responsible for insurance programs. Such activity may be protected by the Noerr-Pennington doctrine. But see *Illinois Podiatry Society, supra* (although physicians may provide price information based on their own experience to government agencies, they may not provide relative fee schedules).

In general, health care providers should be wary of exchanging price information among themselves. An agreement to fix prices may be inferred from the exchange of price information. Even if an agreement is not inferred, a court may conclude that the exchange creates an unacceptably high risk of anticompetitive behavior. In determining whether a particular exchange is unlawful, the courts are likely to emphasize several factors: (1) whether the exchange involves future rather than past prices; (2) whether the buyers and sellers involved in particular transactions are identified; (3) whether the parties that participate in the exchange possess substantial market power; and (4) whether there is any evidence that the exchange stabilized prices. See, e.g., *American Column & Lumber Co. v. United States*, 257 U.S. 377 (1921); *Maple Flooring Manufacturers Ass'n v. United States*, 268 U.S. 563 (1925); *United States v. Container Corp.*, 393 U.S 333 (1969); see also Outline Section One.

II. Indirect price-fixing: boycotts

In addition to direct price-fixing, physicians and other members of the industry may engage in action that indirectly affects the price they receive for their services. Medical societies, trade associations, and other providers may withhold or threaten to withhold their services unless they receive additional reimbursement. Such boycotts, which have been directed at governmental and private third-party insurers, have received a great deal of attention from governmental enforcement agencies.

  A. Medicaid boycotts

  Boycotts or threatened boycotts designed to increase reimbursement levels under Medicaid programs have been challenged by the Department of Justice. For example, the government filed a suit against the Nursing Home Association of Montana, which represents more than two-thirds of the nursing home beds in the state, claiming that the association conspired to raise the price of nursing home services paid under Montana's Medicaid program. The complaint alleged that the association, in conjunction with its members, had jointly refused, and encouraged others to refuse, to enter into contracts with the Montana Department of Social and Rehabilitative Services, except on terms set by the association and its members. The complaint further alleged that the association and its attorneys had acted as the bargaining agent for member nursing homes in negotiating Medicaid contracts with the state. The government and the association have entered into a consent decree in which the defendant agrees that it will not act as an agent for nursing homes in connection with any decision to accept or reject the terms of Medicaid contracts and that it will not advocate or recommend that nursing homes accept or reject a Medicaid contract, reject or discharge Medicaid patients, or threaten not to participate in the Medicaid program. *United States v. Montana Nursing Home Ass'n Inc.*, 1982-2 Trade Cas. ¶ 64,852 (D. Mont. 1982).

The Department of Justice filed a similar suit against the South Carolina Nursing Home Association, claiming that it had conspired to affect the price paid for nursing home services under the South Carolina Medicaid contracts. The government and the association entered into a consent decree virtually identical to the Montana decree. *United States v. Southern Carolina Health Care Ass'n, Inc.*, 1982-2 Trade Cas. ¶ 63,316 (D.S.C. 1980). See also *Michigan State Medical Society*, 3 Trade Reg. Rep. ¶ 21,991 (1983) (FTC order enjoining physicians' joint efforts to affect Medicaid reimbursement).

State enforcement agencies have also challenged threatened Medicaid boycotts. In *Michigan v. Warner-Universal Ambulance Service*, 1980-2 Trade Cas. ¶ 63,536 (Mich. Cir. Ct. 1980), the state of Michigan filed suit against several Michigan ambulance firms, claiming that they had agreed with each other to collectively withdraw from the Michigan Medicaid program because of dissatisfaction with the price paid for ambulance services. A consent decree was entered that enjoined the ambulance services from agreeing to boycott the Michigan Medicaid program. The decree recognized, however, that individual ambulance companies could individually decide not to contract with the program. In *Hawaii v. Hawaii Society of Anesthesiologists, supra,* the state of Hawaii alleged not only that the society had based prices on a relative value guide, but also that the society and its members had threatened to refuse to enter into Medicaid contracts that did not contain terms provided by the association and its members. The state further alleged that the society had acted as an agent for anesthesiologists in connection with any decision to accept to reject Medicaid contracts. In the consent decree, the society agreed that it would not engage in such practices in the future. 1981-2 Trade Cas. ¶ 64,164, at 73,456.

B. Boycotts of state insurance programs
Professional associations and other health care providers may attempt to influence reimbursement levels provided under state insurance programs. Such actions have been challenged by the states under state antitrust laws modeled after the Sherman Act. In *Ohio ex rel. Brown v. Alliance Dental Society*, 1976-1 Trade Cas. ¶ 60,944 (Ohio Ct. Com. Pleas. 1976), the Ohio Attorney General brought an action against an Ohio dentists' association and its members, claiming that they had agreed to refuse to treat persons receiving assistance from the Ohio Department of Public Welfare. The state and the association ultimately entered into a consent decree. Under this decree, the dentists are required to provide care to welfare patients at the reimbursment level in effect at the time the alleged boycott became effective. In the course of adopting the consent decree, the court indicated that the facts alleged in the complaint, if true, would constitute a violation of both the Ohio and federal antitrust laws.

In a similar case, New York filed suit against several individual physicians and a physicians' association. The complaint charged that the defendants had refused to treat nonemergency Workmen's Compensation patients and nonemergency No-Fault Insurance Law patients. The Workmen's Compensation Law provides that treatment for workers who are injured during the course of their employment will be governed by a maximum fee schedule. The No-fault Insurance Law adopts the Workmen's Compensation minimum fee schedule as the maximum fee schedule governing payments to physicians for the treatment of persons injured in automobile accidents. The defendant physicians had urged the state legislature to modify the fee schedule and to eliminate administrative abuses that resulted in payment delays. When their efforts to obtain legislative action failed, they agreed that they would refuse to treat work-related or automobile accident injuries. A New York County Court stated that the boycott was reprehensible, but decided that the medical profession was exempt from liability under New York's antitrust law. This ruling is now on appeal. See *New York v. Roth* 419 N.Y.S. 2d 85 (N.Y. Cty. Ct. 1979). See also *Matter of Application of Hirschorn*, 1978-1 Trade Cas. ¶ 61,876 (N.Y. Cty. Ct. 1979).

C. Boycotts involving private insurers
Health care providers have engaged in concerted action designed to influence the reimbursement policies of private insurers. The FTC

has challenged joint efforts by dentists and dental associations to interfere with insurance companies' cost containment programs. Such programs typically involved insurance company review of X rays and the dentist's diagnosis prior to any costly, nonemergency treatment. The company would limit its benefits to the least expensive yet adequate treatment. The FTC charged that the dental associations collectively withheld dental X rays and encouraged their members to deal with insurers only on terms set by the association. See, e.g., *Indiana Fed'n of Dentists*, 3 Trade Reg. Rep. ¶ 21,992 (1983); *Association of Independent Dentists*, 3 Trade Reg. Rep. ¶ 21,952 (August 1982) (proposed consent order); *Indiana Dental Ass'n*, Docket 9137, 93 F.T.C. 392 (1979) (consent order); *Texas Dental Ass'n*, Docket No. 9139, 3 Trade Reg. Rep. ¶ 21,927 (1982) (proposed consent order). In the consent decrees, the associations agree that they will not engage in such practices in the future.

Hawaii's suit against the anesthesiologist society included a claim that the society had sought to coerce third-party insurers to accept fee schedules it had prepared. The anesthesiologists agreed to stop such efforts. See *Hawaii v. Hawaii Society of Anesthesiologists*, supra. See also *Michigan State Medical Society*, 3 Trade Reg. Rep. ¶ 21,991 (1983) (FTC order enjoining physicians' joint efforts to affect Blue Cross-Blue Shield reimbursement); *New York v. New York State Society of Ophthalmic Dispensers, Inc.*, 1980-1 Trade Cas. ¶ 63,074 (N.Y. Sup. Ct. 1979) (in consent decree, New York Society of Ophthalmic Dispensers agrees not to boycott eyeglass lens and frame manufacturers that participate in employee eye care insurance plans).

D. Boycotts of patients who file malpractice actions

A closely related case, although it does not involve practices directly aimed at affecting reimbursement levels, suggests that physician boycotts will be viewed unfavorably. In *Williams v. St. Joseph Hospital*, 629 F.2d 448 (7th Cir. 1981), plaintiffs alleged that all physicians in Joliet, Illinois, had agreed to refuse to treat any person (or any member of that person's family) who had instituted a malpractice suit against any Joliet doctor. The District Court dismissed. The Seventh Circuit reversed and remanded. It held that the alleged boycott, if it did in fact occur, would violate federal antitrust laws.[4]

E. Implications of boycott decisions

Health care professionals who jointly threaten to withhold services in an effort to affect prices face a serious risk of antitrust liability. The numerous consent decrees provide some evidence of this danger. See *United States v. South Carolina Health Care Ass'n, supra; United States v. Montana Nursing Home Ass'n, Inc., supra; Indiana Dental Ass'n, supra; New York v. New York State Society of Ophthalmic Dispensers, Inc., supra; Hawaii v. Hawaii Society of Anesthesiologists, supra.* The Seventh Circuit's conclusion that physician boycotts of patients who have filed malpractice actions also indicates that such actions will not be viewed favorably by the courts. See *Williams v. St. Joseph Hospital,* 629 F.2d 448 (7th Cir. 1980). Such boycotts, which ordinarily cannot be justified on professional grounds, may even be struck down as *per se* illegal.

It is important to recognize, however, that a distinction can be drawn between group boycotts and an individual decision not to treat certain patients. Only the former is proscribed by the antitrust laws. A distinction can also be drawn between group boycotts and simple efforts to provide advice to government officials responsible for insurance programs, or to private insurers. As was suggested earlier, health care providers should be able to offer suggestions concerning reimbursement policy to government officals under the protection of the Noerr-Pennington doctrine so long as the recommendations are not accompanied by any form of coercion. Most of the consent decrees entered in the boycott cases explicitly permit health care associations to lobby government organizations. Thus, for example, in *United States v. South Carolina Health Care Association, Inc., supra,* the consent decree states that the defendant may represent nursing homes in bona fide judicial or administrative law proceedings, advocate proposed changes in the Medicaid program with federal or state legislative bodies or executive agencies, and disseminate factual information about the Medicaid program to nursing homes. *Id.* at 75,465. See also *Hawaii v. Hawaii Society of Anesthesiologists, supra; United States v. Montana Nursing Home Associations, Inc., supra; Michigan v. Warner-Universal Ambulance Service, supra.* As was also suggested earlier, health care providers acting individually should be able to provide suggestions concerning reimbursement to private insurers. Associations of health care providers may also be able to provide suggestions to insurers. See, e.g., *Virginia Academy of Clinical Psychologists v. Blue Shield of Virginia, supra; United States v. American Society of Anesthesiology, supra;* but see *Illinois Podiatry Society, supra*. Of course, providers should not attempt to force their suggestions on the insurers.

References

1. The District Court had also held that the rule of reason applied. In addition, it found that the interstate commerce requirement was satisfied because the health insurance is an interstate business. It rejected defendants' claim that the establishment of a maximum fee schedule was part of the "business of insurance" and therefore exempt from antitrust liability under the McCarran-Ferguson Act, 15 U.S.C. § 1012 (1978); the agreement did not underwrite or spread any risk unique to the business of insurance. See *Arizona v. Maricopa County Medical Society*, 1979-1 Trade Cas. ¶ 62,694 (D. Ariz. 1979). The latter two rulings were not reviewed by the Ninth Circuit and the Supreme Court.

   At least one other court has rejected the claim that physicians who use an insurance company to fix prices are engaged in the "business of insurance" within the meaning of the McCarran-Ferguson Act. See *Ohio v. Ohio Medical Indemnity, Inc.*, 1978-2 Trade Cas. ¶ 75,115 (S.D. Ohio 1978). But see *Ratino v. Medical Service of the District of Columbia*, 1981-1 Trade Cas. ¶ 64,144 (D. Md. 1981). See also Outline Section Six.

2. See also *Broadcast Music, Inc. v. Columbia Broadcasting System, Inc.*, 441 U.S. 1 (1979). *Broadcast Music* held that the marketing of a right to use copyrighted compositions derived from the entire membership of an association of composers—a blanket license—was not *per se* illegal, even though the sale of the license necessitated literal price-fixing. The decision suggests that the court may be increasingly willing to consider pro-competitive justifications for horizontal restraints.

3. The District Court found that the United States had shown a sufficient nexus with interstate commerce: Anesthesiologists receive substantial portions of their revenues from out-of-state health insurance carriers, or from Medicaid and Medicare; the

guide itself moved across state lines; and the pricing of anesthesiologist services affects insurance premiums, which flow in interstate commerce.
4. In the course of reaching this decision, the court rejected defendants' claim that plaintiffs would not be able to show a substantial impact on interstate commerce. The plaintiffs had alleged that the medical practices of defendant affected interstate commerce because the defendants purchased supplies from out of state, they were members of national associations, and they treated welfare and Medicare patients and received payment from out of state. According to the Seventh Circuit, plaintiffs should be given the opportunity to prove these allegations.

Section six: Antitrust law and cost-containment activities by insurance companies

Insurance companies engage in a number of practices designed to minimize the costs they incur under health insurance policies. For example, they may enter into contracts with health care providers that set maximum reimbursement levels for various services. Under these contracts, the insurance company agrees to reimburse the professional whenever he or she provides services to a policyholder; the amount of reimbursement, however, is limited by ceiling rates contained in the contract. Another example is the use of peer review procedures. An insurance company may decide to sell policies that limit coverage to reasonable charges for necessary care. When a claim for reimbursement is filed, the insurance company submits the claim to a peer review committee, composed of members of the provider's profession. This committee then decides whether the services were necessary and/or the fee reasonable.

Insurance company decisions to establish maximum fee schedules and peer review procedures have been challenged under the antitrust laws. Much of the litigation has focused on the question whether these practices can be considered part of the "business of insurance" within the meaning of the McCarran-Ferguson Act, and are therefore exempt from the antitrust laws. 15 U.S.C. §§ 1011-1015 (1976). Recent Supreme Court decisions suggest that McCarran-Ferguson Act immunity will not be available. However, good arguments can be made that the cost-containment activities are procompetitive and therefore do not violate the antitrust laws.

I. Maximum reimbursement levels

   A. Introduction: techniques for setting maximum reimbursement levels
   There are basically two ways in which an insurance company can set maximum reimbursement levels. (1) An insurance company may simply sell policies in which it agrees that it will indemnify policyholders for their health care expenditures according to a maximum fee schedule. The insurance company does not enter into separate agreements with providers. (2) In addition to entering into contracts with policyholders, an insurance company may enter into separate contracts with health care providers. In those contracts, it agrees that it will reimburse the providers for services they provide to policyholders according to a maximum fee schedule. Where the insurer uses such an arrangement, its contracts with the policyholders ordinarily permit the policyholder to use any provider, regardless of whether the provider has entered into an agreement

with the insurance company. If the policyholders choose a provider who has entered into an agreement with the insurer, they typically incur no out-of-pocket costs, or pay only a small deductible. If the policyholders choose a provider who has not entered into an agreement, they must pay the provider directly and then apply for indemnification from the insurance company.

Agreements between providers and insurance companies that set maximum reimbursement levels have been challenged as violations of the antitrust laws. The lawsuits typically allege that the insurance companies are by themselves attempting to fix the price for providers' services. The lawsuits frequently also include the charge that the insurance company is collaborating with providers who wish to fix the price for their services.

B. Availability of McCarran-Ferguson Act exemption

In virtually all of the cases involving challenges to agreements between insurance companies and providers, the insurance companies have claimed that this practice is part of the "business of insurance" within the meaning of the McCarran-Ferguson Act and is therefore exempt from scrutiny under the antitrust law. For the most part, this defense has not been successful. In *Group Life & Health Insurance Co. v. Royal Drug Co.*, 440 U.S. 205 (1979), the Supreme Court confronted the question whether maximum price agreements entered into by an insurance company and pharmacies were part of the "business of insurance" within the meaning of the act. The insurance company, Blue Shield of Texas, offered policies entitling insured persons to purchase prescription drugs for $2 each from any pharmacy participating in a "pharamacy agreement" with the insurer. Policyholders could also purchase drugs from nonparticipating pharmacies. If they did so, however, they would have to pay the full price charged by the pharmacy and then obtain reimbursement from Blue Shield in an amount no greater than that which the insurer would reimburse a participating pharmacy. The pharmacy agreement, which Blue Shield offered to all Texas pharmacies, provided for a maximum billable amount method of reimbursement. The insurance company determined the maximum it would reimburse participating pharamacies by reference to its own price list. Several nonparticipating pharamacies charged that the pharmacy agreement constituted price-fixing arrangements. The insurer defended on the ground that the pharmacy agreements were part of the business of insurance and therefore exempt from scrutiny under the antitrust laws.

The Supreme Court rejecting this defense. The Court began by stating that a particular practice is part of the business of insurance only if it contains some risk-spreading or underwriting element. It then observed:

> The Pharmacy Agreements [between Blue Shield and participating pharmacies] . . . do not involve any underwriting or spreading of risk, but are merely arrangements for the purchase of goods and services by Blue Shield. By agreeing with pharmacies on the maximum prices it will pay for drugs, Blue Shield effectively reduces the total amount it must pay to its policyholders. The Agreement thus enables Blue Shield to minimize costs and maximize profits. Such cost-saving arrangements may well be sound business practice, and may well inure ultimately to the benefit of policyholders in the form of lower premiums, but they are not the "business of insurance."

Id. at 214 (footnote omitted).

The Court also reasoned that a practice is considered to be part of the business of insurance only if it adjusts the "relationship between insurer and insured, the type of policy which could be issued, its reliability, interpretation, and enforcement." The pharmacy agreements primarily affected the relationship between the insurer and pharmacies, not the insurer and its policyholders. If this were enough, however, then almost every business decision made by an insurance company would be considered to be part of the business of insurance. Finally, the Court noted that, in enacting the McCarran-Ferguson Act, the primary concern of both representatives of the insurance industry and the Congress was that cooperative ratemaking efforts by insurance companies be exempt from the antitrust laws. *Id.* at 221. The pharmacy agreements, however, involved parties wholly outside the insurance industry. *Id.* at 231.

The decision in *Royal Drug* clearly suggests that price agreements with any health care providers—not just those with pharmacies—will not be considered part of the business of insurance. The reasoning used by the Court in analyzing the pharmacy agreements applies with equal force to maximum fee contracts with other providers: they also can be characterized simply as arrangements for the purchase of goods and services; they do not adjust the relationship between the insurer and the insured but rather the relationship between the insurer and the providers; and they involve parties wholly outside the insurance industry.

In fact, lower courts have held that price agreements between insurers and physicians are not part of the business of insurance. In *Arizona v. Maricopa County Medical Society*, 1979-1 Trade Cas. ¶ 67,694 (D. Ariz. 1979), the district court found that the establishment of a maximum fee schedule by a county medical society did not constitute part of the business of insurance, even though the schedule was used by an insurance company controlled by the society. The fee schedule did not underwrite or spread any risk peculiar to the business of insurance.[1]

A similar conclusion was reached in *Ohio v. Ohio Medical Indemnity, Inc.*, 1978-2 Trade Cas. ¶ 75,115 (S.D. Ohio 1978). In that case, Ohio claimed that the Ohio State Medical Association, as the owner of an insurer, Ohio Medical Indemnity Inc., conspired to fix the price of physicians' goods and services by setting reimbursement levels. The district court found that the price-fixing was not part of the business of insurance. Although the alleged conspiracy did affect the rates paid by Ohio Medical Indemnity's policyholders, the overall impact of the conspiracy was much broader: it determined the price and availability of physicians' goods and services to all users and potential users of those services. See also *Kartell v. Blue Shield of Massachusetts*, Trade Cas. 1982-2 ¶ 64,842 (D. Mass. 1982) (Blue Shield's agreement with physicians requiring them to accept the fee paid by Blue Shield as payment in full for covered services is not part of the "business of insurance" under the McCarran-Ferguson Act.[2]

C. The merits of antitrust challenges to maximum reimbursement practices

An insurer's liability for establishing maximum reimbursement levels depends on whether the insurer relies simply on indemnification agreements or whether it has entered into separate agreements with providers. Liability also depends on the extent to which the providers themselves were involved in setting the maximum reimbursement levels.

1. Maximum reimbursement levels contained in indemnification agreement with policyholder

   Assuming that the insurer is not controlled by providers, it may legitimately include maximum reimbursement levels in its insurance policies. If it is controlled by providers, however, there is a serious risk that it will be held liable as a participant in a price-fixing conspiracy.

2. Including maximum reimbursement amounts in provider agreements: no physician control
Implications of Maricopa County. The Supreme Court's recent decision in *Arizona v. Maricopa County Medical Society, supra,* discusses the use of insurance company maximum reimbursement schedules in agreements with health care providers. In that case, the defendant medical society established a maximum fee schedule, which it then used in contracts with health insurers. Under these contracts, the insurers agreed to reimburse society members for health services provided to the insurers' policyholders at rates not exceeding those set forth in the maximum fee schedule. The Supreme Court held that the establishment of the maximum fee schedule by the physicians constituted price-fixing and was illegal *per se*. The Court rejected the physicians' claim that the fee schedule was actually procompetitive because it helped insurers reduce costs and lower premiums. The Court conceded that an insurer's ability to estimate its costs would be impeded if it could not rely on a fee schedule. The schedule did not have to be set by physicians, however. The insurance company could set the ceiling rates itself, with much less impact on competition.

The decision in *Maricopa County* implicitly suggests that independent efforts by insurance companies to establish their own maximum reimbursement levels should enjoy relaxed scrutiny under the antitrust laws—assuming that the insurance company is not controlled by providers and thus cannot be viewed as the vehicle for a horizontal price-fixing conspiracy. As the Court apparently recognized, including maximums in provider agreements may increase competition: the use of maximum fees will reduce insurance company costs and lower premiums. Indeed, because the practices may have procompetitive consequences, a strong argument can be made that the rule of reason should be applied.

Even if a rule of reason analysis is employed, however, there is a slight risk of antitrust liability. For example, the insurance company may control a large portion of the market for insurance. If it possesses a large market share, health care providers who have entered into an agreement with the insurer but who treat both policyholders and nonpolicyholders may feel some pressure to charge nonpolicyholders the same fees that are contained in the provider agreements. In addition, health care providers who have not entered into provider agreements may feel compelled to do so. As a result, the provider agreement may have a stabilizing effect on prices. In addition, the provider agreement may expand the insurer's market power: As the number of providers who enter into provider agreements increases, the insurer's ability to sell its policies may increase. It is conceivable that a court would conclude that these anticompetitive effects outweighed the procompetitive effects of the agreement. The outcome of a particular case is likely to depend on a careful analysis of the agreement between the health care provider and the insurer, the market power possessed by the insurer, and the effect of the agreement on competition in that market. This analysis will be fairly complicated because three sets of participants are involved: the health insurer, the insurance policyholder, and the providers.

Other cases. Several decisions confirm that the courts will hesitate before condemning insurance company decisions to establish maximum reimbursement by means of provider agreements. In *Medical Arts Pharmacy v. Blue Cross & Blue Shield*, 675 F.2d 502 (2nd Cir. 1982), the Second Circuit concluded that insurer-pharmacy agreements virtually identical to those at issue in *Royal Drug* did not violate the antitrust laws. Under Blue Cross's prescription drug program, subscribers, representing approximately 9 percent of Connecticut's population, could obtain prescription drugs from licensed pharmacies at little or no cost beyond the prepayment of premiums. A contract between Blue Cross and the individual subscribers determined the level of benefits for each insured, and a second contract between Blue Cross and the pharmacy set the terms under which a participating pharmacy would provide prescription drugs to the subscribers.

The subscriber contract permitted the insured to obtain prescription drugs from either a participating or nonparticipating pharmacy. If the insured purchased the drugs from a nonparticipating pharmacy, he paid the full price charged by the pharmacy and then obtained reimbursement from Blue Cross in an amount no greater than that which Blue Cross would reimburse a participating pharmacy. If, on the other hand the subscriber selected a participating pharmacy, he generally received the needed drug at no out-of-pocket expense. Blue Cross would then reimburse the pharmacy at a rate established in the pharmacy agreement. The pharmacy agreement, which Blue Cross unilaterally instituted and offered to all Connecticut pharmacies, provided for a "maximum billable amount" method of reimbursement. Blue Cross determined the maximum it would reimburse participating pharmacies by reference to its own price lists or to average wholesale prices.

Medical Arts Pharmacy, which did not enter into a pharmacy agreement, charged that the agreements were price-fixing arrangements proscribed by the Sherman Act. The Second Circuit rejected the pharmacy's claim that the price-fixing agreements were comparable to maximum resale price maintenance or horizontal price-fixing, and therefore *per se* illegal. According to the Second Circuit, Blue Cross was simply a purchaser of the prescription drugs. The *per se* rule applies to agreements to fix the price to be charged in transactions with third parties, not between the contracting parties themselves. Even if Blue Cross were not characterized as a purchaser, but rather as an indemnitor or third-party payor, the *per se* rule should not be applied. Its prescription drug plan differs significantly from the vertical arrangements to restrict resale prices or horizontal agreements among competitors to fix prices. Unlike such practices, the pharmacy agreements were arguably procompetitive. "Prepaid drug insurance plans potentially promote competition and efficiency, for example, by countering the normal insensitivity of drug prices. Pharmacy agreements are ancillary to the otherwise valid commercial efforts of Blue Cross to design the most efficient insurance coverage for subscribers." *Id.* at 506 (citations omitted).

The Second Circuit then applied the rule of reason. It found that the plaintiff pharmacy had failed to present any facts supporting its allegation of a "buyer's conspiracy," or its claim that there was a negative impact on competition.

Medical Arts made no claim that the prices Blue Cross pays to participating pharmacies in any way affect the prices they charge for the prescription drugs provided to non-Blue Cross customers, the prices they charge for non-drug items, or any prices charged by nonparticipating pharmacies. And appellants nowhere make any claim that Blue Cross' market share of less than 10 percent of the drug purchasers' market gave Blue Cross monopsony power with which it might be capable of obtaining agreements with anticompetitive effect. *Id.* at 507. Under the circumstances, no antitrust violation had been proved.[3]

Another case, *Blue Cross and Blue Shield of Michigan v. Michigan Ass'n of Psychotherapy*, 1980-2 Trade Cas. ¶ 63,351 (E.D. Mich. 1980), upheld a pricing agreement between outpatient psychiatric clinics and Blue Cross and Blue Shield of Michigan. In 1979, Blue Cross sought to change its reimbursement policies for mental health services provided to its subscribers. It terminated its existing contracts with outpatient psychiatric clinics and offered them the opportunity to enter into new standard contracts. These new contracts provided that the clinic would furnish mental health care services covered by Blue Cross health care plans to subscribers and obtain reimbursement from Blue Cross. The contract set reimbursement rates in accordance with a maximum rate schedule established by Blue Cross's board of directors. The contract further provided that reimbursement would be limited to the lesser of a provider's billed charge or the ceiling rate. The contract also contained a clause prohibiting the clinic from billing patients not enrolled in the Blue Cross plan at a lower rate than it billed patients who were enrolled.

A number of outpatient clinics entered into these new contracts. Other clinics objected, claiming that the new reimbursement policy violated Section 1 of the Sherman Act. The contract would have the effect of establishing a fixed price for psychotherapy services provided to Blue Cross members and would establish a fixed minimum price equal to Blue Cross's reimbursement rate for mental health patients not covered by Blue Cross.

The District Court found that the contract was neither *per se* illegal, nor illegal under the rule of reason. It quickly disposed of the claim that the contract fixed prices for services provided to Blue Cross members. Although the new agreements between Blue Shield and the participating clinics did set maximum prices that Blue Cross will pay for covered services, this was not a violation of the antitrust laws: Rather, it was simply a contractual arrangement between buyer and seller. The District

Court also disposed of the claim that the new contract fixed the prices to be charged because it established a minimum charge for services rendered to non-Blue Cross members equal to Blue Cross's maximum rates. According to the District Court, the contract simply anticipated that providers would charge nonmembers less than the ceiling rates and required that Blue Cross be given the benefit of the low rates. The new contracts would not have a chilling effect on the rate structure of mental health care clinics, since participating clinics were certainly not compelled to charge non-Blue Cross members rates equivalent to the Blue Cross members' rates.

The reasoning employed in this case is somewhat less sophisticated than that employed in *Medical Arts Pharmacy*. If Blue Cross and Blue Shield of Michigan had substantial market power, it is quite possible that its new contract would have had a chilling effect on the prices charged by mental health care clinics. As a practical matter, they would be required to charge all patients the same rates set by Blue Cross. Of course, this anticompetitive effect might have been outweighed by the pro-competitive effect of the maximum rate agreement. In any event, the *Michigan Association of Psychotherapy* decision does suggest that courts will be fairly reluctant to strike down price agreements between insurers and providers.

Other courts have concluded that insurance company reimbursement arrangements should be tested under the rule of reason, but have not yet decided whether the particular arrangement at issue should survive the rule of reason. In *Manasen v. California Dental Service*, 1981-1 Trade Cas. ¶ 63,959 (N.D. Cal. 1980), California dentists in private practice sued California Dental Service (CDS), a nonprofit corporation that sells prepaid dental insurance. CDS covers approximately 20 to 30 percent of all persons in California who have purchased prepaid dental insurance. CDS provides these subscribers with dental services by means of provider agreements with dentists who agree to accept their "usual, customary, and reasonable" fee as full payment for their services. Participating dentists are paid directly for any dental work performed for CDS subscribers. CDS sets a maximum fee for all services provided by participating dentists at a rate which would satisfy 90 percent of the dentists in the same geographical area. CDS rules prohibit participating dentists from charging non-CDS patients less than the usual fee they have filed with CDS. If a subscriber sees a nonparticipating dentist, the patient must pay that dentist. CDS then indemnifies the patient. This indemnification is ordinarily at a lower percentage of the total fee than that allowed to patients who see participating dentists. The plaintiff dentists argued that the maximum fee schedule constituted price-fixing, and that the practice of indemnifying patients who see nonparticipating dentists at a lesser rate constituted a boycott. The District Court refused to hold that these practices were *per se* illegal; rather, it decided that the rule of reason should apply.

In *Kartell v. Blue Shield of Massachusetts*, 1982-2 Trade Cas. ¶ 64,842 (D. Mass.), which was decided after *Maricopa County*, the District Court relied on *Medical Arts Pharmacy* to hold that Blue Shield's agreement with physicians requiring them to accept the fee paid by Blue Shield as payment in full should be analyzed under the rule of reason. The court observed that Blue Shield was the ultimate payor for the physician's services and thus that the case was unlike *per se* illegal vertical arrangements to fix the price to be charged in transactions with third parties.

3. Including maximum reimbursement amounts in provider agreements; providers control the insurer

The decision in *Maricopa County* clearly holds that physicians may not themselves set the maximum fee levels included in provider agreements. Presumably, an insurance company that was controlled by physicians would also be subject to antitrust liability if it attempted to include maximum reimbursement levels in its agreements with providers. In fact, such an attempt might be treated as illegal *per se:* The insurance company would simply be viewed as the vehicle for a horizontal maximum price-fixing conspiracy.

II. The use of peer review by insurance companies

A. Availability of the McCarran-Ferguson Act exemption

In *Union Labor Life Insurance Co. v. Pireno*, 102 S. Ct. 3002 (1982), the Supreme Court held that the use of a peer review committee by an insurance company did not constitute part of the business of insurance.[4] As required by New York law, Union Labor Life Insurance issued health insurance policies covering certain policyholder claims for chiropractic treatments. Some policies limited the company's liability to "reasonable charges for necessary medical care and treatments." To determine whether particular treatments were necessary and the charges reasonable, the insurer relied on the New York State Chiropractic Association's Peer Review Committee. The Committee was composed of ten practicing New York chiropractors. On a number of occasions, the insurer referred chiropractic treatments performed by Pireno to the Peer Review Committee. The committee concluded that several treatments were unnecessary and several charges unreasonable. Pireno sued the insurance company and the chiropractic association, claiming that peer review practices violated Section 1 of the Sherman Act because it was used as a vehicle to fix the price that chiropractors would be permitted to charge for their services. The insurance company defended on the ground that its use of the committee constituted the business of insurance within the meaning of the McCarran-Ferguson Act. The Supreme Court rejected this claim.

Relying on *Royal Drug*, the Court stated that three criteria should be applied to determine whether a particular practice was part of the business of insurance: (1) whether the practice has the effect of transferring or spreading a policyholder's risk; (2) whether the practice is an integral part of the relationship between the insurer and the insured; and (3) whether the practice is limited to entities within the insurance company. With respect to the first criterion, the Court found that the arrangement played no part in the spreading and underwriting of the policyholder's risk. Peer review takes place only after the risk has already been transferred by means of the policy; it functions only to determine whether the risk of the insured's loss falls within the policy limits. As for the second criterion, the Court reasoned that the use of the peer review committee is distinct from the insurer's contract with its policyholders; it constitutes a separate arrangement between the insurer and third parties not engaged in the business of insurance. Finally, with respect to the third criterion, the Court observed that the arrangement involves parties outside the insurance industry, namely, practicing chiropractors on the peer review committee. Thus, it does not lie at the center of the legislative concern underlying the McCarran-Ferguson exemption in the underwriting of risks. More importantly, such arrangements may prove contrary to the spirit of the McCarran-Ferguson Act, because they have the potential to restrain competition in noninsurance markets.

B. The merits of antitrust challenges to peer review committees
   1. Insurance company liability in peer review cases
   The use of peer review committees can be procompetitive. They help an insurance company to avoid paying for needless or unnecessarily expensive treatment and thus reduce costs and lower premiums.[5] Because the peer review procedure may be procompetitive, a good argument can be made that the rule of reason applies when such practices are challenged and that, in ordinary circumstances, they should be upheld. In fact, the Antitrust Division of Justice has approved the peer review committees challenged in *Pireno*. See Antitrust Implications of Chiropractic Peer Review Committees, 8 Am. J.L. & Med. 45 (1982).

   Insurance companies that establish peer review procedures may still face a slight risk of antitrust liability if they use the procedure to set maximum fees. As was discussed at pp. 5–7 *supra*, maximum fee arrangements may be anticompetitive, depending on market conditions. There is also some risk that an insurance company would be named as co-conspirator in a case charging price-fixing on the part of the providers who are members of the peer review committee. If the insurance company is controlled by physicians, the insurance company might be held liable. This risk could be avoided altogether if the individuals conducting the peer review committee are employed directly by the insurance company. If they are employees and do not have their own practice, they would not be competitors of the physicians whose fees they are reviewing and thus would not have any direct interest in fixing prices.

   2. Physician liability in peer review cases
   The Federal Trade Commission has issued an advisory opinion discussing the Iowa Dental Association's proposal to establish a program for peer review of dental fees. The association wished to institute a peer review program to aid the cost containment efforts of insurers and to assist patients in the resolution of fee-related disputes with dentists. Under the program, a patient, an insurer, or a dentist involved in a particular fee dispute may request a determination by a peer review panel composed of members of the dental association. Participation is voluntary and all determinations will be purely advisory.

The decision of each peer review panel would be based solely on the facts and circumstances of the particular case and would not be disseminated beyond the parties involved in that case. The association would not collect information on dental fees or conduct fee surveys. The FTC concluded that this program, in and of itself, would not violate Section 5 of the FTC Act. *Iowa Dental Association,* 3 Trade Reg. Rep. ¶ 21,918 (April 1982) (advisory opinion).

Because this peer review program was initiated by a professional association rather than by an insurer, the advisory opinion does not discuss in detail the potential liability of insurance companies who rely on peer review procedures. However, the opinion contains a useful analysis of the potential problems faced by health care professionals who participate in a peer review program. The FTC warned that "great care must be taken to assure that [the program's] purpose remains legitimate and that it does not produce anticompetitive effects." *Id.* at 22,271. The program must remain voluntary and advisory. Moreover, the program should not allow determinations about particular past fee disputes to become generalized in future fee or reimbursement decisions. Peer review must be treated as a means of mediating specific fee disputes rather than a process for the collective sanctioning of fee levels or particular practices. It is essential that dissemination of the decisions be strictly limited.

The FTC also warned that assessments of the difficulty of a procedure should be based on the individual expertise of particular members. The association risks antitrust liability if it develops benchmarks such as relative price scales. Peer review should not be used to discipline dentists who engage in advertising or other forms of competition or to discourage innovative practices. To avoid unlawful coercion of third-party payors, the association should make it clear that it is not conferring preferred status on insurers who participate in the program. It should also avoid using the program to determine whether a third-party payor's reimbursement program is reasonable.[6]

In general, providers who participate in peer review run little risk of antitrust liability if they confine their review to the question of whether a particular service was necessary. The risk of liability increases if they also review fees for reasonableness. This risk can be minimized, however, if they follow the guidelines set forth in the FTC letter.

References
1. Although this case ultimately reached the Supreme Court, the Court did not confront the question whether the schedule was part of the business of insurance. *Arizona v. Maricopa County Medical Society*, 102 S. Ct. 2450 (1982).
2. In *Ratino v. Medical Service of the District of Columbia*, 1981-1 Trade Cas. ¶ 64,144 (D. Md. 1981), the district court held that an insurance company's fee schedule for reimbursing physicians for medical services rendered to policyholders, along with the company's fee review procedures, did constitute part of the business of insurance. The continued validity of this holding is in doubt, however. The district court relied heavily on the Fourth Circuit's decision in *Bartholomew v. Virginia Chiropractic Association*, 612 F.2d 812 (4th Cir. 1979), which held that the use of a peer review committee by an insurance company constituted the business of insurance. *Bartholomew* was reversed by the Supreme Court last term in *Union Labor Life Insurance Co. v. Pireno*, 102 S. Ct. 3002 (1982). See pp. 14–19 *infra*.
3. See also *Feldman v. Health Care Service Corp.*, No. 78 C-2621 (N.D. Ill. 1982) (upholding prepaid prescription drug plan against similar challenge); *Sausalito Pharmacy, Inc. v. Blue Shield of California*, 1981-1 Trade Cas. ¶ 63,885 (N.D. Cal. 1981), *aff'd* 677 F. 2d 47 (9th Cir. 1982) (per curiam).
4. In so holding, it affirmed the Second Circuit, which had also held that peer review did not constitute the business of insurance. See *Pireno v. New York State Chiropractic Ass'n*, 650 F.2d 387 (2d Cir. 1981). The Second Circuit was in conflict with the Fourth Circuit's ruling in *Bartholomew v. Virginia Chiropractors Association, Inc.*, 612 F.2d 812 (4th Cir. 1979) (peer review procedure used by health insurance carriers in conjunction with state chiropractors' association constitutes part of the business of insurance). See also *Ratino v. Medical Service of the District of Columbia*, Trade Cas. 1981-1 ¶ 64,144 (D. Md. 1981) (relying on *Ballard* to hold that a medical insurance provider, a hospital, a physician's organization, and several doctors serving on the organization's peer review committees were immune from antitrust laws).

5. The Federal Trade Commission believes that similar cost-containment activities by insurers are very desirable. It has enjoined efforts by health care providers to interfere with activities very similar to those described in this section. See *Michigan State Medical Society*, 3 Trade Reg. Rep. (CCH) ¶ 21,991 (1983); *Indiana Federation of Dentists*, Docket No. 9118, 3 Trade Reg. Rep. (CCh) ¶ 21,992 (1983); *Indiana Dentists Association*, 92 F.T.C. 392 (1979) (consent order); *Texas Dental Association*, Docket No. 9137, 3 Trade Reg. Rep. (CCH) ¶ 21,927 (proposed consent order, June 8, 1982). In each of these cases, dental associations had attempted to boycott insurance companies that were reviewing the provision of services to determine whether the services were reasonable and necessary. The review was conducted by insurance company employees rather than by peer review committees.
6. The FTC also discussed the use of the peer review program to resolve dentist-patient disputes where no third-party payor is involved. According to the FTC, the association should be particularly careful not to let the peer review process set particular "reasonable" fee levels for general use by its members. The patient should be informed that the process is voluntary and advisory, and should be given a hearing.

Index

A

ABMS. *See* American Board of Medical Specialties
Accreditation
  due process requirement, 27–44
  fear of antitrust liability, 103
  FTC comment on medical school accrediting program, 56
  involving discrimination and exclusion, 66
  legal aspects of, 1–5
  liability in tort for activities, 103–109
  as method of quality control, 65–66
  protection of privacy, 147–49
  related to employment decisions, 76
  related to standards, 66
  residency program requirements, 91–94
  as self-regulatory function, 49

Accreditation agencies, guidance on antitrust liability, 48
Accreditation Council for Graduate Medical Education approval of residency training programs, 89
Accreditation process, extravagent representations in, 106–107
Accreditation and review procedures for residency training programs, 89–91
Accreditation standards
  analyzed as potentially anticompetitive, 12
  antitrust challenges to, 7–9
ACGME. *See* Accreditation Council for Graduate Medical Education
Advertising, prohibition on challenged by FTC, 52–53
Agreements among competitors as potential violations, 188–92
Albemarle Paper Co. v. Moody, on job-relatedness as requirement for testing validity, 73, 74

American Board of Family Practice,
   experience with recertification,
   167
American Board of Internal Medicine
   approach to recertification,
   165-66
   experience with recertification,
   166-67
American Board of Medical
   Specialties
   coping with federal regulation of
   examination procedures, 3
   need for insurance, 2
American Educational Research
   Association, 130
   on standards for tests, 68
American Medical Association
   antitrust challenge to ethical
   canons, 52-53
   decision re restriction on
   advertising, 20
   investigations by FTC on
   physicians' advertising, 3
   restriction on advertising, 20
*American Medical Association v.
   United States*, 9
American Psychological Association,
   130
   on standards for tests, 68
*American Society of Mechanical
   Engineers, Inc. v. Hydrolevel
   Corp.*, antitrust liability case, 8,
   53-54
Anglo-American judical system
   founded on principle of reasonableness, 66
Anticompetitive conduct by
   hospitals, 216
Anticompetitive practices, as
   violations of antitrust laws, 17
Anticompetitive restraints
   judged by rule of reason or *per se*
   rules, 11
   tested in lawsuits, 7-9

Antitrust aspects of confidentiality,
   138
Antitrust challenges
   to denial of hospital staff
   privileges, 235-48
   to exclusive physician
   arrangements, 235
   to maximum reimbursement
   practices, 273-79
   to peer review committees, 281-83
Antitrust courts, concern with
   private certification systems, 179
Antitrust/health care analysis, recent
   developments, 15-16
Antitrust issues
   in hospital staff privileges, 7
   raised in physician-hospital contracts, 6
Antitrust law
   and cost-containment activities,
   270-83
   disputes involving medical and
   hospital practice, 18
   enforcement of, 184-85
   "learned professions exemption," 18
   potent form of market regulation,
   17
   potential threat to specialty certification practices, 20
   prohibiting anticompetitive practices, 17
   purpose of, 1
   related to medical specialty
   certification (Klein), 17-26
Antitrust policy, 183
Antitrust statutes, summary of,
   183-84
Antitrust violations
   Goldfarb v. Virginia State Bar,
   49-50
   minimum legal fee schedules,
   49-50
*Applying Antitrust Law to Medical
   Credentialing* (Kissam), 4

Arizona v. Maricopa County Medical Society
  as professional association antitrust case, 51
  on restraints of trade, 11-12
Association of American Medical Colleges protesting testing legislation, 130
Association membership
  as economic necessity, 32-33
  as prerequisite to practice, 34

B

Becker, Carl, 48
Beiglet, Jerome S., M.D., on disclosure of confidential information, 137-52
Bennett Mechanical Comprehension Test, use in employee selection, 73
Benson, John A. Jr., M.D., on recertification, 163-74
Blackmun, Justice Harry on violation of antitrust laws, 54
Board for Certification in Pedorthics, certification program of occupational competency, 56
Board of Curators of the University of Missouri v. Horowitz
  in application of due process requirement, 37-40
  on constitutional due process, 27
Boycotts
  implications of court decisions, 267-68
  as indirect price-fixing devices, 263-68
  involving private insurers, 265-66
  of patients who file malpractice actions, 266
  of state insurance programs, 265
Brandeis, Justice Louis, 136, 138
  on restraint of competition, 51

Brookins v. Bonnell, 31
"Business of insurance" exemption under McCarran-Ferguson Act, 271-73

C

Candidates for licensure
  from foreign medical schools, 157
  as graduates of accredited schools 155-57
  passing a licensing examination, 158-59
  personal attributes, 154
Certification
  from antitrust perspective, 20
  application of antitrust analysis to, 178
  under Consumer-Patient Radiation Health and Safety Act of 1981, 59
  current standard in jeopardy, 171
  dominated by physician organizations, 180
  due process requirement, 27-44
  eligibility criteria, 23
  ensuring future competence, 163
  as form of "commercial speech," 22
  "grandfathering" provisions of, 179
  importance of due process, 2
  involving discrimination and exclusion, 66
  legal aspects of, 1-5
  liability in negligence cases, 105
  liability in tort for activities, 103-109
  a method of quality control, 65-66
  not exempt from antitrust laws, 23
  as prerequisite to practice, 34
  protection of privacy, 147-49
  recognition of eligible applicants, 23

recognition and enforcement components, 21
related to employment decisions, 76
related to standards, 66
residency program requirements, 91–94
as self-regulatory function, 49
standards for, 171
structural fairness as antitrust protection, 23
Certification and accreditation, due process in, 27–44
Certification and accreditation agencies, defense of evaluation procedures, 82–83
use of trademarks and trade names, 112–13
Certification and collective marks acceptance for registration, 117–19
registration of 116–17
in sales of services, 113–14
statutory protection for, 115–16,
Certification evaluation procedures, responsibility for validation of, 76
Certification agencies, guidance on antitrust liability, 48
Certification marks, examples, 125
Certification or accreditation activities, liability in tort for, 103–109
Certification organizations, difference from commercial entities, 104
Certification organizations, protection of trademarks, 112–13
Certification process
consequences of extravagent representations, 106–107
need for records, 105
reasonableness of, 105
relevance of Tarasoff rule, 105
Certifying process, anticompetitive potential of, 177
Challenges to licensing boards (Cramblett), 153–61
Charitable immunity, doctrine of, 104
Chicago Board of Trade v. United States, on restraints on competition, 12
Civil Rights Act of 1964, application to employment, 67
Clayton Act, 183–84
Closed hospital medical staff, interest in by FTC, 6
Collective marks as certification marks, 114
Collective membership marks, examples, 125
Collins v. American Optometric Association, on consequences of extravagent representations, 106–107
Commission to Evaluate Foreign Medical Schools, 157
Competition among hospitals or other health facilities, 210–18
Competition among physicians, 235–54
Concurrent validity in testing, 70
Confidentiality
antitrust aspects of, 138
defined, 137–38
of doctor-patient relationship, 137
Confidential information, disclosure of, 137–52
Construct validity in testing, 71–72
Consumer fraud related to standardized testing legislation, 127–36
Consumer-Patient Radiation Health and Safety Act of 1981, in certification of professional persons, 59
Consumer protection
related to standardized testing legislation, 127–36
in testing legislation, 127–36

Content validity
  criticism of, 81
  in tests of knowledge or skill, 69-70
Continental T.V., Inc. v. GTE Sylvania, Inc., rule of reason test in anticompetitive practices, 12
Continuing education
  "a categorical imperative of contemporary medicine," 169
  need for in professional organizations, 168-69
Cost-containment activities and antitrust law, 270-83
Council of Postsecondary Accreditation, 180
Court cases
  on protection of trademarks, 121-23
  related to educational testing, 77-80
Court decisions ruling against employment tests, 74
Courts
  encountering psychological testing, 65
  inconsistent in decisions on employment test validity, 75
Cramblett, Henry G., M.D., on challenges to licensing boards, 153-61
Creations of new medical specialties, 175-76
Credentialing
  denial of individual certification, 57
  encompassing certification and accreditation, 48-49
  federal involvement in, 59-61
  FTC interest in, 19
  legal aspects of, 49-61
  legal challenges to, 55-61
  Marrese v. American Academy of Orthopaedic Surgeons, 58-59
  by professional associations, 48-49
  public information about, 181
  as self-regulation in lieu of government regulation, 49
  U.S. Department of Justice challenges to, 55
  Veizaga v. National Board for Respiratory Therapy, 57-58
Criterion-related validity in testing, 70

D

Debra P. v. Turlington, on functional literacy examinations, 79, 81
Defenses against antitrust action, 200-209
Directory of Medical Specialists, 164
Directory of Residency Training Programs (AMA), 89
Disclosure of confidential information (Beigler), 137-52
Disclosure provisions in testing legislation, 128-29
Division of markets among competitors, 189-90
Doctor-patient relationship, confidentiality of, 137
Due process
  applied to certification and accreditation, 27-28
  arising from Fifth and Fourteenth Amendments, 28
  Board of Curators v. Horowitz, 37-40
  in certification and accreditation (Feldman), 27-44
  as constitutional requirement, 27-28
  disciplinary criteria versus academic criteria, 31-32
  interests of individual against state, 30

in public and private organizations, 37-40
related to "fairness doctrine," 27-28
state action requirement, 28-32

E

Economic Policy Office of the Antitrust Division of the United States Department of Justice, on tolerant treatment of vertical restraints, 13
Educational testing, 77-80
court cases related to, 77-80
and courts, 65
courts on basic skills testing programs, 79-80
interest in standardized legislation for, 131
problem of validation, 78
related to certification and accreditation agencies, 77
trends, 77
Educational test takers, protection for, 77
EEOC. *See* Equal Employment Opportunity Commission
Eliason Corp. v. National Sanitation Foundation, on legitimacy of standard making, 8
Employee selection procedures
influence of *Uniform Guidelines*, 67-68
use of Professional and Administrative Career Examination, 75
use of tests, 72
Employment discrimination cases reaching the Supreme Court, 67
Employment testing
court challenges to, 72-76
and courts, 65
history and trends in, 72

Title VII, Civil Rights Act of 1964, 67
Equal Employment Opportunity Commission
Guidelines on Employment Testing Procedures, 67
influence on specialty boards, 3
Erdmann, James B., Ph.D., on standardized testing legislation: consumer protection or consumer fraud?, 127-36
Essentials of Accredited Residencies in Graduate Medical Education (Accreditation Council for Graduate Medical Education), 87
general requirements of, 91-94
Establishing new specialties (Weary), 175-82
legal issues, 4-5
Ewing, Joseph Neff Jr., J.D., on standards affecting training programs, 87-102
Examinations
for licensure, 158-59
need for validity and reliability, 3
subject to federal regulation, 3
Exchange of information among competitors, 192-93
Extravagent representations
in certification and accreditation process, 106-107
consequences of, 106-107
court cases concerning, 106-107

F

Fairness. *See* Procedural fairness; Substantive fairness
Falcone criteria, 31
Falcone v. Middlesex County Medical Society
on membership decisions by private associations, 32, 33, 34, 35

Falcone procedural fairness doctrine in membership decisions, 32–35
Fashion Originators' Guild of America, Inc. v. Federal Trade Commission, on restraints of trade, 11
Federal antitrust challenges, analysis of, 7–16
Federal antitrust laws, rule of reason analysis, 11–14
Federal funds and research grants contingent on approved residency program, 87–88
Federal regulation
 qualifying specialists through certification, 170
 over specialty boards, 3
Federal Trade Commission
 authority over professional associations, 55
 concerns with accrediting agencies, 181–82
 on credentialing programs, 56
 in enforcement of antitrust laws, 17
 on illegal self-regulation practices, 49
 on illegality of AMA ethical canons, 52–53
 influence on specialty boards, 3
 interest in closed hospital medical staff, 6
 interest in credentialing, 177
 interest in physician-hospital contracts, 6
 investigation of medical specialty boards, 19
 investigations of health care field, 3–4
Federal Trade Commission Act, 184
Federation of State Medical Boards
 on accreditation of foreign medical schools, 157

Feldman, Albert J., L.L.B., on due process in certification and accreditation, 17–44
Feminist Women's Health Center, Inc. v. Mohammed on antitrust actions, 15–16
Foreign medical schools
 difficulties of accreditation, 157
 licensing of graduates, 154
Frankfurter, Justice Felix on protection of trademarks, 111
Freedom of Information Act, 141
FTC. *See* Federal Trade Commission

G

Goldfarb v. Virginia State Bar
 as antitrust violation case, 49–50
 landmark decision on "learned professionals exemption," 8, 18, 22
 as professional association antitrust case, 51
Government
 secrecy trend in, 141
 trend toward intrusiveness by, 141
Governmental organizations, requirement of due process, 27–28
Government regulation
 of employment testing, 67–72
 need for, 46
 versus self-regulation, 45–46
 threat of antitrust actions, 47
 trend to deregulation, 47
Graduate medical education, accreditation council for, 88
"Green Book," requirements of accredited residencies, 89
Griggs v. Duke Power Co., challenge to employment testing, 72, 73, 74
Group boycotts among competitors, 190–91

H

Hanberry v. Hearst Corporation, on advertising misrepresentation, 107
Health care delivery system, impact of antitrust laws, 18–19
Health care industry, pricing in, 256–70
Health facilities, competition among, 210–18
Health practitioners, analysis of competition among, 177
Horizontal restraints, suspect under antitrust legislation, 188
Hospital Building Co. v. Trustees of Rex Hospital, on restraints of trade, 16
Hospital practice
  disputes under antitrust laws, 18
  impact of antitrust laws, 18
Hospitals
  challenges under antitrust laws, 228–31
  competition among, 210–18
Hospital staff privileges
  current developments, 5–16
  denial of, 235–48
  standards of JCAH, 5

I

Insurance companies
  cost-containment activities by, 27–83
  use of peer review by, 279–83
Insurance protection for specialty boards, 2

J

Jacobs, Jerald A., J.D., on the principle of reasonableness, 45–63
JCAH. *See* Joint Commission on Accreditation of Hospitals
Jefferson Parish Hospital District No. 2 v. Hyde, on antitrust medical staff arrangements, 15
Job-relatedness as criterion in employment testing, 73
Joint Commission on Accreditation of Hospitals, standards for hospital medical staff, 5
Judicial hearing, circumstances for in due process, 31–32
Judicial intervention, "expulsion" versus "application" cases, 33–37
Judicial review of liability for certification or accreditation activities (Willett), 103–109

K

Klein, Joel I., J.D., on antitrust laws and medical specialty certification, 17–26
Klor's, Inc. v. Broadway-Hale Stores, Inc., on restraints of trade, 11
Kronen v. Pacific Coast Society of Orthodontists, 36

L

Lanham Act (1946), federal Trademark Act, 111–13
Larry P. v. Riles, on validity of standardized IQ test, 77–78
Learned professions exemption, 185–87
  related to antitrust laws, 18
Legal aspects of certification and accreditation (Rankin), 1–5
Legislation on standardized testing, 127–36
Legislative and judicial developments concerning privacy, 145–49
Lerner, Arthur, Assistant Director of

Index 293

FTC Bureau of Competition, 19
Liability in tort for certification or accreditation activities (Willett), 103-109
Liaison Committee on Medical Education
 accreditation of medical graduates by, 154
 defects in accrediting program, 56
Licensing boards, challenges to, 153-61
Licensure, qualifications for, 153
Licensure by specialty, dangers of, 173
Limited practitioners. *See* Nonphysician health care workers
Litigation involving exclusive contracts between physicians and hospitals, 6
Lloyd, John S., Ph.D., on validity and reasonableness, 65-85

M

McCarran-Ferguson Act
 "business of insurance" exemption, 271-73
 exemption from antitrust laws, 205-209
Manual for Trademark of Examining Procedure, 117
Marrese v. American Academy of Orthopaedic Surgeons, use of reasonableness and fairness tests in credentialing dispute, 58-59
Marjorie Webster Junior College v. Middle States Association of Colleges and Secondary Schools,
 on accreditation, 22, 23
 on restraints of trade, 22, 23
Maximum fee schedules suspect under antitrust laws, 270

Maximum reimbursement levels set by insurance companies, 270-79
Medicaid boycotts, 263
Medical College Admission Test (MCAT), 128
Medical information, use in law enforcement, 139-40
Medical Knowledge Self-Assessment Program of the American College of Physicians, 166
Medical licensing boards
 challenges to disciplinary actions, of, 160
 ensuring competence of licensees, 160-61
 responsibility of, 153
Medical licensure, challenges to prerequisites to, 154-59
Medical organizations, challenge of due process, 27-28
Medical practice
 impact of antitrust laws, 18
 need for continuing education, 169
Medical practitioners, ensuring competence of, 160-61
Medical profession, trademark issues in, 111
Medical residency training programs, standards for, 87-94
Medical specialists, need for continuing cognitive skills, 164
Medical specialties, proliferation of new specialties, 175
Medical specialty boards
 adoption of recertification examinations, 166
 adoption of recertification programs, 163-64
 from antitrust perspective, 20
 approval of residency programs, 87
 in atmosphere of antitrust enforcement, 21
 certification not state action, 29

concern over antitrust actions, 19
historical developments in legal issues, 2–5
importance of due process for, 2
increasing federal regulation of, 3
influence of Equal Employment Opportunity Coordinating Council, 3
information-providing function, 20
investigation by Federal Trade Commission, 19
need for insurance, 2
potentially anticompetitive practices, 20
protection of trade names and trademarks, 2
role of as procompetitive bodies, 20
significance of medical malpractice crisis, 2
Medical specialty certification
  related to antitrust laws, 17–26
  related to trade names and trademarks, 111–25
  role of trade names and trademarks (Vittum), 111–25
Medical specialty groups, dissemination of relative value scales by, 260
Medical staff, antitrust implications for in hospital privileges, 5
Membership rules, fairness requirements, 34–35
Mergers, suspect under Clayton Act, 195–98
Mergers and acquisitions among hospitals, 210
Michigan State Medical Society, on arrangements peculiar to health care field, 15
Mishiwaka Rubber and Woolen Mfg. Company v. S. S. Kresge Co., on protection of trademarks, 111
Monopolies, violations of Sherman Act, 187–88
Monopolization as violation under Sherman Act, 14

N

National Association of Insurance Commissioners'"Insurance Information and Privacy Protection Model Act," 140
National Audio-Visual Association, Inc., role in credentialing rules, 55–56
National Commission for Health Certifying Agencies on nonphysician health professionals, 180
National Council on Measurement in Education, 130
  on standards for educational and psychological tests, 68
National Education Association on standardized testing, 135
National Health Lawyers Association on FTC challenge to specialty boards, 19
National Society of Professional Engineers v. United States
  as antitrust violation case, 50
  on learned professions exemption, 8
New medical specialties
  candidates' qualifications, 178
  creation of, 176
  establishing, 175–82
  issues in recognition of, 177
  need for definition of scope, 178
Nixon v. Condon test on state action by associations, 29
Noerr-Pennington doctrine 25, 201, 202
  in lobbying for certification, 25
Nonphysician health care workers legal issues involved, 159

proliferation of, 159
related to cost containment, 159-60
Northern Pacific Railway v. United States, on *per se* rules, 11

O

Occupational licensing as state function, 48

P

PACE. *See* Professional and Administrative Career Examination
Paralegal Institute, Inc. v. American Bar Association, challenge to accreditation standards, 23
Parsons College v. North Central Association of Colleges and Secondary Schools, 30
Peer review cases, physician liability in, 281-83
Peer review committees, antitrust challenges to, 281-83
Per se test of antitrust liability, 51
Per se violations, 185
Physician referrals, potential anticompetitive consequences of, 321-32
Physicians
  agreements involving insurance companies, 220-28
  competing with nonphysicians, 220
  competition among, 235-54
  concern for failure of recertification, 165
  denial of medical malpractice insurance, 221-22
  need for continuing education, 169
  price-fixing by, 256-59
  qualifying for new medical specialties, 175-76
  value of recertification for, 169-70
Physicians' organizations, practice restrictions by, 248-54
Pinsker v. Pacific Coast Society of Orthodontists, 33, 34
Predictive validity in testing, 70
Price agreements among competitors, 188-89
Price discrimination, suspect under Robinson-Patman Act, 198-200
Price-fixing by health care professionals, 256-60
The principle of reasonableness (Jacobs), 45-63
Privacy
  defined, 138
  erosion of, 139-41
  judicial decisions on, 146-47
  protective legislation for, 145-46
Privacy Protection Act of 1980, on protection of the media, 140
Private associations
  fairness in membership decisions, 32-36
  judicial intervention in, 32
  membership as economic necessity, 33
  membership as privilege, 32-33
  propriety of membership decisions, 32-34
  as quasi-governmental entities, 47
Private insurers, boycotts of, 265-66
Private medical regulation
  current challenge to, 26
  due process issue, 27-28
Privilege, defined, 137
Procedural fairness in membership and certification decisions, 35-36
Professional associations
  credentialing function, 48-49
  due process applications, 32-40
  elevation of professional standards, 35

insulation from antitrust liability, 48
not a state entity, 29
requirements for self-regulatory activities, 47–48
Professional and Administrative Career Examination (PACE), in employee selection, 75
Professional certifying bodies, risk to in enforcement activities, 24
Professional credentialing. *See* Credentialing
Professional engineers as professional association antitrust case, 51
Professional organizations
 analysis of vertical restraints, 13
 antitrust implications of certification by, 178–79
 distaste for antitrust challenges to, 179
 per se rule versus rule of reason, 13–14
 requirements for continuing education, 169
Professional self-regulation. *See* Self-regulation
Protection of trademarks under federal Trademark Act, 111–13
Proving agreement among competitors, 191–92

R

Radiology services, limitations on access to, 232–33
Rankin, James W., J.D.
 on current developments affecting hospital staff privileges, 5–16
 on legal aspects of certification and accreditation, 1–5
Reasonableness
 in cases involving employment and educational testing, 80–81
 defined, 66
 practical guidelines on, 59–61
 principle of, 45–63
Reasonableness test of antitrust liability, 51
Recertification
 ABMS guidelines for, 168
 advantages to physician, 170
 difficulty of publicizing value of, 170–71
 legal issues in, 4
 linkage to reregistration by license, 172
 private and voluntary nature of, 173–74
 qualification resulting from, 169
 reasons for, 163
 requirement of unlimited medical licensure, 172
 standards for, 171
 trend toward indispensability, 166
Recertification (Benson), 163–74
Recognition component of certification process as exempt from antitrust laws, 21–22
Red Diamond Supply, Inc. v. Liquid Carbonic Corp., on vertical and horizontal restraints, 10
Relative value scales, suspect as price-fixing devices, 260–63
Residency programs
 accreditation process, 89–91
 antitrust considerations, 90–91
 chronological development of, 88–89
 general requirements for, 91–94
 need for, 87
 numbers of, 89
 responsibility of the hospital, sample document, 95–102
Right to Financial Privacy Act, 141
Robinson-Patman Act, 184
The role of trade names and trademarks in medical specialty certification (Vittum), 111–25

Rule of reason
  applied to professional services, 8
  contrasted with *per se* rule, 12
  minimalist test of accreditation standards, 24
Rule of reason doctrine in antitrust cases, 23
Rule of reason violations, 185

S

Salter v. New York State Psychological Association, on professional association and state action, 29
Secrecy in government activities, 141–44
Self-regulated bodies, ethical obligations of, 47
Self-regulation
  advantages of, 46
  antitrust implications of, 49–55
  application of *per se* antitrust analysis, 52
  illegal practices in, 49–55
  nature of, 47
  political climate favorable to, 61
  by professional associations, 46
  as quasi-governmental, 45
  related to due process safeguards, 47
Sherman Act, 183
  definition of monopolizing offenses, 14
  provisions of Section I, 9
  related to hospital staff privileges, 7
  on restraint of trade, 51
Smith v. North Michigan Hospital, on rule of reason, 10
Specialties, establishing, 175–82
Specialty boards. *See* Medical specialty boards
Specialty certification, need for, 21

Standard Oil Co. of New Jersey v. United States, 9
Standardized testing, improvement of, 134
Standardized testing legislation
  codifying sponsors' testing practices, 129
  concerns of proponents of, 134
  as consumer protection issue, 135
  Harrington Bill, 130
  influence on medical profession, 130–31
  objectives of, 132–33
  remedies offered, 128–30
  responsibilities of test sponsors, 128–29
Standardized testing legislation: consumer protection or consumer fraud? (Erdmann), 127–36
Standardized tests, weakening of, 132–33
Standards affecting training programs (Ewing), 87–102
Standards for Educational and Psychological Tests (1974), 68
Standards for educational and psychological tests, 68, 130
  on content validity, 69–70
Standards for medical residency training programs, 87–94
Standards for recertification, 171
Stanford-Binet Intelligence Scale, in educational testing, 78
State action in due process requirement, 28–32
State insurance programs, boycotts of, 265
Substantive fairness in membership rules, 34–35

T

Tarasoff v. Regents of University of California, on reasonableness of

certification process, 105
Tarasoff rule, relevance in certification process, 105
Testing legislation. *See* Standardized testing legislation
Testing standards related to validity, 68-69
Tort liability
  in accreditation procedures, 103-109
  for certifying organizations, guidelines for, 107-109
  misrepresentations, 104, 106
  negligence claims, 104, 105
Trademarks
  defined, 112
  federal registration of, 119-20
  importance of protection of, 121-24
  remedies for infringement, 120-21
  statutory protection for, 111-25
Trade names, defined, 112
Trade names and trademarks
  protection of for specialty boards, 2
  role in medical specialty certification, 111-25
Training programs
  standards affecting, 87-102
See also Medical residency training programs
Treister v. Academy of Orthopaedic Surgeons, 33, 34
"Truth-in-testing" legislation, 4, 127

U

Uniform Guidelines on Employee Selection Procedures, 67
  adoption of testing standards, 68
  on construct validity, 71-72
  on content validity, 70
  influence on licensure and certification, 67-68
  minimum technical standards for validity studies, 68
  on validity of testing or selection procedures, 70-72
Union labels as collective marks, 115
United States Dental Institute v. American Association of Orthodontists, on accreditation, 24
United States v. Trenton Potteries Co., on restraints of trade, 11
United States v. United States Gypsum Co., on *per se* restraints, 11
Unlimited medical licensure required for recertification, 172
U.S. Department of Justice
  business review procedure, 55, 56
  concern in violations of antitrust laws, 17
  on illegal self-regulation practices, 49
  on physician-hospital contracts, 6
U.S. Office of Education
  recognition of accrediting agencies, 180
  recognition of credentialing organizations, 56, 59
U.S. Supreme Court
  on *American Society of Mechanical Engineers, Inc. v. Hydrolevel Corp.*, 53, 54
  on antitrust aspects of confidentiality, 138
  Arizona v. Maricopa County Medical Society, 50-51
  challenge to employment testing, 72-73
  challenging self-regulation, 49-55
  on constitutional due process, 37-39
  on disclosures of census lists, 145
  Dos Santos case, 6
  on due process requirement, 28
  on elements of due process, 28

employment discrimination cases, 67
on exclusionary rule, 144
Goldfarb v. Virginia State Bar, 49–50
on hospital staff privileges, 6
on job relatedness and employment tests, 73–74
National Society of Professional Engineers v. United States, 50
on restraints *per se* unlawful, 11–12
ruling on anticompetitive restraints, 8
use of *per se* test of antitrust liability, 51
use of reasonableness test, 51
on validity of employment testing procedures, 75–76

V

Validity
in cases involving employment and educational testing, 80–81
defined, 66–67
in educational testing, 77–78
types of, 69
Validity and reasonableness (Lloyd), 65–83
Validity studies, minimum standards for, 68
Veizaga v. National Board for Respiratory Therapy, on certification, 24
as federal antitrust case, 57–58
Vertical v. horizontal restraints, determinations under Sherman Act, 10–11
Vertical restraints as antitrust violations, 193–95
Virginia Academy of Clinical Psychologists v. Blue Shield of Virginia, on violations of antitrust laws, 25
Vittum, Daniel W. Jr., J.D., on the role of trade names and trademarks in medical specialty certification, 111–25

W

Weary, Peyton E., M.D., on establishing new specialties, 175–82
Wechsler Intelligence Scale for Children, in educational testing, 78
Weiss v. New York Hospital, on violations of Sherman Act, 14
Wilk v. American Medical Association, on unlawful restraint of trade, 7–8, 9
Will, George, on "big government," 45
Willett, David E., J.D., on judicial review: liability in tort for certification or accreditation activities, 103–109
Wonderlic Personnel Test, use in employee selection, 73

Z

Zurcher v. Standford Daily, on protection of media privacy, 140

Index to Cases Cited

A

Abbott Laboratories v. Portland Retail Druggist Association, 199
Academy of Ambulatory Foot Surgery v. American Podiatry Association, 201, 253
Addyston Pipe & Steel Co. v. United States, 190
Albemarle Paper Co. v. Moody, 73, 74
Aloe Creme Laboratories, Inc. v. American Society for Aesthetic Plastic Surgery, Inc., 118
American Academy of Orthopaedic Surgeons, 260
American Association of Orthodontists, 189
American Automobile Ass'n v. National Automobile Ass'n, 122
American College of Obstetricians and Gynecologists, 260
American College of Radiology, 189, 260
American Column & Lumber Co. v. United States, 263
American Dental Association, 249
American Medical Association v. Federal Trade Commission, 189, 249, 250
American Medical Association v. United States, 9, 52
American Medicorp, Inc. v. Humana, Inc., 197, 212, 213, 215
American Motor Inns, Inc. v. Holiday Inns, Inc., 245
American Society of Anesthesiologists, Inc., 251
American Society of Mechanical Engineers v. Hydrolevel Corp., 8, 53, 54, 55
American Tobacco Co. v. United States, 188, 246

302 Legal Aspects of Certification and Accreditation

Anderson v. Banks, 79
Anglin v. Blue Shield, 209
Application of Beatrice Foods Company, 120
Arizona ex rel. Corbin v. Arizona Radiological Society, 251
Arizona v. Maricopa County Medical Society, 11, 50, 51, 52, 54, 187, 188, 189, 227, 235, 242, 243, 256, 258, 259, 261, 273, 274
Association of Independent Dentists, 249, 266

B

Ballard v. Blue Shield of Southern West Virginia, 221, 224, 225
Barr v. National Right to Life Committee, Inc., 205
Bartholomew v. Virginia Chiropractors Association, 208
Bates v. State Bar of Arizona, 200, 249
Blue Cross and Blue Shield of Michigan v. Michigan Ass'n of Psychotherapy, 227, 278
Blue Cross of Washington and Alaska v. Kitsap Physician Services, 250, 253
Blue Shield of Virginia v. McCready, 185, 221
Board of Curators of the University of Missouri v. Horowitz, 27, 37–39
Boddicker v. Arizona State Dental Association, 190, 252, 254
Broadcast Music, Inc., v. Columbia Broadcasting System, 189
Brookins v. Bonnell, 31
Broward County Medical Association, 249
Brown Shoe Co. v. FTC, 194
Bruce's Juices, Inc. v. American Can Co., 198
Brunswick Corp. v. Pueblo Bowl-O-Matic, Inc., 245
Bryant, 76

C

California Medical Ass'n, 260
California Motor Transport Co. v. Trucking Unlimited, 202, 216
California Retail Liquor Dealers Association v. Midcal Aluminum, Inc., 200, 214
Cantor v. Detroit Edison Co., 200
Capital Temporaries, Inc. v. Olsten Corp., 195
Cardio-Medical Associates, Ltd. v. Crozer-Chester Medical Center, 205, 230, 236
Carl Zeiss Stiftung v. V.E.B. Carl Zeiss, Jena, 122
Cement Manufacturers Protective Association v. United States, 192–93
Chicago Board of Trade v. United States, 12, 185, 240
Chiropractic Society v. Radiological Society of New Jersey, 232
Citizen Publishing Co. v. United States, 197
City of Fairfax v. Fairfax Hospital Association, 210, 215
City of Lafayette v. Louisiana Power, 214
Coca-Cola Co. v. Howard Johnson Co., 122
Collins v. American Optometric Association, 106

Communications Satellite Corp. v. Comcet, Ind., 112
Community Communication Co. v. City of Boulder, 201
Community of Roquefort v. William Faehndrich, Inc., 122
Continental T.V., Inc. v. C GTE Sylvania, Inc., 12, 193
Contra Sokol v. University Hospital, 244, 245
Cowen v. New York Stock Exchange, 190
Crane v. Inter-Mountain Health Care Inc., 204, 230

D

Debra P. v. Turlington, 79, 81
Denver v. Santa Barbara Commun. Dialysis Center, 216
Dos Santos (case), 6
Douglas Fir Plywood Ass'n, 115
Dr. Miles Medical Co. v. John D. Park & Sons, 193

E

E. A. McQuade Tours, Inc. v. Consolidated Air Tour Manual Committee, 9
Eastern Railroads Presidents Conf. v. Noerr F Motor Freight, Inc., 216
Eastern Railroads Presidents Conference v. Noerr Motor Freight, Inc., 202, 216
Eastern States Retail Lumber Dealers Association v. United States, 193
Eliason Corp. v. National Sanitation Foundation, 8
Elizabeth Hospital Inc. v. Richardson, 203

F

Falcone v. Middlesex County Medical Society, 31, 32, 33, 34, 35
Fashion Originators' Guild of America, Inc. v. Federal Trade Commission, 11, 190
Federal Prescription Service v. American Pharmaceutical Association, 203
Federal Trade Commission v. Consolidated Foods, 198
Federal Trade Commission v. Fred Meyer, Inc., 198
Federal Trade Commission v. Procter & Gamble, 198
Feldman v. Jackson Memorial Hospital, 204, 228, 229
Feminist Women's Health Center, Inc. v. Mohammed, 15, 202, 254
Firefighters Institute for Racial Equality v. City of St. Louis, 76
Forbes Health System Medical Staff, 250
Fultner Enterprises, Inc. v. United States Steel Corp., 194

G

General Electric v. Gilbert, 74
General Shale Products Corp. v. Struck Construction Co., 200
Gold Cross Ambulance v. City of Kansas City, 217
Goldfarb v. Virginia State Bar, 8, 18, 22, 49, 51, 52, 54, 186, 189, 200, 235
Gough v. Rossmore Corp., 194, 240
Griggs v. Duke Power Co., 72, 73, 74
Group Life Health Insurance Co. v. Royal Drug Co., 206, 207, 222
Guardians Association of New York

City v. Civil Service Commission, 76
Gulf Oil Corp. v. Copp Paving Co., 199

H

Hahn v. Oregon Physician's Service, 207, 220, 223, 224
Hanberry v. Hearst Corporation, 107
Hartford Empire Co. v. United States, 190
Hatley v. American Quarter Horse Ass'n, 9
Hawaii v. Hawaii Society of Anesthesiologists, Inc., 261, 264, 266, 267
Health Care Equalization Committee v. Iowa Medical Society, 201, 207, 221, 223, 224, 225, 228, 229, 232
Hoberman v. Lock Haven Hospital, 30
Hobson v. Hansen, 77
Hoffman v. Delta Dental Plan, 204, 207, 209
Hoffman v. Garden City, 243
Hollander, 77
Horowitz. See Board of Curators of the University of Missouri v. Horowitz
Hospital Building Co. v. Trustees of Rex Hospital, 16, 202, 204, 211, 216, 217, 230, 236
Huber Baking Co. v. Stroehmann Brothers Co., 114
Huron Valley Hospital v. City of Pontiac, 188, 201, 214, 215
Hyde v. Jefferson Parish Hospital District No. 2, 195, 204, 236, 237, 238–39, 241, 242

I

Illinois Brick Co. v. Illinois, 185
Indiana Dental Ass'n, 267
Indiana Fed'n of Dentists, 266
In Re Florida Citrus Commission, 116
In Re Institute of Certified Professional Business Consultants, 119
In Re Monsanto Co., 116
In Re National Society of Cardiopulmonary Technologists, Inc., 119
In Re Professional Photographers of Ohio, Inc., 119
Interstate Circuit, Inc. v. United States, 191
Iowa Dental Association, 282

J

Jefferson City Pharmaceutical Association, Inc. v. Abbott Laboratories, 200
Jefferson Parish Hospital District No. 2 v. Hyde, 15

K

Kartell v. Blue Shield of Massachusetts, 273, 279
Kiefer-Stewart v. Joseph E. Seagram & Sons, 193
Klamath Lake Pharmaceutical Association v. Klamath Medical Service Bureau, 195, 207, 209
Klor's, Inc. v. Broadway-Hale Stores, Inc., 11, 190, 243
Kreuzer v. American Academy of Periodontology and American Dental Association, 252
Kronen v. Pacific Coast Society of Orthodontists, 36

L

Larry P. v. Riles, 77, 78
Levin v. Joint Commission on Accreditation of Hospitals, 190, 229
Liberty Glass Co. v. Allstate Insurance Co., 207
Luevano v. Campbell, 75

M

McCready v. Blue Shield of Virginia, 225
McElhinney v. Medical Protective Company, 236, 243, 246
McKesson & Robbins v. Phillips Chemical Co., 123
McLain v. Real Estate Board of New Orleans, Inc., 204, 230, 236
Malini v. Singleton and Associates, 204, 236
Manasen v. California Dental Service, 278
Maple Flooring Manufacturers Ass'n v. United States, 192, 263
Maricopa. *See* Arizona v. Maricopa County Medical Society
Marjorie Webster Junior College, Inc. v. Middle States Ass'n of Colleges and Secondary Schools, Inc., 9, 22, 23
Marrese v. American Academy of Orthopaedic Surgeons, 58
Martin B. Glauser Dodge Co. v. Chrysler Corp., 240
Matter of Application of Hirschorn, 265
Medical Arts Pharmacy of Stamford, Ind. v. Blue Cross and Blue Shield of Connecticut, Inc., 191, 275, 278, 279
Medical Services Corp. of Spokane County, 191, 250

Michigan State Medical Society, 15, 264, 266
Michigan v. Warner-Universal Ambulance Service, 264, 267
Minnesota State Medical Ass'n, 260
Mishawaka Rubber and Woolen Mfg. Company v. S. S. Kresge Co., 11
Mishler v. St. Anthony's Hospital System, 204
Molinas v. National Basketball Association, 190
Mulhearn v. Rose-Neath Funeral Home, Inc., 207

N

Nara v. American Dental Association, 205
National Gerimedical & Gerontology Center v. Blue Cross, 205, 213
National League of Cities v. Usery, 217
National Science Foundation v. National Sanitation Foundation Testing Laboratory, Inc., 118
National Society of Professional Engineers v. United States, 8, 50, 51, 52, 54, 186, 190, 235, 240
National Trailways Bus System v. Trailway Van Lines, 115
Neeld v. National Hockey League, 9
New Jersey v. Nurses Private Duty Registry, 259, 261
New York v. American Medical Association, 228, 229, 232
New York v. New York State Society of Ophthalmic Dispensers Inc., 266, 267
New York v. Roth, 191, 265
Nixon v. Condon, 29

North Carolina v. P.I.A. Asheville, Inc., 214
Northern Pacific Railway v. United States, 11, 183
Nurse Midwifery Associates v. B. K. Hibbet, 221, 223, 224, 228

O

Ohio ex rel. Brown v. Alliance Dental Society, 265
Ohio ex rel. Brown v. JCAH, 229, 230
Ohio v. Ohio Medical Indemnity, Inc., 273
Olmstead v. United States, 136
Oreck v. Whirlpool Corp., 194, 240

P

Packard Motor Car Co. v. Webster Motor Car Co., 193
Paralegal Institute, Inc. v. American Bar Association, 23
Parents in Action on Special Education (PASE) v. Hannon, 78
Parker v. Brown, 200, 214
Parsons College v. North Central Association of Colleges and Secondary Schools, 30
Phoenix Baptist Hospital v. Samaritan Health Services, 203, 215, 216
Pinsker v. Pacific Coast Society of Orthodontists, 33, 34
Pireno v. New York State Chiropractic Association, 208
Pireno. See Pireno v. New York State Chiropractic Association [OR] Union Labor Life Insurance Co. v. Pireno
Portland Retail Druggists Association v. Kaiser Foundation Health Plan, 195

Powsner v. St. Joseph Mercy Hospital of Detroit, 241, 247
Prestonettes v. Coty, 112
Princeton Community Phone Book, Inc. v. Bates, 249
Proctor v. State Farm Mutual Automobile Insurance Co., 208

R

Radiant Burners, Inc. v. Peoples Gas and Light Co., 243
Ratino v. Medical Service of District of Columbia, 209
Red Diamond Supply, Inc. v. Liquid Carbonic Corp., 10
Riggal v. Washington County Medical Society, 203
R. M. Hollingshead Corp. v. Daview-Young Soap Co., 115
Robinson v. Magovern, 190, 204, 236, 237, 238, 244, 245, 247
Royal Drug. See Group Life Health Insurance Co. v. Royal Drug Co.

S

Salter v. New York State Psychological Association, 29
Santos v. Columbus-Cuneo-Cabrini Medical Center, 237, 238, 240, 248
Sausalito Pharmacy, Inc. v. Blue Shield of California, 201
Saxlehner v. Eisner & Mendelson Co., 123
Siegel v. Chicken Delight, Inc., 194
Slavek v. American Medical Association, 229, 232
Slavek v. Pennsylvania, 232
SmithKline Corp. v. Eli Lilly & Co., 195, 237
Smith v. Northern Michigan Hospital, Inc., 241

Index to Cases Cited **307**

Spears Free Clinic and Hospital v. Cleeve, 203
St. Bernard Hospital v. Hospital Service Association, 207
St. Paul Fire & Marine Ins. Co. v. Barry, 223
St. Paul Life Insurance Co. v. Barry, 208
Standard Oil Co. of New Jersey v. United States, 9, 188
Stella v. Mercy Hospital, 245

T

Tampa Electric Co. v. Nashville Coal Co., 194, 238
Tarasoff v. Regents of University of California, 105
Texas Dental Ass'n, 266
Theatre Enterprises v. Paramount Film Distributing Corp., 191, 244
Times-Picayune Publishing Co. v. United States, 188, 195, 237
Timken Roller Bearing Co. v. United States, 189
Treister v. Academy of Orthopaedic Surgeons, 33, 34

U

Underwriters Laboratories, Inc. v. United Laboratories, Inc., 120, 121, 123
Union Labor Life Insurance Co. v. Pireno, 148, 207, 208, 222, 279, 281
United Mine Workers v. Pennington, 202, 216
United States v. Aluminum Co. of America, 187
United States v. American Medical Association, 190
United States v. American Pharmaceutical Ass'n and Michigan Pharmaceutical Ass'n, 259
United States v. American Society of Anesthesiologists, 189, 193, 207, 259, 261, 262, 268
United States v. Arnold Schwinn, 193
United States v. College of American Pathologists, 251
United States v. Container Corp. of America, 189, 192, 199, 245, 263
United States Dental Institute v. American Association of Orthodontists, 24, 191, 202, 253, 254
United States v. E. I. du Pont de Nemours & Co., 188, 237
United States v. Gasoline Retailers Association, 189
United States v. General Dynamics, 196
United States v. Greater Buffalo Press, 195
United States v. Grinnell Corp., 188, 246
United States v. Halifax Hospital Medical Center and Volusia County Medical Society, 250
United States v. Hospital Affiliates International, Inc., 204, 212
United States v. Illinois Podiatry Society, Inc., 260, 262, 268
United States v. Jerrold Electronics, 195
United States v. Loew's, Inc., 194
United States v. Montana Nursing Home Ass'n, Inc., 264, 267
United States v. Parke-Davis, 193
United States v. Penn-Olin Chemical, 196, 198
United States v. Philadelphia National Bank, 195, 196, 205, 238

United States v. Socony Vacuum Oil Co., 188
United States v. Group Life & Health Insurance Co. v. Royal Drug Co., 207, 271, 272, 275, 280
United States v. South Carolina Health Care Association, 191, 264, 267
United States v. South-Eastern Underwriters Association, 203
United States v. Topco Associates, Inc. 189
United States v. Trenton Potteries Co., 11
United States v. United Shoe Machinery Corp., 187
United States v. United States Gypsum Co., 11, 245
United States v. Von's Grocery, 197

V

Vandervelde v. Put & Call Brokers & Dealers Association, 189
Vanguard Justice Society v. Hughes, 76
Van Winkle, 114
Veizaga v. The National Board for Respiratory Therapy, 24, 57, 76
Virginia Academy of Clinical Psychologists v. Blue Shield of Virginia, 25, 191, 201, 202, 206, 208, 220, 221, 222, 223, 227, 228, 258, 259, 262, 268

W

Washington v. Davis, 74
Weiss v. York Hospital, 14, 238, 246, 248
White and White, Inc. v. American Hospital Supply Co., 217
Whitfield v. Illinois Board of L2 Law Examiners, 30
Wigdor, 74
Wilk v. American Medical Association, 7, 9, 228, 229, 231, 232, 233
Williams v. Kleaveland, 243, 244
Williams v. St. Joseph Hospital, 266, 267
Wolf v. Jane Phillips Episcopal Memorial Medical Center, 203

Z

Zamiri v. William Beaumont Hospital, 236
Zazzali v. New Jersey Pharmaceutical Ass'n, 259
Zurcher v. Standford Daily, 140

DE